The Comparative Reader

COMPARATIVE STUDIES

Series Editor: John T. Kirby

Volume 1. John T. Kirby (ed.). *The Comparative Reader: A Handlist of Basic Reading in Comparative Literature.*

THE COMPARATIVE READER

A Handlist of Basic Reading in Comparative Literature

EDITED BY JOHN T. KIRBY

CHANCERY PRESS
NEW HAVEN
1998

Chancery Press
Post Office Box 3395
New Haven, Connecticut 06515-0795

Copyright © 1998 by Chancery Press

Library of Congress Cataloging-in-Publication Data

The Comparative reader : a handlist of basic reading in comparative
   literature / edited by John T. Kirby.
         p.   cm. — (Comparative studies; volume 1)
      Includes bibliographical references.
      ISBN 1-890657-00-X. — ISBN 1-890657-01-8 (pbk.)
      1. Literature, Comparative — Bibliography.   I. Kirby, John T.
   Z6514.C7C66   1998
   [PN871]
   016.809 — dc21   97-50495
                                                          CIP

              2 4 6 8 9 7 5 3 1

      This book is set in Bembo, with titling in Gill Sans
         Printed in the United States of America
            Cover design by Grant King

For Robert and Janice, with love

The Comparative Reader

TABLE OF CONTENTS

INTRODUCTION AND ACKNOWLEDGMENTS

> Of the making of many books there is no end.
> — Ecclesiastes 12:12

> Comparisouns doon offte gret greuaunce.
> — John Lydgate, *The Fall of Princes*

Comparative Literature / Comparative Studies

It is no exaggeration to say that the Humanities are under siege, or that, within this field, the state of Comparative Literature is particularly precarious. How could it fail to be otherwise, when there is no scholarly consensus on what qualifies as 'literature,' or even on what may be classified as a 'text'? But in a number of ways, Comparative Literature — like my own especial purview of Classics — epitomizes the Humanities as a whole. 'What is it *for?*' is the ruthless teleological inquisition of today's bottom-liner. My first (perhaps defensive) response is: What is beauty for? What is the 'use' of a flower, or of a sunset? But, upon reflection, I think that other rejoinders, both academic and pragmatic, present themselves. As for the academic: if, as Alexander Pope opined, the proper study of mankind is man, then it would be illiberal indeed to cordon off the Humanities from study — that field which most squarely contemplates, in Cicero's wonderful term, *humanitas* — all that makes us human. As for the pragmatic: the 'use' (if such were needed) of such humanistic study displays itself, not only in the aggregation (for its own sake) of information within this field, but also in the way it trains the mind to *think*: just as, they say, there is no sweeter sound to hear than the utterance of one's own name, so too there is no topic that focuses the attention like that of the human condition itself — particularly in narrative. In fact, as research into the processes of human thought continue, it becomes clearer than ever that narrativity is at the very basis of how we think, reason, and feel.[1] Indeed Mark Turner has recently gone so far as to contend that story actually precedes language.[2] Not every student of literature will go on to be a professor of literature; but presumably every one of them needs to know, not only how to think, but how and why she thinks as she does. For this, one can do no better than to study literature. And — in this age where 'multiculturalism' has finally begun to receive the attention it deserves — for understanding alterity, and how and why others think as they do, one can do no better than to study Comparative Literature.

But once again we stub our toes on that word, Literature. Do we mean by this '*belles-lettres*' in the most traditional sense? Or, as more radically defined, 'The Record of Culture' in all its broadest applications? I personally know professional scholars willing to defend both the extreme positions just mentioned, as well as a host of others who occupy more intermediate positions along the spectrum. Often this question becomes politicized as the site of acrimonious conflict. Some departments, to make room for the non-verbal text, have renamed themselves 'Comparative Studies.' Indeed, at least one graduate program now offers a full doctorate in Visual Culture.[3]

I would like to propose, and not entirely for its shock value, that we consider Classical Studies itself as a paradigm for the most forward-looking of comparative curricula: the ideal of *Altertums-*

---

[1] On this, see especially Danto 1985; Fisher 1987; Ricœur 1984–1988; Turner 1991 and 1996; Freedman and Combs 1996.

[2] Turner 1996.

[3] See Heller 1996.

wissenschaft, especially as conceived by Wilamowitz and his epigones,[4] explicitly embraced not only the 'great masterworks' of Greek and Latin *belles-lettres*, but also the humblest papyrus laundry-lists, the most humdrum official inscriptions, and the most salacious graffiti. Nor is this all. Wilamowitz, a scion of the old Prussian nobility, could never be accused of trendiness; but his vision of *Altertumswissenschaft* also required scrutiny of non-verbal 'texts' such as painting, sculpture, and architecture. Literally every shred of available evidence was, for Wilamowitz, precious information in assembling a rounded view of the ancient cultures — not excluding their arts, their political, religious, and philosophical systems, or their approaches to history and science: in short, Wilamowitz and his school sought to know everything that could be known about the ancient Greeks and Romans. And this approach, imported to America by German-trained scholars, became the foundation of the discipline of Classics as we know it here today.

I mention these historical details, not solely as a way for rooting for the home team, but also in order to draw attention to the fact that while such a holistic approach might, under the rubric of 'Comparative Studies,' seem subversive or radically anti-intellectual to some, it actually has, in the tradition of the *Totalitätsideal* of Wilamowitz, a gilt-edged pedigree — signed and sealed, as it were, in the pinnacle of the Ivory Tower. What was missing, of course, in the era of 'pure philology,' was a sensitivity (sometimes) to the political situating of the extant remains of ancient literature, and (almost universally) to the ideological underpinnings and political implications of the scholar's own approach. What one did tend to find, which will not sit so well with today's scholarship, was a kind of complacent positivism about the results of textual criticism or about historical 'fact.' But all these, of course, are just

[4] See e.g. Wilamowitz 1982, and in particular the introduction (by Hugh Lloyd-Jones) to that edition, which (while warmly appreciative) does not exclude critique of Wilamowitz's approach.

the sorts of issues that have come to the fore in literary study in our times — in the field of Classics as in the modern literatures.

Readers, Readers

As Terentianus Maurus wrote long ago, *habent sua fata libelli*: each book has its own fate, according to the various uses that its readers make of it. I envision at least three types of reader for this one:

• First, and closest to home, those students (like my own at Purdue) who will need basic reading lists for the study of Comparative Literature. At Purdue, every candidate for the Master of Arts in Comparative Literature must sit for four comprehensive written examinations, one each on three areas of her own choosing, plus a fourth one on a required set of 'foundational' texts from a variety of ancient cultures. Each of these areas is represented in *The Comparative Reader* by a list (or, in one case, a set of sub-lists) that I call a 'module.' The 'foundational' texts are listed in the module entitled, with a nod toward Edward Said, 'Beginnings?'; the three elective areas are to be chosen from the remaining modules.

• Teachers of Comparative Literature who desire a prototype, at least, for their own curricula, may want to adopt (or adapt) Purdue's modular system. In the best of all possible academic institutions, the study of Comparative Literature would know no bounds; unfortunately, outside the realm of dreams, most colleges and universities do have limitations of personnel and program. Purdue is no exception. But this school will lack what that one has, and will have what that one lacks; accordingly I have tried to gather between these covers modules that will account for most of the national literatures and at least some of the topical areas with which academic comparatists occupy themselves today. I am acutely aware that not all national literatures are accounted for here — we have (as yet) included no modules for Czech or Filipino or Korean literatures, for example. But we have made a start, and more than that, I think; and it is my hope that others who are in a position to offer other comparable options may find our system a viable model, or at least a base upon which to build.

• While this book is written by and (primarily) for those who are about the business of Comparative Literature within the academy, it is my hope that readers not currently pursuing an academic degree may also find it useful. Someone, for example, who is putting together a lifetime reading plan may well want to consult *The Comparative Reader* for ideas about where to begin and what path to take. Less ambitiously, someone who just wants to expand her knowledge about a given culture, or to be guided to some 'books that have made a difference,' might profitably browse these pages. For such readers, blissfully free of curricular obligations and requirements, *The Comparative Reader* will function less as an itinerary than as a road-map: the possibilities are unstructured and, potentially, limitless.

One could also imagine less salubrious uses for this book — for example, if the reader were to look to it as a sort of yardstick of the competence that is now known in some quarters as 'cultural literacy,' which brings up a topic I shall return to in a moment: the Literary Canon.

How to Use This Book

In most cases, each module is organized as simply as possible: every item listed is required to be read, and items have been arranged alphabetically by author, chronologically by author, chronologically by publication, or by one of these conventions after having been grouped according to genre. Where a contributor has deemed it important to stipulate a particular edition or translation,[5] such par-

---

[5] At Purdue, a student who chooses a national literature as a third area is permitted to read that module's texts in English translation. This assumes that the first and second areas are themselves also national literatures.

A few of the modules — e.g. those for Hungarian and Near Eastern studies — represent literatures taught on a limited basis or not at all at Purdue. For this reason, they are represented here solely in English translation. Other institutions may well have faculty capable of teaching

ticulars are specified. When no edition or translation is stipulated, it is to be assumed that any currently-available, commercially-published version is acceptable.

In some cases, a module will include a small list of reference-works marked 'for consultation as needed.' In such cases, of course, these items are not considered part of the material on which the candidate is to be examined; they are included purely as ancillae for the inquisitive reader. Some lists will also include suggestions for further reading; these too are optional and not part of the materials for examination.

Special mention ought perhaps to be made of the options we have included for the study of literary theory. Students at Purdue begin the M.A. program with an introductory semester-long 'Proseminar' that focuses on the comparative method and on the various schools of theory. Often this exposure will engender an abiding interest in one or more of these schools; for students who wish to make this an area of specialization, there are two options. One is to use the overview-module, which offers a broad variety of theoretical schools. The other is to use the longer module, which is itself divided into a number of smaller sub-lists. The student using this module will first read the basic overview-texts listed at the beginning of the module; then, selecting any three of the theoretical approaches listed, she will read the ten or so items listed for each of those. This affords the option of pursuing a few schools of literary theory in some depth.

In a few cases — Feminist Histories and Theories, Queer Studies, Psychoanalysis, Rhetoric, Semiotics, and Visual Culture — what might simply have been included as sub-lists within the larger Literary Theory module have instead been expanded to the status of complete modules. This reflects the richness of these schools as critical approaches and/or their particular cultivation by Purdue faculty (which our students will want especially to exploit). Of

---

such literatures in the original languages, and their students will of course not need recourse to translations.

course each of the other theoretical schools listed — and some not listed at all here — could be similarly expanded in order to maximize the strengths of a given faculty.

Canon Fodder

I may as well now return to an issue that I have already raised, and address some questions that some of my readers are doubtless already pondering: What about the literary canon? Even though the scope of this book extends well beyond the limitations of Western culture, doesn't the creation of such lists *ipso facto* reinscribe the canon, or at least the notion of canonicity? And does this not lay the baleful groundwork for perpetuating the marginalization of those who are already repeatedly marginalized?

These are not trivial questions, and I do not address them lightly. Indeed, as a classicist — one who specializes, at least partly, in what Bernard Knox has called 'The Oldest Dead White European Males'[6] — I ponder these questions continually.

It appears to me that, on analogy with the gestures of expansion and contraction, there are two basic tendencies in the structuring of human knowledge of this sort. The first tendency, the *aggregative*, may best be represented by the production of encyclopaedias. This practice is itself an ancient one; we see it evinced in the massive (and endlessly entertaining) *Historia naturalis* of Pliny the Elder. More modern examples include the *Encyclopédie* of Diderot and the *Oxford English Dictionary*. The second tendency, the *selective*, focuses not on inclusivity but on exclusivity. It is true that the making of any list that does not pretend to completeness is by nature exclusionary, and that when time and space are limited, the inclusion of this author or title means that that one must be left out. By the same token, the demands of time within the academy (and, by extension and analogy, of human lifespan) require that choices be made. At Purdue, training in Comparative Literature at the M.A. level is that of basic competence in the student's own

---

[6] Knox 1993.

selection of areas: to use an optical metaphor, the view at this level is as if through a wide-angle lens. Later, at the Ph.D. level, the student switches as it were to a zoom lens, exploring her chosen areas in greater depth. For this reason, we set no fixed reading-lists for the doctoral level; each doctoral student draws up a set of reading-lists in consultation with her advisor or major professor, and is subsequently examined on these 'customized' lists. But at the M.A. level, we have striven to introduce some standardization within what is already an extraordinarily flexible and malleable system of choices.

I have asked my contributors to limit themselves strictly in drawing up their modules. In order for the M.A. student to be able to sit for written examinations (typically) by the end of her fourth semester of study, we have endeavored to keep each module within a realistic range — the equivalent, usually, of between thirty and forty books. Such a limit, even so, is quite ambitious and requires considerable discipline; it is understood that, under ordinary circumstances, a substantial number of these texts will have been studied as part of the student's coursework for the M.A.

In view of such merciless restrictions, many, many titles and authors of undeniable importance have had to be excluded. These choices must be thought of as reflecting not so much the personal predilections of the contributors as the instructions I gave them: namely, to put together a short list of items, in any given area, that the prospective Master of Arts in Comparative Literature absolutely ought to know. In certain cases the stipulation 'in Comparative Literature' may have led to specific inclusions (and thereby to exclusions) whose rationale might not be immediately obvious. This is certainly the case, for example, with the modules for Classical Studies: were I designing a reading-list for a straight M.A. in Greek, for example, I would probably not be inclined to make the *Cratylus* of Plato more of a priority than the whole of Thucydides. But, given its tremendous importance in the history of literary theory, the Platonic dialogue belongs indisputably in this module. Similarly, the modern Rhetoric list excludes many important items in composition-theory that any M.A. candidate *in Rhetoric* would be required to read; but this module is a Rhetoric list *for Comparative Literature*. Hence its peculiarities. The same could probably be said, *mutatis mutandis*, for a number of the other modules as well.

If, then, as Donne's verse has it, comparisons are odious, selection can only be more so. But in our defense — and I will say that I think my contributors have done a valiant and a splendid job of fulfilling their draconian charge — I can only say, first, that one must begin somewhere; second, that I am confident that these modules represent as good a place (or set of places) as any from which the budding comparatist might begin; and third, that we have not intended these lists to be graven in stone: they represent our best judgments at this point in time, in culture, and in the development of the discipline. In all likelihood we shall feel the need to revise them before too long; and, with any luck, we may also be able to add new modules as our own program grows. In the meantime, here we stand.

To return to the topic of canonicity. In the formation of what we now call literary canons,[7] there are (attendant upon the aggregative and selective tendencies I have already mentioned) a number of interactive phenomena, which include what we may call *judgment, preservation*, and *reproduction*.[8] By 'judgment' I mean the evaluation of whether a text is worth particular attention. It is inevitable that such judgments will be made; the question is by whom, and under what circumstances. By 'preservation' I mean the decision to retain a text for rereading; by 'reproduction' I mean the publication and dissemination of texts that have been preserved in the sense just explained. The salient question in

---

[7] This modern notion of the canon is substantially different from the ancient, as O'Sullivan 1997 perspicuously demonstrates.

[8] My discussion here, it will be seen, owes a certain debt to Guillory 1995.

connection with preservation and reproduction is *why* such actions are taken.

New acts of judgment follow upon preservation and reproduction; and so the circle continues. As Guillory well observes,

> ... the process we call canon-formation first appeared in ancient schools in connection with the social function of disseminating a knowledge of how to read and write. The selection of texts was a means to that end, not an end in itself. ... The problem of the canon is a problem of syllabus and curriculum, the institutional forms by which works are preserved as *great* works.'[9]

The academic problem of the canon today does not hinge on the question of basic literacy, but it indeed remains (to a great extent) a pedagogical one: What texts shall we teach to our students, and how, and why? Moreover, one of the most important aspects of a text's reception would be the history of its position in (or outside) the canon.

One would be hard-put to find a better articulation of the issues at stake than this by Edmund White:

> I myself am in favor of desacralizing literature, of dismantling the idea of a few essential books, of retiring the whole concept of the canon. A canon is for people who don't like to read, people who want to know the bare minimum of titles they must consume in order to be considered polished, well rounded, civilized. Any real reader seeks the names of more and more books, not fewer and fewer.
>
> The notion of a canon implies that we belong to something called Western Civilization that is built on a small sacred library and that that library is eternal and universal and important in the way no individual reader can ever be. I would say that every part of such an

[9] Guillory 1995:240 (emphasis his).

assumption is misguided.... Even the hierarchy inherent in the concept of a canon must be jettisoned.... the canon, even among the most conservative readers, shifts from one generation to the next. Look at the Harvard Five-Foot Shelf of Classics, once considered definitive. Few people today read Charles Dana's *Two Years Before the Mast* or Whittier's poetry, but for my grandparents such books were unquestionably canonical, as was *The Pilgrim's Progress* or William Dean Howell's *The Rise of Silas Lapham*.[10]

But despite all the recent ideological opposition that canonicity has received, the 'general reader' (if there is such a creature) persists in just this sort of exclusionary practice. If anything, as we approach the turn of the century, such activity has intensified. I would cite the following examples, all from within the past two years, as ready evidence:

• A major exhibition mounted by the New York Public Library, in which one hundred fifty-nine works were displayed in celebration of the Library's first one hundred years. For this exhibition, all the librarians on staff were asked to suggest books that 'had had a significant influence, consequence, or resonance during the Library's first 100 years.'[11] A commemorative volume was published, listing (with some alterations, based on the suggestions and objections of visitors to the exhibition) these books.[12]

• A book by David Denby, which reached the *New York Times* Best Seller List, that details his latter-day revisitation of his college studies at Columbia, and more specifically of a number of 'great books' such as the *Aeneid* of Vergil and the *Divine Comedy* of Dante.[13]

• A recent issue of the *New York Times Book Review* dedicated to its own hundredth anniversary, in which over seventy 'significant

[10] White 1994:375–376.
[11] Diefendorf 1996:4.
[12] Diefendorf 1996.
[13] Denby 1996.

reviews' from the *Review*'s first hundred years were reprinted. This issue, the first page proclaims, purports to celebrate '100 years … of Dostoyevsky, Conrad, Lawrence, Joyce, Freud, Kafka, Dreiser, Fitzgerald, Hemingway, Orwell, Salinger, Mailer, Bellow, Updike, Morrison, Rushdie, Woolf, Wolfe, Wolfe, Wolf and thousands more, authors who changed the world and authors the world forgot.'[14] A perusal of the table of contents, however, shows that the reviews reprinted are virtually without exception of books one might easily term canonical. And yet — and this is more to the point — even if they were not, the very act of including them in such an issue of the *Review* is one of canon-making.

• The fourth edition of Clifton Fadiman's *Lifetime Reading Plan* (coedited with John S. Major), listing and commenting on 233 items from Homer to Richard Wright.[15]

It seems to me that this exclusionary practice is one that comes from the heart, if not of our nature, then certainly of our culture: we are canon-making creatures. Whatever our feeling about canons, they are not about to go away.[16] For this reason, I maintain that the canon itself should be an important object of careful scrutiny for any student of Comparative Literature.

While we have consciously attempted *not* to reinscribe in *The Comparative Reader* a canon of writers who merely reiterate the

[14] McGrath 1996:1.
[15] Fadiman 1997.
[16] For more on the vexed issue of the canon, see (among many others) Fowler 1979, Fiedler 1981, Guillory 1993 and 1995, von Hallberg 1985, LaCapra 1989, Harris 1991, Lauter 1991, Bloom 1994, and Levine 1996. Some of the cultural issues at stake are examined in chapter 4 of Nussbaum 1997, which should be read by every single person interested in the study of Comparative Literature.

I should mention that some of my contributors have felt a certain discomfort with the whole list-making project, and generously agreed to humor me here only because of the specific needs of our own program. (One of them, Aparajita Sagar, took exception not only to the notion of lists, but also to my alternative approach to canonicity as outlined in these pages.) To these protestors I am especially grateful; and I want to make sure that their dissenting voices are duly noted.

dominant paradigm or hegemonic discourse of their own cultural milieux, we have also recognized that one must understand the dominant paradigm regardless of whether one proposes to embrace or to challenge it. Derrida, for example, did not undertake his deconstruction of Western metaphysics without first reading Plato and Aristotle — in Greek. Consequently, to those who wish to subvert the Canon, I would say: First you must know it, intimately, just as General Patton is said to have focused his attention each night on a portrait of Feldmarschall Rommel. To this end, and also for those of a stalwartly traditional cast, there is plenty of 'canonical' literature, Western and otherwise, represented in these modules — enough for the interested reader to be able to trace a history of a given culture's literary heritage.

At the same time, there are also plenty of non-canonical texts listed here. For those who are interested in reading 'against the grain' in a variety of ways, we have been careful to include authors and titles that have historically been chronically excluded from such curricula. Moreover — and the most traditional teachers of Comparative Literature may frown at this — we have included modules that represent *areas of study* rather than purely *national literatures* narrowly construed. The reasons for this, quite simply, are that students will want to focus on them, and that hiring institutions will want them to be able to teach them. In any case, these areas in particular — for example, Feminist Theories, Postcolonial Studies, or Queer Studies — are especially fruitful venues for the study of the subaltern. Those concerned with 'balance' will find some relief in the required 'Beginnings?' module, which ensures that every student will read some texts that are resolutely traditional. And, of course, those constructing programs of study along the most traditional lines are free to exclude the more avant-garde modules from their curricula.[17]

---

[17] For some historical sense of the disparate philosophies underpinning various approaches to Comparative Literature, the reader is directed to

As I have said, thirty-five or so items is a harsh limit to impose. Some educators may wish to paint with a broader stroke than we have done, augmenting each module and allowing the student some leeway in choosing which items to read. In the end, for the sake of simplicity and clarity, I opted not to take such a route in this list. There is nothing to stop the student from reading other titles in addition to those listed here! On the contrary, these modules should be considered as bare bones, as minimal guidelines, as springboards to further investigation — during doctoral study and beyond. There is nothing canonical or exclusionary about them in that sense. Indeed, nothing would delight me more than to learn that, having read one play by Sophocles, the student cannot resist reading the other six. When such things happen, you may be sure that the intellectual adventure is in full swing.

Acknowledgments

This book is obviously the work of many hands, and my first debt of thanks is to each of those contributors whose expertise these modules represent. Most of them are, or have been, Purdue faculty, who in virtually every case have/had a very real and substantial ongoing commitment to the education and nurturing or our Comparative Literature students; those students themselves best know the generosity and wisdom of their mentors. In addition to these, we have a number of distinguished contributors from other institutions. I am most grateful to these colleagues as well for sharing their expertise with us in this collaborative effort. We could not have produced the volume without their contributions.

In my role as editor of this volume, I am also indebted to the additional advice and assistance of a number of colleagues and friends. Certainly I am grateful to Djelal Kadir and Edith Clowes, my predecessors in the Purdue chair of Comparative Literature, as their own M.A. lists have served as a prototype for this one. For

---

(e.g.) Clements 1978; Koelb 1988; Guillén 1993; and the valuable collections of manifesti and essays in Bernheimer 1995 and Kadir 1995.

special additional thanks I must single out Beate Allert, Ann Astell, Becky Brown, Pat Curd, Connie Dunbar, Robert Freeman, Paul Halsall, Patty Hart, Grant King, Edward and Jean Kirby, Janice Lauer, Vincent Leitch, Howard Mancing, Floyd Merrell, Neil O'Sullivan, Carol Poster, Victor Raskin, Kip Robisch, Bill Rohlfing, Joe Salmons, Laura Salsini, Ed Schiappa, Deborah Starewich, Anthony Tamburri, and Pan Welland.

— *John T. Kirby*

WORKS CITED IN THE NOTES

Bernheimer, Charles (1995) ed. *Comparative Literature in the Age of Multiculturalism*. Baltimore: Johns Hopkins University Press.

Bloom, Harold (1994). *The Western Canon: The Books and School of the Ages*. NY: Harcourt Brace.

Clements, Robert J. (1978). *Comparative Literature as Academic Discipline: A Statement of Principles, Praxis, Standards*. NY: The Modern Language Association of America.

Danto, Arthur C. (1985). *Narration and Knowledge*. NY: Columbia University Press.

Denby, David (1996). *Great Books: My Adventures with Homer, Rousseau, Woolf, and Other Indestructible Writers of the Western World*. NY: Simon & Schuster.

Diefendorf, Elizabeth (1996) ed. *The New York Public Library's Books of the Century*. NY: Oxford University Press.

Fadiman, Clifton (1997) and John S. Major. *The New Lifetime Reading Plan: The Classic Guide to World Literature, Revised and Expanded*. NY: HarperCollins, 4th edition 1997.

Fiedler, L. (1981), and H. Baker, edd. *English Literature: Opening Up the Canon*. Baltimore: Johns Hopkins University Press.

Fisher, Walter R. (1987). *Human Communication as Narration: Toward a Philosophy of Reason, Value, and Action.* Columbia: University of South Carolina Press.

Fowler, Alastair (1979). 'Genre and the Literary Canon.' *New Literary History* 11:97–119.

Freedman, Jill (1996) and Gene Combs. *Narrative Therapy: The Social Construction of Preferred Realities.* NY: Norton.

Guillén, Claudio (1993). *The Challenge of Comparative Literature.* Cambridge MA: Harvard University Press.

Guillory, John (1993). *Cultural Capital: The Problem of Literary Canon Formation.* Chicago: University of Chicago Press.

— (1995). 'Canon.' Pp. 233–249 in Frank Lentricchia and Thomas McLaughlin, edd., *Critical Terms for Literary Study.* Chicago: University of Chicago Press 1990, 2nd edition 1995.

Hallberg, Robert von (1985) ed. *Canons.* Chicago: University of Chicago Press.

Harris, Wendell V. (1991). 'Canonicity.' *PMLA* 106:110–121.

Heller, Scott (1996). 'Rochester is Only University Offering Ph.D. in Visual Culture.' *The Chronicle of Higher Education*, 19 July 1996, p. A15.

Kadir, Djelal (1995) ed. *Comparative Literature: States of the Art.* Special issue of *World Literature Today* (69.2, Spring 1995).

Knox, Bernard M. W. (1993). *The Oldest Dead White European Males and Other Reflections on the Classics.* NY: Norton.

Koelb, Clayton (1988) and Susan Noakes, edd. *The Comparative Perspective on Literature: Approaches to Theory and Practice.* Ithaca: Cornell University Press.

LaCapra, Dominick (1989). *Soundings in Critical Theory.* Ithaca: Cornell University Press.

Lauter, Paul (1991). *Canons and Contexts.* NY: Oxford University Press.

Levine, Lawrence W. (1996). *The Opening of the American Mind: Canons, Culture, and History.* Boston: Beacon Press.

McGrath, Charles (1996) ed. *The New York Times Book Review*, 6 October 1996.

Nussbaum, Martha C. (1997). *Cultivating Humanity: A Classical Defense of Reform in Liberal Education*. Cambridge MA: Harvard University Press.

O'Sullivan, Neil (1997). 'Caecilius, The "Canons" of Writers, and the Origins of Atticism.' Pp. 32–49 in William J. Dominik, ed., *Roman Eloquence: Rhetoric in Society and Literature*. London: Routledge.

Ricœur, Paul (1984–1988). *Time and Narrative*. Three volumes. Chicago: University of Chicago Press.

Turner, Mark (1991). *Reading Minds: The Study of English in the Age of Cognitive Science*. Princeton: Princeton University Press.

— (1996). *The Literary Mind*. NY: Oxford University Press.

White, Edmund (1994). 'The Personal is Political: Queer Fiction and Criticism.' Pp. 367–377 in White, *The Burning Library: Essays*. NY: Random House.

Wilamowitz-Moellendorf, Ulrich von (1982). *History of Classical Scholarship*. Baltimore: Johns Hopkins University Press.

The Comparative Reader

'BEGINNINGS?' — A Sampling
of Foundational Texts
from a Variety of Ancient Cultures

The Epic of Gilgamesh [3 versions, ca. 1800–1000 BCE]. Transl. Maureen Gallery Kovacs. Stanford: Stanford University Press 1985.

Homer (Homêros, 8th century BCE). *Iliad: Homer*. Transl. Stanley Lombardo. Indianapolis: Hackett 1996.

— *The Odyssey of Homer*. Transl. Allen Mandelbaum. Berkeley: University of California Press 1990; Bantam edition 1991.

Lao Tzu (6th century BCE). *Tao Te Ching: A New English Version*. Transl. Stephen Mitchell. NY: HarperCollins 1988.

Confucius (K'ung Fu Tzu, 551–479 BCE). *The Analects*. Transl. D.C. Lau. NY: Penguin 1979.

Sophocles (Sophoklês, ca. 496–406 BCE). *Oedipus the King*. In *Sophocles: The Three Theban Plays*, transl. Robert Fagles. NY: Penguin 1984.

Plato (Platôn, ca. 427–347 BCE). *Phaedrus*. Transll. Alexander Nehamas and Paul Woodruff, in John M. Cooper and D. S. Hutchinson, edd., *Plato: Complete Works*. Indianapolis: Hackett 1997.

— *Republic*. Transl. Robin Waterfield. Oxford: Oxford University Press 1993.

— Seventh Letter. Transl. Glenn Morrow, in John M. Cooper and D. S. Hutchinson, edd., *Plato: Complete Works*. Indianapolis: Hackett 1997.

— *Symposium*. Transl. Robin Waterfield. Oxford: Oxford University Press 1994.

Aristotle (Aristotelês, 384–322 BCE). *Poetics*. Transl. Richard Janko. Indianapolis: Hackett 1987.

Bhagavad-Gita (ca. 200 BCE). Transl. Winthrop Sargeant. Albany: SUNY Press 1984.

Ramayana (ca. 200 BCE–200 CE). *The Ramayana of Valmiki: An Epic of Ancient India*. Transl. Robert P. Goldman. 4 volumes. Princeton: Princeton University Press 1984–1994. Read book 1, cantos 66–67; book 2, cantos 7–19; and book 6, cantos 106–110.

Catullus (Gaius Valerius Catullus, ca. 84–54 BCE). Read entire, in *The Poems of Catullus*, transl. C. H. Sisson (NY: Orion Press 1967); *The Poems of Catullus*, transl. Charles Martin (Baltimore: Johns Hopkins University Press 1989); or *The Poems of Catullus*, transl. Guy Lee (Oxford: Oxford University Press 1991).

Vergil (Publius Vergilius Maro, 70–19 BCE). *Aeneid*, transl. Robert Fitzgerald. NY: Random House 1981.

Horace (Quintus Horatius Flaccus, 65–8 BCE). *Odes*. Read entire, in *Horace: The Complete Odes and Epodes*, transl. W. G. Shepherd. NY: Penguin 1983.

Ovid (Publius Ouidius Naso, 43 BCE–?17 CE). *The Metamorphoses of Ovid*, transl. Allen Mandelbaum. San Diego: Harcourt Brace Jovanovich 1993.

Holy Bible, New International Version, (Grand Rapids: Zondervan). Read the following selections:

Hebrew Scriptures
Genesis 1–12, 19, 25, 27, 37, 39–45; Exodus 3–12, 20; Ruth (entire); 1 Samuel 8–10, 16; 2 Samuel 1–7; Esther (entire); Job (entire); Psalms 1, 2, 8, 14, 18–19, 22–24, 27, 42, 46–48, 51, 63, 84, 90, 98, 100, 110, 115, 121, 139; Proverbs (entire); Ecclesiastes (entire); Song of Songs (entire); Isaiah 1–6, 9, 40, 42–43, 53, 55, 60–61, 65; Jeremiah 25, 31, 33; Ezekiel 1–3, 37; Daniel 1–6, 12; Zechariah 9; Malachi 3.

Christian Scriptures
Luke 1–2; Matthew 1–7, 26–28; John (entire); Acts 1–4; Romans (entire); 1 Corinthians 13, 15; Ephesians 6; Philippians 4; Colossians 3; Hebrews (entire); James 2; Revelation (entire).

Qur'an [7th century CE]. *The Koran*, transl. N.J. Dawood. NY: Penguin 1993. Read *Suras* 1, 4, 5, 10, 12, 19, 55, 62, 71, 76.

The Thousand and One Nights [earliest Arabic version ca. 850 CE]. Read Prologue, 'Aladdin and the Enchanted Lamp,' and

Epilogue, in *Tales from the Thousand and One Nights*, ed. N. J. Dawood. NY: Penguin 1973. You may also use the unabridged *Book of the Thousand Nights and a Night* transl. Richard F. Burton (e.g. NY: Heritage Press 1962, 6 volumes in 3).

— *John T. Kirby*

AFRICA I: Contemporary Literatures of West Africa in English or in English Translation

---

Achebe, Chinua. *Things Fall Apart*. NY: Anchor Books 1994.

— *Arrow of God*. NY: Anchor Books 1969.

— *Girls at War and Other Stories*. London: Heinemann 1972.

— *Hopes and Impediments: Selected Essays*. NY: Doubleday 1989.

— and C. L. Innes, edd. *African Short Stories*. Portsmouth: Heinemann 1985.

Balogun, F. Odun. *Adjusted Lives: Stories of Structural Adjustments*. Trenton: Africa World Press 1995.

— *Tradition and Modernity in the African Short Story: An Introduction to a Literature in Search of Critics*. NY: Greenwood Press 1991.

Okpewho, Isidore. *Tides*. London: Longmans 1993.

Okri, Ben. *The Famished Road*. NY: Random House 1993.

— *Songs of Enchantment*. NY: Anchor Books 1993.

Emecheta, Buchi. *The Joys of Motherhood*. Portsmouth: Heinemann 1994.

Niane, D. T. *Sundiata: An Epic of Old Mali*. Transl. G.D. Pickett. London: Longmans 1986.

Aidoo, Ama Ata. *Dilemma of a Ghost and Anowa*. London: Longmans 1965.

— *No Sweetness Here: A Collection of Short Stories*. NY: Longmans 1979.

— *Changes: A Love Story*. NY: Feminist Press 1993.

Ajayi, Omofolabo Soyinka. *Yoruba Dance: The Semiotics of Movement and Yoruba Body Attitude*. Trenton: Africa World Press 1997.

Akwanya, Amechi. *Orimili*. Portsmouth: Heinemann 1991.

Armah, Ayi Kwei. *The Beautiful Ones Are Not Yet Born.* Portsmouth: Heinemann 1969.

Awoonor, Kofi. *This Earth, My Brother.* Portsmouth: Heinemann 1972.

Bâ, Mariama. *So Long a Letter.* Portsmouth: Heinemann 1981.

Echewa, T. Obinkaram. *The Crippled Dancer.* Portsmouth: Heinemann 1986.

Irele, Abiola. *The African Experience in Literature and Ideology.* Bloomington: Indiana University Press 1990.

Kane, Cheikh Hamidou. *Ambiguous Adventure.* Transl. Katherine Woods. Portsmouth: Heinemann 1972.

Nwapa, Flora. *Women Are Different.* Trenton: Africa World Press 1992.

Ousmane, Sembene. *God's Bits of Wood.* Transl. Francis Price. Portsmouth: Heinemann 1970.

Owomoyela, Oyekan, ed. *A History of Twentieth-Century African Literatures.* Lincoln: University of Nebraska Press 1993.

Oyono, Ferdinand. *Houseboy.* Transl. John Reed. Portsmouth: Heinemann 1966.

Ogundipe-Leslie, Molara. *Recreating Ourselves: African Women & Critical Transformations.* Trenton: Africa World Press 1994.

Soyinka, Wole. *Collected Plays 1: A Dance of the Forests, The Swamp Dwellers, The Strong Breed, The Road, The Bacchae of Euripides.* NY: Oxford University Press 1973.

— *Collected Plays 2: The Lion and the Jewel, Kongi's Harvest, The Trials of Brother Jero, Jero's Metamorphosis, Madmen and Specialists.* NY: Oxford University Press 1974.

— *Mandela's Earth and Other Poems.* New York: Random House, 1988.

Tutuola, Amos. *The Palm-Wine Drinkard and His Dead Palm-Wine Tapster in the Dead's Town.* NY: Grove Press 1953.

Also Recommended

Asante, Kariamu Welsh, ed. *African Dance: An Artistic, Historical and Philosophical Inquiry.* Trenton: Africa World Press, 1996.

Harrow, Kenneth W. *Thresholds of Change in African Literature: The Emergence of a Tradition.* Portsmouth: Heinemann 1995.

James, Adeola. *In Their Own Voices: African Women Writers Talk.* Portsmouth: Heinemann 1990.

Kennedy, Ellen Conroy. *The Negritude Poets.* NY: Thunder's Mouth Press 1989.

Kerr, David. *African Popular Theatre from Precolonial Times to the Present Day.* Portsmouth: Heinemann 1995.

Kestloot, Lilyan. *Black Writers in French: A Literary History of Negritude.* Washington: Howard University Press 1991.

Mortima, Mildred. *Journeys Through the French African Novel.* Portsmouth: Heinemann 1990.

Okpaku, Joseph, ed. *New African Literature and the Arts.* 2 volumes. NY: Thomas Y. Crowell 1970.

Okpewho, Isidore. *African Oral Literature: Backgrounds, Character, and Continuity.* Bloomington: Indiana University Press 1992.

Wilkinson, Jane. *Talking with African Writers: Interviews with African Poets, Playwrights & Novelists.* Portsmouth: Heinemann 1992.

— *Pierre-Damien Mvuyekure*

AFRICA II: Contemporary Literatures of East, Central, and Southern Africa in English or in English Translation

Abrahams, Peter. *Mine Boy*. Portsmouth: Heinemann 1963.

Beti, Mongo. *The Poor Christ of Bomba*. Portsmouth: Heinemann 1971.

Brutus, Dennis. *A Stubborn Hope: Selected Poems of South Africa & A Wider World*. Portsmouth: Heinemann 1991.

— *A Simple Lust*. Portsmouth: Heinemann 1973.

Chipasula, Frank. *Whispers in the Winds*. Portsmouth: Heinemann 1991.

Couto, Mia. *Every Man Is A Race*. Portsmouth: Heinemann 1995.

— *Voices Made Night*. Portsmouth: Heinemann 1990.

Gordimer, Nadine. *Crimes of Conscience*. Portsmouth: Heinemann 1991.

— *A Sport of Nature*. NY: Penguin 1987.

— *Selected Stories*. NY: Viking Press 1976.

— *Jump, and Other Stories*. NY: Farrar Straus Giroux 1991.

Head, Bessie. *Maru*. Portsmouth: Heinemann 1972.

— *A Question of Power*. Portsmouth: Heinemann 1974.

— *When Rain Clouds Gather*. Portsmouth: Heinemann 1969.

Hove, Chenjerai. *Bones*. Portsmouth: Heinemann 1990.

— *Shadows*. Portsmouth: Heinemann 1992.

Imbuga, Francis D. *Shrines of Tears*. Nairobi: Longmans 1993.

Laguma, Alex. *A Walk in the Night*. London: Heinemann 1967.

Liyong, Taban lo. *Frantz Fanon's Uneven Ribs*. London: Heinemann 1971.

— *Eating Chiefs: Luvo Culture from Lolwe to Malkal*. London: Heinemann 1970.

Lopes, Henri. *Tribaliks: Contemporary Congolese Stories*. Portsmouth: Heinemann 1988.

Mandela, Nelson. *No Easy Walk to Freedom*. Portsmouth: Heinemann 1973.

Mazrui, Ali A. *The Trial of Christopher Okigbo*. Portsmouth: Heinemann 1971.

Mofolo, Thomas. *Chaka*. Portsmouth: Heinemann 1981.

Mphahlele, Es'kia. *Voices in the Whirlwind*. NY: Hill & Wang 1972.

Mudimbe, V.Y. *The Invention of Africa: Gnosis, Philosophy, and the Order of Knowledge*. Bloomington: Indiana University Press 1988.

Mwangi, Meja. *The Cockroach Dance*. New York: Longmans 1979.

— *Striving for the Wind*. Portsmouth: Heinemann 1992.

Nagenda, John. *The Seasons of Thomas Tebo*. Portsmouth: Heinemann 1986.

Ndebele, Njabulo. *Fools and Other Stories*. NY: Longmans 1983.

Ngara, Emmanuel. *Ideology and Form in African Poetry: Implications for Communication*. Portsmouth: Heinemann 1990.

Ngugi, wa Thiong'O. *Devil on the Cross*. Portsmouth: Heinemann 1982.

— *A Grain of Wheat*. Portsmouth: Heinemann 1968.

— *Matigari*. Portsmouth: Heinemann 1989.

— *The River Between*. Portsmouth: Heinemann 1965.

— *Secret Lives*. Portsmouth: Heinemann 1975.

— *Weep Not Child*. Portsmouth: Heinemann 1964.

— *Decolonizing the Mind: The Politics of Language in African Literature*. Portsmouth: Heinemann 1986.

— *Moving the Center: The Struggle for Cultural Freedoms*. Portsmouth: Heinemann 1993.

Ogot, Grace. *The Promised Land*. Nairobi: East African Publishing House 1966.

p'Bitek, Okot. *Song of Lawino & Song of Ocol*. Portsmouth: Heinemann 1984.

Sam, Agnes. *Jesus Is Indian*. Portsmouth: Heinemann 1995.

Zwelonke, D. M. *Robben Island*. Portsmouth: Heinemann 1973.

Also Recommended: see the list appended to the 'Africa I' module.

— *Pierre-Damien Mvuyekure*

AFRICAN/AMERICAN STUDIES

Bennett, Lerone. *Before the Mayflower: A History of Black America*. Chicago: Johnson Publishing Company 1969, 6th edition 1987.

Boyd, Herb, and Robert Allen, edd. *Brotherman: The Odyssey of Black Men in America*. NY: Ballantine Books 1995.

Collins, Patricia Hill. *Black Feminist Thought: Knowledge, Consciousness, and the Politics of Empowerment*. NY: Routledge 1991.

Cooper, Anna Julia. *A Voice from the South* [1892]. NY: Oxford University Press 1988.

DuBois, W. E. B. *The Souls of Black Folk* [1903]. In Franklin, *Three Negro Classics*.

Ellison, Ralph. *Invisible Man*. NY: Random House 1952.

Fanon, Frantz. *Black Skin, White Masks*. NY: Grove Press 1967, 1991.

Franklin, John Hope, ed. *Three Negro Classics: Up from Slavery, Souls of Black Folk, and Autobiography of an Ex-Colored Man*. NY: Avon Books 1965.

Gates, Henry Louis, Jr., and Cornel West. *Future of the Race*. NY: Alfred A. Knopf 1996.

Giddings, Paula. *When and Where I Enter: The Impact of Black Women on Race and Sex in America*. NY: William Morrow 1984.

Guy-Sheftall, Beverly, ed. *Words of Fire: An Anthology of African American Feminist Thought*. NY: Norton 1995.

Hatch, James V., with Ted Shine, edd. *Black Theatre, U.S.A.: Forty-Five Plays by Black Americans, 1847–1974*. NY: Free Press 1974.

Hayes, Floyd, III, ed. *A Turbulent Voyage: Readings in African American Studies*. San Diego: Collegiate Press 1992.

Hill, Erroll, ed. *The Theatre of Black Americans: A Collection of Critical Essays*. 2 volumes. Englewood Cliffs: Prentice-Hall 1980.

hooks, bell. *Feminist Theory: From Margin to Center*. Boston: South End Press 1984.

Huggins, Nathan I. et al., edd. *Key Issues in the Afro-American Experience*. 2 volumes. NY: Harcourt Brace Jovanovich 1971.

Johnson, James Weldon. *Autobiography of an Ex-Colored Man* [1927]. In Franklin, *Three Negro Classics*.

Joy, James. *The Talented Tenth*. NY: Routledge 1996.

Karenga, Maulana. *Introduction to Black Studies*. Inglewood/Los Angeles: Kawaida Publications 1982, 1987.

Lerner, Gerda, ed. *Black Women in White America: A Documentary History*. NY: Vintage 1972.

Lewis, David Levering, ed. *The Portable Harlem Renaissance Reader*. NY: Viking 1994.

Lorde, Audre. *Sister Outsider: Essays and Speeches*. Freedom: The Crossing Press 1984.

Madhubuti, Haki R. *Black Men: Obsolete, Single, Dangerous? Afrikan American Familes in Transition: Essays in Discovery, Solution and Hope*. Chicago: Third World Press 1990.

Massey, Douglas, and Nancy A. Denton. *American Apartheid: Segregation and the Making of the Underclass*. Cambridge MA: Harvard University Press 1993.

Mohanty, Chandra Talpade, et al., edd. *Third World Women and the Politics of Feminism*. Bloomington: Indiana University Press 1991.

Morrison, Toni. *Beloved*. NY: Plume 1987.

Sapphire. *Push*. NY: Knopf 1996.

Vance, Carole S. *Pleasure and Danger: Exploring Female Sexuality*. Boston: Routledge and Kegan Paul 1984.

Washington, Booker T. *Up from Slavery* [1901]. In Franklin, *Three Negro Classics*.

Williams, Patricia J. *The Alchemy of Race and Rights*. Cambridge MA: Harvard University Press 1991.

Winant, Howard. *Racial Conditions: Politics, Theory, Comparisons*. Minneapolis: University of Minnesota Press 1994.

— *Carolyn E. Johnson*

AUSTRALIAN AND NEW ZEALAND
LITERATURES IN ENGLISH
(excluding Aboriginal and Maori literatures)

Reference Works (for consultation as needed)

Kramer, Leonie, ed. *The Oxford History of Australian Literature*. NY: Oxford University Press 1981.

— and Adrian Mitchell, edd. *The Oxford Anthology of Australian Literature*. NY: Oxford University Press 1985.

Sturm, Terry, ed. *The Oxford History of New Zealand Literature in English*. NY: Oxford University Press 1991.

I. Australian Literature

Fiction

Astley, Thea. *The Well Dressed Explorer*. Sydney: Angus and Robertson 1962.

Carey, Peter. *The Tax Inspector*. New York: Knopf 1992.

Franklin, Miles [Stella Maria Sarah Miles Franklin]. *My Brilliant Career* [1901]. Sydney: Angus and Robertson 1965.

Garner, Helen. *Monkey Grip*. New York: Seaview Books 1977, 1981.

— *True Stories*. Melbourne: Text Publishing 1996.

Herbert, Xavier. *Capricornia* [1937]. Hawthorn, Victoria: Lloyd O'Neil 1971.

Jolley, Elizabeth. *Stories*. NY: Penguin 1989.

Keneally, Thomas. *The Chant of Jimmie Blacksmith*. Sydney: Angus and Roberston 1972.

Lawson, Henry. *The Drover's Wife and Other Classic Stories*. Sydney: Angus and Roberston 1966, 1991.

Praed, Rosa. *Lady Bridget in the Never-Never Land* [1915]. NY: Pandora 1987.

Prichard, Katharine Susannah. *Coonardoo, The Well in the Shadow*. London: J. Cape 1929.

— *Happiness; Selected Short Stories*. Sydney: Angus and Robertson 1967.

Richardson, Henry Handel [Ethel Florence Lindesay Robertson]. *The Getting of Wisdom* [1910]. Port Melbourne: Minerva/Reed Books, 1977.

Stead, Christina. *The Man Who Loved Children* [1940]. NY: Avon Books 1966.

White, Patrick. *Voss*. NY: Penguin 1960.

— *The Burnt Ones*. NY: Viking Press 1964.

Poetry

Dawe, Bruce. *Beyond the Subdivisions*. Melbourne: Cheshire 1969.

Hope, A.D. [Alec Derwent]. *Collected Poems, 1930–1965*. NY: Viking Press 1966.

Malouf, David. *Neighbors in a Thicket*. St. Lucia, Queensland: University of Queensland Press 1974.

Murray, Les A. *The Daylight Moon*. Manchester: Carcanet 1988.

Paterson, A.B. ('Banjo'). 'The Man From Snowy River.' In *The Collected Verse of A.B. Paterson*. Sydney and London: Angus and Roberston 1946.

Slessor, Kenneth. *Poems*. Sydney: Angus and Robertson, 2nd edition 1957. Originally published in 1944 as *One Hundred Poems, 1919–1939*.

Wright, Judith. *Collected Poems 1942–1970*. Sydney: Angus and Robertson 1971.

II. New Zealand

Fiction

Ashton-Warner, Sylvia. *Spinster* [1958]. London: Virago 1980.

Frame, Janet. *The Lagoon: Short Stories*. Christchurch: Caxton Press 1951.

Mansfield, Katherine. *Bliss and Other Short Stories*. NY: Knopf 1923.

Sargeson, Frank. *Joy of the Worm*. London: MacGibbon and Kee 1969.

Shadbolt, Maurice. *The New Zealanders: A Sequence of Stories*. Christchurch: Whitcombe and Tombs 1959.

Poetry

Adcock, Fleur. *Selected Poems*. Oxford: Oxford University Press 1983.

Campbell, Alistair. *Collected Poems, 1947–1981*. Martinborough: A. Taylor 1981.

Curnow, Allen. *Allen Curnow, Selected Poems 1940–1989*. London: Penguin 1990.

Manhire, Bill. *Zoetropes: Poems 1972–1982*. Sydney: Allen and Unwin 1984.

— *Melissa Deutsch Scott*

BRITISH LITERATURE (Including Some Texts Written in English by Irish Writers)

Abbreviations

Ashfield = Ashfield, Andrew, ed. *Romantic Women Poets 1770–1838. An Anthology*. Manchester and NY: Manchester University Press, 1995.

Breen = Breen, Jennifer, ed. *Women Romantic Poets 1785–1832. An Anthology*. Everyman's Library. London: Dent; Rutland: Tuttle, 1992.

Ellmann = Ellmann, R., and R. O'Clair, edd. *The Norton Anthology of Modern Poetry*. 2nd edition. NY and London: Norton, 1988.

Ferguson = Ferguson, Margaret, et al., edd. *The Norton Anthology of Poetry*. 4th edition. NY and London: Norton, 1996.

Gilbert = Gilbert, Sandra M., and Susan Gubar, edd. *The Norton Anthology of Literature by Women: The Tradition in English*. 2nd edition. NY and London: Norton, 1996.

Lonsdale = Lonsdale, Roger, ed. *Eighteenth Century Women Poets. An Oxford Anthology*. Oxford and NY: Oxford University Press, 1990.

Lyric Poetry

Middle English Lyrics: Ferguson 13–16, 63–70.

Skelton, John (?1460–1529). Ferguson 65–67, and *The Oxford Book of Late Medieval Verse and Prose*, ed. Douglas Gray (Oxford: Clarendon Press 1985), 382–391.

Sidney, Sir Philip (1554–1568). Ferguson 188–199.

Shakespeare, William (1564–1616). Ferguson 234–249.

Lanyer, Aemelia (1569–1645). Susanne Woods, ed. *The Poems of Aemelia Lanyer*. Women Writers in English 1350–1850. Oxford: Oxford University Press 1993.

Donne, John (1572–1631). Ferguson 263–290.

Milton, John (1608–1674). Ferguson 354–379.

Pope, Alexander (1688–1744). Ferguson 539–577.

Gray, Thomas (1716–1771). Ferguson 606–613.
Yearsley, Ann (1752–1806). Ashfield 83–89.
Blake, William (1757–1827). Ferguson 670–684.
Williams, Helen Maria (?1762–1827). Ashfield 67–81.
Wordsworth, William (1770–1850). Ferguson 699–714, 721–737.
Wordsworth, Dorothy (1771–1855). Breen 128–134.
Coleridge, Samuel Taylor (1772–1834). Ferguson 739–763.
Hemans Felicia Dorothea (1793–1835). Ashfield 176–198.
Keats, John (1795–1821). Ferguson 831–850.
More, Hannah (1795–1833). Breen 10–24.
Browning, Elizabeth Barrett (1806–1861). Gilbert 373–406.
Tennyson, Alfred Lord (1809–1861). Ferguson 885–911.
Browning, Robert (1812–1889). Ferguson 911–941.
Arnold, Matthew (1822–1888). Ferguson 987–1000.
Hopkins, Gerard Manley (1844–1889). Ellmann 87–108.
Kipling, Rudyard (1865–1936). Ellmann 188–204.
Yeats, William Butler (1865–1939). Ellmann 133–188.
Owen, Wilfred (1893–1918). Ellmann 539–547.
Smith, Stevie (1902–1971). Ellmann 652–660.
Auden, W. H. (1907–1973). Ellmann 732–755.
Lewis, Alun (1915–1944). Ferguson 1466–1469.
Heaney, Seamus (1939–). Ellmann 1515–1534.
Atwood, Margaret (1939–). Gilbert 2215–2221.
Boland, Eavan (1944–). Gilbert 2295–2300.
Fenton, James (1949–). Ellmann 1656–1665.

Drama

Anonymous. *Everyman* (ca. 1490) in A. C. Cawley, ed. *Everyman and Medieval Miracle Plays.* Everyman's Library (new edition). London: Dent; Rutland: Tuttle, 1993.

Sackville, Thomas (1536–1608), and Thomas Norton (1532–1584). *Gorboduc, or Ferrex and Porrex.* In Russell A. Fraser and Norman Rabkin, edd., *Drama of the English Renaissance.* Volume 1: The Tudor Period. NY and London: Macmillan, 1976.

Marlowe, Christopher (1564–1593). *The Tragical History of Doctor Faustus.* In David Bevington and Eric Rassmussen, edd., *Doctor Faustus and Other Plays.* The World's Classics. Oxford: Oxford University Press, 1995.

Shakespeare, William (1564–1616). *The Tragedy of Hamlet Prince of Denmark*. In G. Blakemore Evans et al., edd. *The Riverside Shakespeare*. Boston: Houghton Mifflin 1974.

— *The Tempest*. In G. Blakemore Evans et al., edd., *The Riverside Shakespeare*. Boston: Houghton Miflin 1974.

Jonson, Ben (1572–1637). *Volpone, or The Fox*. In Gordon Campbell, ed., *The Alchemist and Other Plays*. The World's Classics. Oxford: Oxford University Press, 1995.

Wycherly, William (1641–1715). *The Country Wife*. In Peter Dixon, ed., *The Country Wife and Other Plays*. The World's Classics. Oxford: Oxford University Press, 1996.

Gay, John (1685–1732). *The Beggar's Opera*. Edd. Bryan Loughrey and T. O. Treadwell. Penguin Classics. London and NY: Penguin 1987.

Sheridan, Richard Brinsley (1751–1816). *The School for Scandal*. In Eric S. Rump, ed., *The School for Scandal and Other Plays*. Penguin Classics. London and NY: Penguin 1988.

Synge, J. M. (1871–1909). *Riders to the Sea*. In Ann Saddlemeyer, ed., *The Playboy of the Western World and Other Plays*. The World's Classics. Oxford: Oxford University Press, 1995.

Beckett, Samuel (1906–1989). *Endgame*. In *Endgame and Act Without Words*. NY: Grove, 1983.

Osborne, John (1929–). *Look Back in Anger*. In *Look Back in Anger and Other Plays*. Collected Plays, volume 1. NY and Boston: Faber and Faber 1993.

Pinter, Harold (1930–). *The Homecoming*. In *Complete Works: Three*. An Evergreen Book. NY: Grove Weidenfeld 1990.

Kureishi, Hanif (1948–). *Borderline*. In *Outskirts and Other Plays*. London and Boston: Faber and Faber 1992.

Long Narrative Verse

Anonymous (ca. 950 CE). *Beowulf*. In Ruth P. Lehman, transl. *Beowulf: An Imitative Translation*. Austin: University of Texas Press 1988.

— (ca. 1350). *Sir Gawain and the Green Knight*. Transl. Brian Stone. Penguin Classics. NY: Penguin.

Chaucer, Geoffrey (ca. 1343–1400). *The Canterbury Tales*. In Larry D. Benson et al., edd., *The Riverside Chaucer*. Third edition. Boston: Houghton Mifflin 1987. Read: 'The General Prologue'; 'The

Miller's Prologue and Tale'; 'The Wife of Bath's Prologue and Tale'; 'The Pardoner's Prologue and Tale.'

Spenser, Edmund (1552–1599). *The Faerie Queene*, books 1 and 2. In Thomas P. Roche with C. Patrick O'Connell, Jr., edd. *The Faerie Queene*. Penguin Classics. NY: Penguin 1987.

Milton, John (1608–1674). *Paradise Lost*, books 1, 2, and 9. In Stephen Orgel and Jonathan Goldberg, edd., *John Milton*. Oxford Authors. Oxford: Oxford University Press 1991.

Wordsworth, William (1770–1850). *The Prelude* (1805), books 1, 2, 9, and 10. In Jonathan Wordsworth, M. H. Abrams, and Stephen Gill, edd., *The Prelude: 1799, 1805, 1850*. NY and London Norton 1979.

Long Narrative Prose

Behn, Aphra (?1640–1689). *Oroonoko, or The History of a Royal Slave* (1688). In Paul Salzman, ed., *Oroonoko and Other Writings*. The World's Classics. Oxford: Oxford University Press 1994.

Swift, Jonathan (1667–1745). *Gulliver's Travels*. Ed. Paul Turner. The World's Classics. Oxford: Oxford University Press 1987.

Richardson, Samuel (1689–1761). *Pamela; or Virtue Rewarded*. Ed. Peter Sabor. Penguin Classics. NY: Penguin [1981].

Fielding, Henry (1707–1754). *The History of Tom Jones*. Ed. R. P. C. Mutter. Penguin Classics. NY: Penguin 1985.

Sterne, Laurence (1713–1768). The Life and Opinions of Tristram Shandy, Gentleman. Ed. Ian Campbell Ross. The World's Classics. Oxford: Oxford University Press 1983.

Equiano, Olaudah (ca. 1745–1797). *The Interesting Narrative of Olaudah Equiano Written by Himself*. Ed. Robert J. Allison. Bedford Series in History and Culture. Boston: Bedford Books of St Martin's Press, 1995.

Radcliffe, Anne (1764–1823). *The Mysteries of Udolpho*. Ed. Bonamy Dobrée with Frederick Carter. The World's Classics. Oxford: Oxford University Press 1980.

Austen, Jane (1775–1817). *Emma*. Ed. Terry Castle. The World's Classics. Oxford: Oxford University Press 1995.

Dickens, Charles (1812–1870). *Our Mutual Friend*. Ed. Michael Cotsell. The World's Classics. Oxford: Oxford University Press 1990.

Eliot, George (1819–1880). *Middlemarch*. Ed. David Carroll. The World's Classics. Oxford: Oxford University Press 1988.

Conrad, Joseph (1857–1924). *Heart of Darkness.* In Cedric Watts, ed., *The Heart of Darkness and Other Tales.* The World's Classics. Oxford: Oxford University Press 1990.

Joyce, James (1882–1941). *Ulysses: The Corrected Text.* Edd. Hans Walter Gabler et al. NY: Vintage 1986.

Woolf, Virginia (1882–1941). *Orlando: A Biography.* A Harvest Book. NY: Harcourt Brace [1973]).

Byatt, A. S. (1936–). *Possession: A Romance.* NY: Random House 1990.

— *Shaun F. D. Hughes*

CANADIAN LITERATURES
in English or in English Translation

Reference Works (for consultation as needed) and Abbreviations

Atwood = Atwood, Margaret, and Robert Weaver, edd. *The New Oxford Book of Canadian Short Stories*. Oxford: Oxford University Press 1995.

Black = Black, Ayanna, ed. Voices: *Canadian Writers of African Descent*. NY: HarperCollins 1992.

Cagnon, Maurice. *The French Novel of Quebec*. Boston: Twayne 1986.

Doucette = Doucette, L.E., ed. and transl. *The Drama Out of Our Past: Major Plays from Nineteenth Century Quebec*. Toronto: University of Toronto Press 1984.

Jones, Joseph, and Johanna Jones. *Canadian Fiction*. Boston: Twayne 1981.

King = King, Thomas, ed. *All My Relations: An Anthology of Contemporary Canadian Native Fiction*. Norman: University of Oklahoma Press 1992.

Mackenzie, W. Roy. *Ballads and Sea Songs from Nova Scotia*. Hatboro: Folklore Associates 1963.

New, W.H. *A History of Canadian Literature*. NY: New Amsterdam 1989.

Petrone, Penny. *Native Literature in Canada: From the Oral Tradition to the Present*. Toronto: Oxford University Press 1990.

Roy = Roy, G.R., ed. and transl. *Twelve Modern French Canadian Poets*. Westport: Greenwood Press 1976.

Smith = Smith, A.J. M., ed. *The Oxford Book of Canadian Verse*. Toronto: Oxford University Press 1983.

Story, Norah. *The Oxford Companion to Canadian History and Literature*. Toronto: Oxford University Press 1967.

Teleky = Teleky, Richard, ed. *The Oxford Book of French-Canadian Short Stories*. Toronto: Oxford University Press 1983.

Tougas, Gerard. *History of French Canadian Literature*. Transl. Alta Lind Cook. Westport: Greenwood Press 1976.

Weiss, Jonathan. *French-Canadian Theater*. Boston: Twayne 1986.

Criticism

Atwood, Margaret. *Survival: A Thematic Guide to Canadian Literature*. Toronto: McClelland & Stewart 1996.

Frye, Northrop. *The Bush Garden: Essays on the Canadian Imagination*. Toronto: Anansi 1971.

Staines, David, ed. *The Canadian Imagination: Dimensions of a Literary Culture*. Cambridge MA: Harvard University Press 1977.

Wilson, Edmund. *O Canada: An American's Notes on Canadian Culture*. NY: Farrar, Straus and Giroux 1964.

Fiction

Armstrong, Jeanette. 'This is a Story.' King 129–135.

Atwood, Margaret. *Surfacing*. Toronto: McClelland & Stewart 1972.

— 'True Trash.' Atwood 247–266.

Bissoondath, Neil. 'Digging Up the Mountains.' Atwood 421–435.

Blais, Marie-Claire. *A Season in the Life of Emmanuel*. Transl. Derek Coltman. NY: Farrar, Straus and Giroux 1966.

Blue Cloud, Peter. 'Weaver Spider's Web.' King 46–47.

Brand, Dionne. 'Sans Souci.' Atwood 390–397.

Callaghan, Morley. 'All the Years of Her Life.' Atwood 9–13.

Clarke, Austin. 'Letter of the Law Black.' Black 45–55.

Cohen, Leonard. *Beautiful Losers*. Toronto: McClelland & Stewart 1966.

Duncan, Sara Jeanette. *The Imperialist*. Toronto: McClelland & Stewart 1990.

Far, Sui Sin. *Mrs Spring Fragrance and Other Writings*. Edd. Amy Ling and Annette White-Parks. Read pp. 17–41, 66–82, 198–210.

Ferron, Jacques. *Quince Jam*. Transl. Ray Ellenwood. Toronto: Coach House 1977.

Gallant, Mavis. *The Collected Stories of Mavis Gallant*. NY: Random House 1996. Read 'A Day Like Any Other,' 'My Heart is Broken,' 'An Unmarried Man's Summer,' 'The Remission,' 'Ice Wagon Going Down the Street,' 'Linnet Muir.'

Hébert, Anne. 'The Torrent.' Teleky 115–151.

Jasmin, Claude. 'Lulu the Tailor.' Teleky 225–233.

Johnston, Basil H. 'Summer Holidays in Spanish.' King 201–212.

Kattan, Naim. 'The Neighbor.' Teleky 197–203.

Laurence, Margaret. *The Diviners*. Toronto: McClelland & Stewart 1974.

— *The Stone Angel*. Toronto: McClelland & Stewart 1964.

Marchessault, Jovette. 'Song One: The Riverside.' King 175.

Montgomery, Lucy Maud. *Anne of Green Gables*. Toronto: McClelland & Stewart 1989.

Munro, Alice. *The Progress of Love*. Toronto: McClelland & Stewart 1986. Read 'White Dump' and 'The Progress of Love.'

Richler, Mordecai. *The Apprenticeship of Duddy Kravitz*. Toronto: McClelland & Stewart 1974.

Robinson, Hart. 'An Okanagan Indian Becomes a Captive Circus Showpiece in England.' King 1–26.

Ross, Sinclair. *The Lamp at Noon and Other Stories*. Toronto: McClelland & Stewart 1987. Read 'The Lamp at Noon' and 'A Field of Wheat.'

Roy, Gavrielle. *The Tin Flute*. Toronto: McClelland & Stewart 1959.

Tremblay, Michel. 'The Devil and the Mushroom.' Teleky 254–261.

Drama

Davies, Robertson. *At My Heart's Core [and] Overlaid*. Toronto: Simon & Pierre 1991.

Frechette, Louis-Honoré. 'Felix Poutre: A Historical Drama in Five Acts.' Doucette 183–229.

Mair, Charles. *Tecumseh: A Drama*. Toronto: Radisson Society of Canada 1926.

Quesnel, Joseph. 'Anglomania, or Dinner, English-Style.' Doucette 1–31.

Reaney, James. *Colours in the Dark*. Toronto: Macmillan 1961.

Poetry

Atwood, Margaret. *The Journals of Susanna Moodie*. Oxford: Oxford University Press 1970.

Birney, Earle. Smith 219–229.

Charpentier, Gabriel. Roy 3–9.

Crawford, Isabelle Valency. Smith 44–53.

Dumont, Fernand. Roy 11–17.

Garneau, Saint-Dénis. Roy 27–33.

Hébert, Anne. Roy 61–65.

Hine, Daryl. Smith 424–430.

Lampman, Archibald. Smith 71–80.

Layton, Irving. Smith 304–309.

Legris, Isabel. Roy 85–91.

MacKay, L.A. Smith 203–205.

McLachlan, Alexander. Smith 11–12.

McPherson, Jay. Smith 410–413.

Ogundipe-Leslie, Molara. Black 1–5.

Ouellette, Fernand. Roy 93–99.

Pratt, E.J. *Towards the Last Spike: A Verse-Panoraman of the Struggle to Build the First Canadian Transcontinental from the Time of the Proposed Union with British Columbia (1870) to the Hammering of the Last Spike in Eagle Pass (1885)*. Toronto: Macmillan 1952.

Purdy, Al. Selected Poems. Toronto: McClelland & Stewart 1972.

Ross, W.W.E. Smith 175–178.

Scott, Duncan Campbell. Smith 93–104.

Wilkinson, Anne. Smith 279–287.

Nonfiction

Adams, Howard. *Prison of Grass: Canada from a Native Point of View*. Saskatoon: Fifth House Publishers 1975.

Berton, Pierre. *The Impossible Railway: The Building of the Canadian Pacific*. NY: Knopf 1972.

Campbell, Maria. *Halfbreed*. Toronto: McClelland & Stewart 1973.

Leacock, Stephen. *The Bodley Head Leacock*. Ed. J.B. Priestley. London: The Bodley Head 1957. Read (from *Literary Lapses*) 23–24; (from *Sunshine Sketches*) 97–146; 'The New Education,' 323–329.

Moodie, Susanna. *Roughing It in the Bush, or, Forest Life in Canada*. Toronto: McClelland & Stewart 1970.

McLuhan, Marshall. *The Essential McLuhan*. NY: Basic Books 1995.

Mowat, Farley. *The World of Farley Mowat*. Ed. Peter Davison. Boston: Little, Brown & Co. 1980.

Traill, Catherine Parr. *The Backwoods of Canada: Being Letters from the Wife of an Emigrant Officer Illustrative of the Domestic Economy of British America*. Toronto: McClelland & Stewart 1989.

— *Carol Poster*

CELTIC LITERATURES I:
Irish and Scottish

Reference Works (for consultation as needed) and Abbreviations

Bradley = Bradley, Anthony, ed. *Contemporary Irish Poetry: An Anthology*. Berkeley: University of California Press 1980.

Craig, Cairns, ed. *The History of Scottish Literature. Volume 4: Twentieth Century*. Aberdeen: Aberdeen University Press 1987.

Deane = Deane, Seamus, ed. *The Field Day Anthology of Irish Writing*. 3 volumes. Derry: Field Day Publications 1991.

Gifford, Douglas, ed. *The History of Scottish Literature. Volume 3: Nineteenth Century*. Aberdeen: Aberdeen University Press 1987.

Harrington = Harrington, John T., ed. *Modern Irish Drama*. NY: W.W. Norton & Co. 1991.

Hart, Francis Russell. *The Scottish Novel from Smollett to Spark*. Cambridge MA: Harvard University Press 1978.

Hook, Andrew, ed. *The History of Scottish Literature. Volume 2: 1660–1800*. Aberdeen: Aberdeen University Press 1987.

Jack, R.D.S., ed. *The History of Scottish Literature. Volume 1: Medieval and Renaissance*. Aberdeen: Aberdeen University Press 1987.

Mercier = Mercier, Vivian, ed. Great Irish Short Stories. NY: Dell 1964.

Watson, Roderick. *The Literature of Scotland*. NY: Schocken Books 1985.

I. Irish Literature

Selections from Deane (Various Genres)

Volume 1: Pages 1–223, 274–394, 465–499, 662–670, 726–745, 816–821, 993–997, 1053–1079, 1070–1300.

Volume 2: Pages 1–114, 516–541, 556–561, 720–830, 950–963.

Volume 3: Pages 20–22, 49–170, 380–680.

Fiction

Carleton, William. 'The Horse Stealers.' Mercier 74.

Edgeworth, Maria. *Castle Rackrent*. NY: Garland 1978.

Joyce, James. *A Portrait of the Artist as a Young Man*. Boston: Bedford Books of St Martin's Press 1993.

Lavin, Mary. 'Brigid,' 'The Nun's Mother.' Mercier 329–356.

Moore, George. 'Julia Cahill's Curse,' 'So On He Fares.' Mercier 106–123.

Muirchu Maccu Mactheni, 'How St Patrick Obtained Armagh.' Mercier 19–22.

O'Brien, Flann. *At Swim Two Birds*. London: McGibbon & Kee 1960.

Ó Conaire, Pádraic. 'The Woman on Whom God Laid His Hand.' Mercier 191–201.

O'Connor, Frank. 'Peasants,' 'The Man of the World.' Mercier 279–296.

O'Faolin, Sean. 'The Fur Coat,' 'Two of a Kind.' Mercier 261–278.

O'Flaherty, Liam. 'Lovers,' 'The Blow.' Mercier 237–260.

Stephens, James. 'Three Women Who Wept.' Mercier 202–214.

Drama

Beckett, Samuel. *Waiting for Godot*. NY: Grove Press 1956.

Behan, Brendan. *The Quare Fellow*. Harrington 255–310.

Boucicault, Dion. *London Assurance*. NY: Norton 1984.

Gregory, Lady Isabella Augusta. *Spreading the News*. Harrington 108–150.

O'Casey, Sean. *Juno and the Peacock*. Harrington 204–253.

Synge, John Millington. *The Playboy of the Western World*. Harrington 73–118.

Yeats, William Butler. *Collected Plays of W.B. Yeats*. London: Macmillan 1934. Read *The Only Jealously of Emer, Cathleen ni Houlihan*, and *A Full Moon in March*.

Epic/Mythology/Folktale

Gregory, Lady Isabella Augusta, transl. and arr. *Gods and Fighting Men: The Story of the Tuatha De Danaan and of the Fianna of Ireland*. NY: Scribner's 1904. Read pp. 1–15, 73–120, 159–247, and 430–460.

Leahy, A.H. *Heroic Romances of Ireland*. NY: Lemma Publishing Co. 1974. Read 'The Sick-Bed of Cuchulain.'

Poetry
Boland, Eavan. Bradley 343–348.

Clarke, Austin. Bradley 37–60.

Fallon, Padraic. Bradley 78–87.

Hartnett, Michael. Bradley 296–309.

Heaney, Seamus. *Sweeney Astray.* London: Faber & Faber 1983.

— (in) Bradley 260–278.

Kavanaugh, Patrick. Bradley 66–77.

Kinsella, Thomas. Bradley 176–197.

Mahon, Derek. Bradley 310–325.

Montague, John. Bradley 198–224.

Muldoon, Paul. Bradley 375–380.

Murphy, Richard. *The Battle of Aughrim and The God Who Eats Corn.* London: Faber & Faber 1968. Read 'The Battle of Aughrim.'

Ni Chuilleanain, Eilean. Bradley 326–331.

O'Connor, Frank. Bradley 61–65.

O'Grady, Desmond. Bradley 249–254.

Prose (fiction and nonfiction)
Gregory, Lady Isabella Augusta. 'Our Irish Theatre.' Harrington 377–385.

Moore, George. *Hail and Farewell.* Ed. Richard Cave. Toronto: Macmillan 1976.

II. Scottish Literature

Fiction
Dunn, Douglas, ed. *The Oxford Book of Scottish Short Stories.* Oxford: Oxford University Press 1995.

Hogg, James. *The Private Memoirs and Confessions of a Justified Sinner.* Oxford: Oxford University Press 1969.

Scott, Sir Walter. *The Heart of Midlothian.* NY: E.P. Dutton 1961.

Stevenson, Robert Louis. *Kidnapped.* NY: Dodd, Mead & Co. 1949.

Drama
Brown, Ian, and Mark Fisher. *Made in Scotland: An Anthology of New Scottish Plays.* London: Methuen 1995.

Hayward, Brian. *Galoshins: The Scottish Folk Play*. Edinburgh: Edinburgh University Press 1992.

Tobin, Terence. *Plays by Scots 1660–1800*. Iowa City: University of Iowa Press 1974.

Poetry

Kerrigan, Catherine, ed. *An Anthology of Scottish Women Poets*. Edinburgh: Edinburgh University Press 1991.

Kratzmann, Gregory, ed. *Colkelbie Sow and the Talis of the Fyve Bestes*. NY: Garland 1983.

Macpherson, James. *The Poems of Ossian and Related Works*. Edinburgh: Edinburgh University Press 1996.

Scott, Tom, ed. *The Penguin Book of Scottish Verse*. Harmondsworth: Penguin 1970.

Prose (fiction and nonfiction)

Mackenzie, Agnes Mure, ed. *A Garland of Scottish Prose*. Glasgow: The House of Grant 1956.

Muir, Edmund. *Scot and Scotland: The Predicament of the Scottish Writer*. London: Routledge & Sons 1936.

— *Carol Poster*

CELTIC LITERATURES II:
Breton, Cornish, Manx, Welsh

Reference Works (for consultation as needed) and Abbreviations

Arnold, Matthew. *On the Study of Celtic Literature and Other Essays.* NY: E.P. Dutton 1916. Read 'On the Study of Celtic Literature.'

Sharp = Sharp, E.A., and J. Matthay, edd. *Lyra Celtica: An Anthology of Representative Celtic Poetry.* Edinburgh: John Grant 1932.

Rhys, John. *Celtic Folklore: Welsh and Manx.* 2 volumes. Oxford: The Clarendon Press 1901.

I. Breton Literature

Anonymous. Early Breton Poems: 'The Dance of the Sword,' The Lord Nan and the Fairy, 'Alain the Fox,' 'Bran.' Sharp 53–63.

— Medieval Breton Poems: 'The Poor Clerk,' 'The Secrets of the Clerk,' 'Love Song.' Sharp 331–337.

Helias, Pierre-Jakez. *The Horse of Pride: Life in a Breton Village.* Transl. and abridged by June Guicharnaud. New Haven: Yale University Press 1978.

Hervé-Noël le Breton. 'Hymn to Sleep,' 'The Burden of Lost Souls.' Sharp 338–341.

Le Braz, Anatole. *The Land of Pardons.* Transl. Frances M. Gostling. London: Methuen 1906.

Leo-Kermorvan. 'The Return of Taliessin.' Sharp 348–350.

Souvestre, Emile. *Popular Legends of Brittany.* Translated by a Lady. Boston: Crosby, Nichols, & Co. 1859.

Rumble, Thomas C. *The Breton Lays in Middle English.* Detroit: Wayne State University Press 1965.

Tiercelin, Thomas C. 'By Menec'hi Shore.' Sharp 351.

Timma, Lenora, ed. and transl. *A Modern Breton Political Poet: Anjela Duval. A Biography and Anthology.* Lewiston: Edwin Mellen Press 1990.

Weingartner, Russell, ed. and transl. *Graelent and Guingamor: Two Breton Lays.* NY: Garland 1985.

II. Cornish Literature

Primary

Anonymous. 'Merlin the Diviner,' 'The Pool of Pilate.' Sharp 44–46.

Harris, Markham, transl. *The Cornish Ordinalia: A Medieval Dramatic Trilogy.* Washington: Catholic University of America Press 1969.

— transl. *The Life of Meriasek: A Medieval Cornish Miracle Play.* Washington: Catholic University of America Press 1977.

Hawker, Stephen. 'Featherstone's Doom,' 'Trebarrow.' Sharp 319–320.

Neuss, Paula, ed. and transl. *The Creacion of the World: A Critical Edition and Translation.* NY: Garland 1983.

Quiller-Couch, A.T. 'The Splendid Spur,' 'The White Moth.' Sharp 317–318.

Rowse, A.L. *A Cornish Childhood.* London: Jonathan Cape 1942.

— ed. *A Cornish Anthology.* London: Macmillan 1968.

Stephens, Ricardo. 'Witch Margaret,' 'A Ballad,' 'Hell's Piper.' Sharp 312–328.

Secondary

Ellis, P. Berresford. *The Cornish Language and Its Literature.* London: Routledge and Kegan Paul 1974.

Murdoch, Brian. *Cornish Literature.* Cambridge: D.S. Brewer 1993.

III. Manx Literature

Primary

Brown, Thomas Edward. *The Poems of T.E. Brown.* Liverpool: University Press of Liverpool 1952.

— *The Letters of Thomas Edward Brown.* Ed. Sidney T. Irwin. Liverpool: University Press of Liverpool 1952.

Caine, Hall. 'Graih my Chree.' Sharp 309–314.

— *The Manxman.* NY: D. Appleton & Co. 1895.

— *The Deemster: A Romance of the Isle of Man.* Chicago: Rand, McNally & Co. 1894.

— *My Story.* NY: D. Appleton & Co. 1908.

Clague, John. *Cooinaghtyn Manninagh: Manx Reminiscences.* Castletown: M.J. Blackwell 1911.

Secondary

Sutton, Max Keith. *The Drama of Storytelling in T.E. Brown's Manx Yarns.* Newark: University of Delaware Press 1991.

Tobias, Richard C. *T.E. Brown.* Boston: Twayne 1978.

IV. Welsh Literature

Primary

Clancy, Joseph P, ed. *Medieval Welsh Lyrics.* NY: St Martin's Press 1965. Read pp. 107–270.

— ed. *The World of Kate Roberts. Selected Stories 1925–1981.* Philadelphia: Temple University Press 1991.

Dafydd ap Gwilym. *The Poems.* Transl. and comm. Richard Morgan Loomis. Binghamton: Medieval and Renaissance Texts Society 1982.

Ford, Patrick K., transl. *The Mabinogi and Other Medieval Welsh Tales.* Berkeley: University of California Press 1977.

Garlick, Raymond, and Roland Mathias, edd. *Anglo-Welsh Poetry 1480–1990.* Bridgend: Seren Books 1982.

Gruffydd, W.J. *The Years of the Locust.* Transl. D. Myrddin Lloyd. Llandysul: Gomer Press 1976.

Jones, Gwyn. *The Oxford Book of Welsh Verse in English.* Oxford: Oxford University Press 1977.

— and Islwyn Ffowc Elis, edd. *Classic Welsh Short Stories.* Oxford: Oxford University Press 1992.

McKenna, Catherine A. *The Medieval Welsh Religious Lyric: Poems of the Gogynfeirdd, 1137–1282.* Belmont: Fors & Bailie Publishers 1991.

Thomas, Dylan. *Under Milk Wood.* NY: New Directions 1954.

— *The Collected Stories*. NY: New Directions 1971. Read 'A Child's Christmas in Wales.'

Secondary

Breeze, Andrew. *Medieval Welsh Literature*. Dublin: Four Courts Press 1997.

Jarman, A.O.H., and Gwilym Rees Hughes, edd. *A Guide to Welsh Literature*. 2 volumes. Swansea: Christopher Davies 1979.

— Carol Poster

CHINESE LITERATURE, Traditional and Modern

Reference Works (for consultation as needed)

C.T. Hsia, C. T. *The Classic Chinese Novel.* NY: Columbia University Press 1968.

— *A History of Modern Chinese Fiction.* New Haven: Yale University Press, 2nd edition 1971.

Nienhauser, William H., Jr., ed. *Indiana Companion to Traditional Chinese Literature.* Bloomington: Indiana University Press 1986.

I. Traditional Chinese Literature

Suggested anthologies of English translations (other translations to be used as noted in the list):

Birch, Cyril, ed. *Anthology of Chinese Literature.* 2 volumes. NY: Grove Press 1972.

— ed. *Stories from a Ming Collection.* NY: Grove Press 1958.

Chaves, Jonathan, transl. *The Columbia Book of Later Chinese Poetry: Yüan, Ming and Ch'ing Dynasties (1279-1911).* NY: Columbia University Press 1986.

Kao, Karl S. Y., ed. *Classical Chinese Tales of the Supernatural and the Fantastic.* Bloomington: Indiana University Press 1985.

Waley, Arthur, transl. *Chinese Poems.* London: Unwin Books 1961.

Ma, Y. W., and Joseph S. M. Lau, edd. *Traditional Chinese Stories: Themes and Variations.* NY: Columbia University Press 1978.

Mair, Victor H., ed. *The Columbia Anthology of Traditional Chinese Literature.* NY: Columbia University Press 1994.

Owen, Stephen, ed. and transl. *An Anthology of Chinese Literature: Beginnings to 1911.* NY: Norton 1996.

Watson, Burton, transl. *The Columbia Book of Chinese Poetry: From Early Times to the Thirteenth Century.* NY: Columbia University Press 1984.

Poetry (i): Shih *Poetry*

Shih-ching (*The Book of Songs*). For translations, see Arthur Waley, transl., *The Book of Songs* (NY: Grove Press 1985). Read 'Kuan chü' (no. 1), 'Ye yu ssu chün' (no. 23), 'Mang' (no. 58), 'Hsi yu ch'ang-ch'u' (no. 148), 'Huang niao' (no. 131), 'Shuo shu' (no. 113), 'Ch'i yüeh' (no. 154).

Ch'ü Yüan (ca. 340 BCE–278 BCE), *Ch'u-tz'u*. For translations, see David Hawkes, transl. *The Songs of the South* (NY: Penguin 1985). Read 'Li sao.'

Yüeh-fu ballads. Read 'Chan ch'eng nan,' 'Mo shang sang.'

Ku-shih shih-chiu shou ('Nineteen Old Poems'). Read 'Hsing hsing ch'ung hsing hsing,' 'Hsi pei yu kao lou,' 'Ch'ü ch'e shang-tung men.'

Ts'ao Chih (192–232 CE). Read 'Tsa shih' nos. 1 and 6; 'Ye t'ien huang-chüeh hsing.'

T'ao Yüan-ming (365–427). 'Ho Kuo chu-po' no. 1, 'Kuei yüan t'ien chü' no. 1, 'Yin chiu' no. 5.

Hsieh Ling-yün (385–433). 'Yü Nan-shan wang Pei-shan ching hu chung chan-t'iao,' 'Teng ch'ih shang lou.'

Wang Wei (701–761 CE). 'Kuan lieh,' from 'Wang-ch'uan chi': 'Lu ch'ai,' 'Luan chia lai,' 'Tsa shih' ('Chün tzu ku hsiang lai'), 'Chung-nan pieh-yeh.'

Li Po (701–762 CE). *Ku feng* no. 1 ('Ta yah …'), 'Chiang chin chiu,' from 'Ch'iu-p'u ko' (nos. 14, 15): 'Lu huo …,' 'Pai fa …,' 'Tzu ch'ien,' 'Lin-lu ko.'

Tu Fu (712–770 CE). 'Wang yüeh'; 'Ping chü hsing,' 'Yüeh ye,' 'Ch'iu hsing pa shou' (no. 1), 'Chiang-nan feng Li Kui-nien.'

Wang An-shih (1021–1086 CE). 'Shu Hu-yin Hsien-sheng pi er shou.' (Chinese texts in Kao Pu-ying, *T'ang Sung shih chü-yao*.)

Su Shih (1037–1101 CE). 'Chou chung ye ch'i,' 'La-jih yu Ku-shan.' (Chinese texts in Kao Pu-ying, *T'ang Sung shih chü-yao*.)

Huang T'ing-chien (1045–1105 CE). 'T'i Lo-hsing-ssu.' (Chinese texts in Kao Pu-ying, *T'ang Sung shih chü-yao*.)

Poetry (ii): Lyrics in Tz'u *Form*

Su Shih (1037–1101 CE). 'Shui-tiao ko-t'ou': 'Ming yüeh chi shih yu'; 'Nien-nu chiao': 'Ta chiang tung ch'ü'; 'Lin chiang hsie': 'Ye yin ….'

Li Ch'ing-chao (1084–ca. 1151 CE). 'Sheng sheng man': 'Hsün-hsün mi-mi'; 'Ju meng ling': 'Ch'ang chi ….'

Drama

Kuan Han-ch'ing (ca. 1240–ca. 1320 CE). *Tou O yüan*. For a translation, see Shih Chung-wen, *Injustice to Tou O*. Cambridge: Cambridge University Press 1972.

Long Narrative

Ts'ao Hsüeh-ch'in (1715–1763 CE; alt. dates, 1724–1764). *Hung-lou meng*. There are various translations; the most recent and complete is David Hawkes and John Minford, transll., *The Story of the Stone*. 5 volumes. NY: Penguin 1973–1986.

Short Narrative

Ts'ao P'i (?187–226). *Lieh i chuan*: 'Chiang Chi wang erh.'

Kan Pao (fl. first half of the 3rd century). *Sou shen chi*: "Tung Yung,' 'T'ien shang Yü-nü.'

Tao Ch'ien (?365–427). *Sou shen hou chi*: 'Hsü Hsüan-fang nü.'

Shen Chi-chi (ca. 742–ca. 805). 'Chen chung chi.'

Yüan Chen (775–831). 'Ying-ying chuan.'

Shen Ya-chih (?782–?831). 'Feng Yan chuan.'

Hsüeh Yung-juo (fl. 830). 'Ku-jen ch'i.'

Feng Meng-lung (1574–1646). 'Chiang Hsing-ko ch'ung hui chen-chu-shan' ('The Pearl Shirt Reëncountered'), 'Kuan-yüan sou wan feng hsien-nü.'

P'u Sung-ling (1640–1715). *Liao-chai chih-i*: 'Ying-ning,' 'Huang ying,' 'Hua pi.'

II. Modern Chinese Literature

Anthologies: Various Genres

Anderson, Jennifer, and Theresa Munford, transll. *Chinese Women Writers: A Collection of Short Stories by Chinese Women Writers of the 1920s and 30s*. Hong Kong: Joint Publishing Co. 1985.

Gunn, Edward. *Twentieth-Century Chinese Drama: An Anthology*. Bloomington: Indiana University Press 1983.

Goldblatt, Howard, ed. *Chairman Mao Would Not Be Amused: Fiction from Today's China*. NY: Grove 1995.

Lau, Joseph S. M., et al, edd. *Modern Chinese Stories and Novellas, 1919–1949*. NY: Columbia University Press 1981.

— and Howard Goldblatt, edd. *The Columbia Anthology of Modern Chinese Literature*. NY: Columbia University Press 1996.

Liu Ts'un-yan and John Minford, edd. *Chinese Middlebrow Fiction: From the Ch'ing and Early Republican Eras*. Hong Kong: Chinese University Press 1984.

Tai, Jeanne, ed. *Spring Bamboo: A Collection of Contemporary Chinese Short Stories*. NY: Random House 1989.

Wang, David Der-wei, and Jeanne Tai, edd. *Running Wild: New Chinese Writers*. NY: Columbia University Press 1994.

Yeh, Michelle, ed. and transl. *Anthology of Modern Chinese Poetry*. New Haven: Yale University Press 1992.

Individual works

Bei Dao. *Notes from the City of the Sun: Poems by Bei Dao*. Ed. and transl. Bonnie McDougall. Ithaca: Cornell University Press 1983.

Ding Ling. *I Myself Am a Woman: Selected Writings of Ding Ling*. Ed. Tani E. Barlow with Gary J. Bjorge. Boston: Beacon Press 1989.

Lao She. *Rickshaw: The Novel Lo-to Hsiang Tzu* [1936]. Transl. Jean M. James. Honolulu: University of Hawaii Press 1979.

Liu E. *The Travels of Lao Ts'an*. Transl. Harold Shadick. Ithaca: Cornell University Press 1966.

Lu Xun. *Diary of a Madman and Other Stories*. Transl. William Lyell. Honolulu: University of Hawaii Press 1990.

Mao Dun. *Rainbow*. Transl. Madeleine Zelin. Berkeley: University of California Press 1992.

Shen Congwen. *The Chinese Earth*. Transl. Ching Ti and Robert Payne. NY: Columbia University Press 1947.

Wang Anyi. *Love in A Small Town*. Transl. Eva Hung. Hong Kong: Rendition Books 1988.

Xiao Hong. Tales *of Hulan River*. Transl. Howard Goldblatt. Hong Kong: Joint Publishing Co. 1988.

— *Daniel Hsieh and Yingjin Zhang*

CONTEMPORARY LITERARY AND CRITICAL THEORY I: A Selected Bibliography

NOTE: Students choosing a theoretical component as one of their areas of study may select this module, the following one, *or* one of the following: Cultural Studies; Feminist Histories and Theories; Philosophy of Aesthetics; Psychoanalysis; Rhetoric I, II, or III; or Semiotics.

Basic Reference Works (for consultation as needed)

Groden, Michael, and Martin Kreiswirth, edd. *The Johns Hopkins Guide to Literary Theory and Criticism*. Baltimore: Johns Hopkins University Press 1994.

Marshall, Donald G. *Contemporary Critical Theory: A Selected Bibliography*. NY: Modern Language Association of America 1993.

Preminger, Alex, and T. V. F. Brogan, edd. *The New Princeton Encyclopedia of Poetry and Poetics*. Princeton: Princeton University Press 1993.

Anthologies

Adams, Hazard, ed. *Critical Theory Since Plato*. Fort Worth: Harcourt Brace Jovanovich, 2nd edition 1992.

Davis, Robert Con, and Ronald Schleifer, edd. *Contemporary Literary Criticism: Literary and Cultural Studies*. NY: Longman, 3rd edition 1994.

Overviews

Best, Steven, and Douglas Kellner. *Postmodern Theory: Critical Interrogations.* NY: Guilford Press 1991.

Eagleton, Terry. *The Ideology of the Aesthetic.* Oxford: Blackwell 1990.

Graff, Gerald. *Professing Literature: An Institutional History.* Chicago: University of Chicago Press 1987.

Leitch, Vincent. *American Literary Criticism form the 1930s to the 1980s.* NY: Columbia University Press 1988.

Influential Figures and Texts

Bakhtin, Mikhail. *The Dialogic Imagination: Four Essays.* Austin: University of Texas Press 1981.

Barthes, Roland. *S/Z.* NY: Hill and Wang 1974.

Baudrillard, Jean. *Simulations.* NY: Semiotext(e) 1983.

Benjamin, Walter. *Illuminations.* NY: Schocken 1969.

Bloom, Harold. *The Anxiety of Influence: A Theory of Poetry.* NY: Oxford University Press 1973.

Butler, Judith. *Gender Trouble: Feminism and the Subversion of Identity.* NY: Routledge 1990.

Deleuze, Gilles, and Félix Guattari. *Anti-Oedipus: Capitalism and Schizophrenia.* Minneapolis: University of Minnesota Press 1983.

Derrida, Jacques. *Dissemination.* Chicago: University of Chicago Press 1981.

Foucault, Michel. *Discipline and Punish: The Birth of the Prison.* NY: Random House 1977.

Freud, Sigmund. *The Interpretation of Dreams.* Transl. James Strachey. NY: Basic Books 1955.

Frye, Northrop. *Anatomy of Criticism: Four Essays.* Princeton: Princeton University Press 1957.

Gramsci, Antonio. *Selections from the Prison Notebooks of Antonio Gramsci.* NY: International Publishers 1971.

Heidegger, Martin. *Poetry, Language, Thought.* NY: Harper & Row 1971.

Jameson, Fredric. *The Political Unconscious*. Ithaca: Cornell University Press 1979.

— *Postmodernism, or, the Cultural Logic of Late Capitalism*. Durham: Duke University Press 1991.

Kristeva, Julia. *Revolution in Poetic Language*. NY: Columbia University Press 1984.

Lacan, Jacques. *Ecrits: A Selection*. NY: Norton 1977.

Man, Paul de. *Allegories of Reading: Figural Language in Rousseau, Nietzsche, Rilke, and Proust*. New Haven: Yale University Press 1979.

Said, Edward. *Orientalism*. NY: Pantheon 1978.

Silverman, Kaja. *The Subject of Semiotics*. NY: Oxford University Press 1983.

Wellek, René, and Austin Warren. *Theory of Literature*. NY: Harcourt Brace Jovanovich, 3rd edition 1962.

— *Vincent B. Leitch*

CONTEMPORARY LITERARY AND CRITICAL THEORY II: Various Schools

The field of 'Literary Theory' is impossibly vast — indeed, it might better be termed 'Literary Theories' — and, moreover, its bibliography is changing faster than one can enunciate the innovations. This module can hope to do no more than to offer *some* categories or schools of theory that readers may find useful, and then to list *some* of the texts that have proved to be important in those categories. (Certain approaches that might well have been listed here, including Feminist Histories and Theories, Psychoanalysis, Queer Studies, Rhetoric, Semiotics, and Visual Culture, have been separated out into modules of their own. Other possible categories have been conflated — my 'reader-oriented' section represents the conflation of what are usually thought of as several distinct schools — and some possible categories have been omitted altogether in this book.)

To master the field of Literary Theory completely is likely impossible even for those who make it their life's task. At the M.A. level, the important thing is to *begin*: to select a few areas of interest and to make one's way toward a working familiarity with some of the basic texts in those schools of thought. The acquisition of knowledge in this realm is palpably cumulative; what seems at first opaque and impenetrable becomes, in time, increasingly accessible, as one begins to acquire the vocabularies of these theorists and to understand the various ways in which they approach their tasks.

This module includes fourteen categories, three of which are for special authors whose work is both unusually prolific and unusually resistant to categorization. The student selecting this module as one of her areas should read *all* the books listed under 'Basic Overviews,' plus the titles listed for any *three* of the fourteen categories. Once again, it must be stressed that such choices make only for a beginning in this massive field. But the longest journey, as the ancient proverb has it, begins with but a single step.

Reference Works (for consultation as needed)
Colapietro, Vincent M. *Glossary of Semiotics*. NY: Paragon House 1993.

Ducrot, Oswald, and Tzvetan Todorov. *Encyclopedic Dictionary of the Sciences of Language*. Baltimore: Johns Hopkins University Press 1979.

Guerin, Wilfred, et al., edd. *A Handbook of Critical Approaches to Literature*. NY: Oxford University Press, 3rd edition 1992.

Makaryk, Irena R., ed. *Encyclopedia of Contemporary Literary Theory: Approaches, Scholars, Terms*. Toronto: Univeristy of Toronto Press 1993.

Marshall, Donald G. *Contemporary Critical Theory: A Selective Bibliography*. NY: Modern Language Association of America 1993.

Preminger, Alex, and T. V. F. Brogan, edd. *The New Princeton Encyclopedia of Poetry and Poetics*. Princeton: Princeton University Press 1993. Abridged as T. V. F. Brogan ed., *The New Princeton Handbook of Poetic Terms*. Princeton: Princeton University Press 1994.

Prince, Gerald S. *A Dictionary of Narratology*. Lincoln: University of Nebraska Press 1987.

Basic Overviews
Best, Steven, and Douglas Kellner. *Postmodern Theory: Critical Interrogations*. NY: Guilford Press 1991.

Eagleton, Terry. *Literary Theory: An Introduction*. Minneapolis: University of Minnesota Press 1983, 2nd edition 1996.

Leitch, Vincent. *American Literary Criticism from the 30s to the 80s*. NY: Columbia University Press 1988.

Cognitive Science
Babuts, Nicolae. *The Dynamics of the Metaphoric Field: A Cognitive View of Literature*. Newark: University of Delaware Press 1992.

Collins, Christopher. *The Poetics of the Mind's Eye: Literature and the Psychology of Imagination*. Philadelphia: University of Pennsylvania Press 1991.

Esrock, Ellen J. *The Reader's Eye: Visual Imaging as Reader Response*. Baltimore: Johns Hopkins University Press 1994.

Hobbs, Jerry R. *Literature and Cognition*. Stanford: Center for the Study of Language and Information 1990.

Holland, Norman N. *The Critical I*. NY: Columbia University Press 1992.

Johnson, Mark. *The Body in the Mind: The Bodily Basis of Meaning, Imagination, and Reason*. Chicago: University of Chicago Press 1987.

Lakoff, George. *Women, Fire, and Dangerous Things: What Categories Reveal about the Mind*. Chicago: University of Chicago Press 1987.

Lakoff, George, and Mark Johnson. *Metaphors We Live By*. Chicago: University of Chicago Press 1980.

Lakoff, George, and Mark Turner. *More Than Cool Reason: A Field Guide to Poetic Metaphor*. Chicago: University of Chicago Press 1989.

Rosenblatt, Louise M. *Literature as Exploration*. NY: Modern Language Association 1995.

Turner, Mark. *Reading Minds: The Study of English in the Age of Cognitive Science*. Princeton: Princeton University Press 1991. Read 'Professing English' and 'Envoi: Cognitive Rhetoric and Literary Criticism.'

— *The Literary Mind*. NY: Oxford University Press 1996.

Deconstruction

Culler, Jonathan. *On Deconstruction*. Ithaca NY: Cornell University Press 1982.

Derrida, Jacques. *Dissemination*. Chicago: University of Chicago Press 1981.

— *Margins of Philosophy*. Chicago: University of Chicago Press 1982.

— *Of Grammatology*. Baltimore: Johns Hopkins University Press 1976.

— *Positions*. Chicago: University of Chicago Press 1981.

— *The Post Card: From Socrates to Freud and Beyond*. Chicago: University of Chicago Press 1987.

Ellis, John. *Against Deconstruction*. Princeton: Princeton University Press 1989.

Hartman, Geoffrey. *The Fate of Reading and Other Essays*. Chicago: University of Chicago Press 1975.

Leitch, Vincent. *Deconstructive Criticism: An Advanced Introduction*. NY 1983.

Man, Paul de. *Allegories of Reading: Figural Language in Rousseau, Nietzsche, Rilke, and Proust*. New Haven: Yale University Press 1979. Read 'Semiology and Rhetoric.'

— *Blindness and Insight: Essays in the Rhetoric of Contemporary Criticism*. NY: Oxford University Press 1971; second revised edition Minneapolis: University of Minnesota Press 1983. Read 'Criticism and Crisis.'

— *The Resistance to Theory*. Minneapolis: University of Minnesota Press 1986. Read 'The Resistance to Theory.'

Linguistics for Littérateurs

Benveniste, Emile. *Problems in General Linguistics*. Coral Gables: University of Miami Press 1971. Read chapters 18–20.

Clark, Herbert H. *Using Language*. Cambridge: Cambridge University Press 1996.

Culler, Jonathan. *Ferdinand de Saussure*. NY: Penguin 1976, second edition 1986.

Kristeva, Julia. *Language: The Unknown. An Initiation into Linguistics*. NY: Columbia University Press 1989.

Lakoff, George, and Mark Johnson. *Metaphors We Live By*. Chicago: University of Chicago Press 1980.

Lyons, John. *Chomsky*. Hassocks: Harvester Press 1977.

Ortony, Andrew, ed. *Metaphor and Thought*. Cambridge: Cambridge University Press 1979, 2nd edition 1993.

Saussure, Ferdinand de. *Course in General Linguistics*. Transl. Wade Baskin. NY: McGraw-Hill 1966. (The preferred French edition is *Cours de linguistique générale*. Edition critique préparée par Tullio de Mauro. Paris: Payot 1994.)

Schauber, Ellen, and Ellen Spolsky. *The Bounds of Interpretation: Linguistic Theory and Literary Text*. Stanford: Stanford University Press 1986.

Sperber, Dan, and Deirdre Wilson. *Relevance: Communication and Cognition*. Cambridge MA: Harvard University Press 1986.

Whorf, Benjamin Lee. *Language, Thought, and Reality: Selected Writings of Benjamin Lee Whorf*. Ed. John B. Carroll. Cambridge MA: MIT Press 1956.

Marxist Theory

Althusser, Louis. *Lenin and Philosophy and Other Essays*. NY: Monthly Review Press 1971. Read 'Ideology and Ideological State Apparatus.'

Benjamin, Walter. *Illuminations*. NY: Schocken 1977. Read 'The Work of Art in the Age of Mechanical Reproduction.'

Craig, David, ed. *Marxists on Literature: An Anthology*. Baltimore: Penguin 1975.

Deleuze, Gilles, and Félix Guattari. *Anti-Oedipus: Capitalism and Schizophrenia*. Minneapolis: University of Minnesota 1983.

Eagleton, Terry. *Ideology: An Introduction*. NY: Verso 1991.

Goldmann, Lucien. *Towards a Sociology of the Novel*. London: Tavistock 1975.

Gramsci, Antonio. *The Southern Question*. West Lafayette: Bordighera 1995.

Jameson, Fredric. *The Political Unconscious*. Ithaca NY: Cornell University Press 1979.

Lukács, Georg. *Realism in Our Time: Literature and the Class Struggle*. NY: Harper and Row 1964.

Marcuse, Herbert. *The Aesthetic Dimension: Toward a Critique of Marxist Aesthetics*. Boston: Beacon 1978.

Marx, Karl, and Friedrich Engels. *Marx and Engels on Literature and Art*. St. Louis: Telos Press 1973.

Rose, Peter W. *Sons of the Gods, Children of Earth: Ideology and Literary Form in Ancient Greece*. Ithaca NY: Cornell University Press 1992. Read chapter 1.

Williams, Raymond. *Marxism and Literature*. NY: Oxford University Press 1977.

Narratology

Bal, Mieke. *Narratology: Introduction to the Theory of Narrative*. Toronto: University of Toronto Press 1985.

Barthes, Roland. 'Introduction to the Structural Analysis of Narrative.' In *Image, Music, Text*, ed. Stephen Heath. NY: Hill & Wang 1977.

Booth, Wayne. *The Rhetoric of Fiction*. Chicago: University of Chicago Press 1961, 2nd edition 1983.

Chatman, Seymour. *Story and Discourse: Narrative Structure in Fiction and Film*. Ithaca NY: Cornell University Press 1978.

— *Coming to Terms: The Rhetoric of Narrative in Fiction and Film.* Ithaca NY: Cornell University Press 1990.

Genette, Gérard. *Figures of Literary Discourse.* NY: Columbia University Press 1982.

— *Narrative Discourse: An Essay in Method.* Ithaca NY: Cornell University Press 1980.

Martin, Wallace. *Recent Theories of Narrative.* Ithaca NY: Cornell University Press 1986.

Onega, Susana, and José Ángel García Landa. *Narratology.* London: Longman 1996.

Prince, Gerald S. *A Grammar of Stories: An Introduction.* The Hague: Mouton 1973.

Rimmon-Kenan, Shlomith. *Narrative Fiction: Contemporary Poetics.* London: Methuen 1983.

Sturgess, Philip J. M. *Narrativity: Theory and Practice.* Oxford: Clarendon Press 1992.

New Criticism

Brooks, Cleanth. *The Well Wrought Urn: Studies in the Structure of Poetry.* NY: Reynal & Hitchcock 1947.

Empson, William. *Seven Types of Ambiguity.* London: Chatto & Windus 1930.

Leavis, F. R. *New Bearings in English Poetry: A Study of the Contemporary Situation.* London: Chatto & Windus 1932.

Lentricchia, Frank. *After the New Criticism.* Chicago: University of Chicago Press 1980.

Ransom, John Crowe. *The New Criticism.* Norfolk: New Directions 1941.

Richards, I. A. *Practical Criticism.* London: NY: Harcourt, Brace 1929.

Tate, Allen. *Collected Essays.* Denver: A. Swallow 1959.

Wellek, René, and Austin Warren. *Theory of Literature.* London: Cape, 3rd edition 1966.

Wimsatt, W. K., and Monroe Beardsley. *The Verbal Icon.* Lexington: University of Kentucky Press 1954.

— and Cleanth Brooks. *Literary Criticism: A Short History.* NY: Knopf 1957.

Phenomenology

Derrida, Jacques. *Speech and Phenomena, and Other Essays on Husserl's Theory of Signs.* Evanston: Northwestern University Press 1973.

Detweiler, Robert. *Story, Sign, and Self: Phenomenology and Structuralism as Literary Critical Methods*. Philadelphia: Fortress Press 1978.

Gadamer, Hans-Georg. *Truth and Method*. NY: Crossroad 1975.

Hegel, G. W. F. *Phenomenology of Spirit*. Oxford: Clarendon Press 1977.

Heidegger, Martin. *Poetry, Language, Thought*. NY: Harper & Row 1971

— *The Basic Problems of Phenomenology*. Bloomington: Indiana University Press 1982

Husserl, Edmund. *Cartesian Meditations: An Introduction to Phenomenology*. Dordrecht: Kluwer 1960.

Ingarden, Roman. *The Cognition of the Literary Work of Art*. Evanston: Northwestern University Press 1973.

Merleau-Ponty, Maurice. *Phenomenology of Perception*. London: Routledge 1962.

Spiegelberg, Herbert. *The Phenomenological Movement: A Historical Introduction*. The Hague: Nijhoff, 3nd edition 1982.

Postmodern Thought

Arac, Jonathan. *Critical Genealogies: Historical Situations for Postmodern Literary Studies*. NY: Columbia University Press 1987.

Baudrillard, Jean. *Selected Writings*. Ed. Mark Poster. Stanford: Stanford University Press 1988.

Bové, Paul A., ed. *Early Postmodernism: Foundational Essays*. Durham: Duke University Press 1995.

Foster, Hal, ed. *The Anti-Aesthetic: Essays on Postmodern Culture*. Port Townsend: Bay Press 1983.

Hassan, Ihab. *The Postmodern Turn: Essays in Postmodern Theory and Culture*. Columbus: Ohio State University Press 1987.

Hutcheon, Linda. *The Politics of Postmodernism*. London: Routledge 1989.

Jameson, Fredric. *Postmodernism, or, the Cultural Logic of Late Capitalism*. Durham: Duke University Press 1991.

Kaplan, E. Ann, ed. *Postmodernism and Its Discontents: Theories, Practices*. NY: Verso 1988.

Lyotard, Jean-François. *The Postmodern Condition: A Report on Knowledge*. Minneapolis: University of Minnesota Press 1984.

McHale, Brian. *Postmodernist Fiction*. NY: Routledge 1987.

Reader-Oriented Theories

Bleich, David. *Subjective Criticism*. Baltimore: Johns Hopkins University Press 1978.

Eco, Umberto. *The Open Work*. Cambridge MA: Harvard University Press 1989.

Fish, Stanley. *Is There a Text in This Class? The Authority of Interpretive Communities*. Cambridge MA: Harvard University Press 1980.

Hirsch, E. D., Jr. *Validity in Interpretation*. New Haven: Yale University Press1967.

Holub, Robert C. *Reception Theory: A Critical Introduction*. London: Methuen 1984.

Iser, Wolfgang. *The Act of Reading: A Theory of Aesthetic Response*. Baltimore: Johns Hopkins University Press 1978.

Jauss, Hans-Robert. 'Levels of Identification of Hero and Audience.' *New Literary History* 5 (1973–1974) 283–317.

— *Toward an Aesthetic of Reception*. Minneapolis: University of Minnesota Press 1982.

Suleiman, Susan R., and Inge Crosman, edd. *The Reader in the Text: Essays on Audience and Interpretation*. Princeton: Princeton University Press 1980.

Tompkins, Jane P. *Reader-Response Criticism: From Formalism to Post-Structuralism*. Baltimore: Johns Hopkins University Press 1980.

Russian Formalism

Bann, Stephen, and John E. Bowlt, edd. *Russian Formalism: A Collection of Articles and Texts in Translation*. NY: Barnes & Noble 1973.

Bennett, Tony. *Formalism and Marxism*. London: Methuen 1979.

Ehrlich, Victor. *Russian Formalism: History–Doctrine*. New Haven: Yale University Press, 3rd edition 1981.

Jakobson, Roman. *Language in Literature*. Cambridge MA: Harvard University Press 1987 (read chapters 7, 8, 10, 24).

Lemon, Lee T., and Marion J. Reis, edd. *Russian Formalism*. Lincoln: University of Nebraska Press 1965.

Matejka, Ladislav, and Krystyna Pomorska, edd. *Readings in Russian Poetics: Formalist and Structuralist Views*. Cambridge MA: MIT Press 1971.

Merquior, J. G. *From Prague to Paris: A Critique of Structuralist and Post-Structuralist Thought*. London: Verso 1986.

Propp, Vladimir. *Morphology of the Folktale*. Austin: University of Texas Press, 2nd edition 1968.

Steiner, Peter. *Russian Formalism: A Metapoetics*. Ithaca: Cornell University Press 1984.

Striedter, Jurij. *Literary Structure, Evolution, and Value: Russian Formalism and Czech Structuralism Reconsidered*. Cambridge: Harvard University Press 1989.

Structuralism

Barthes, Roland. *The Semiotic Challenge* (NY: Hill & Wang 1988). Read Part One (pp. 11–148).

Culler, Jonathan. *Structuralist Poetics: Structuralism, Linguistics, and the Study of Literature*. Ithaca NY: Cornell University Press 1975.

— *Ferdinand de Saussure*. NY: Penguin Books 1977.

Dosse, François. *History of Structuralism*. 2 volumes. Transl. Deborah Glassman. Minneapolis: University of Minnesota Press 1997.

Jakobson, Roman. *Language in Literature*. Cambridge MA: Harvard University Press 1987 (read chapters 7, 8, 10, 24).

Lévi-Strauss, Claude. *Structural Anthropology*. NY: Basic Books 1963. Read 'The Structural Study of Myth.'

Macksey, Richard, and Eugenio Donato, edd. *The Languages of Criticism and the Sciences of Man: The Structuralist Controversy*. Baltimore: Johns Hopkins University Press 1972.

Merquior, J. G. *From Prague to Paris: A Critique of Structuralist and Post-Structuralist Thought*. London: Verso 1986.

Saussure, Ferdinand de. *Course in General Linguistics*. NY: McGraw-Hill 1966.

Scholes, Robert. *Structuralism in Literature: An Introduction*. New Haven: Yale University Press 1974.

Sturrock, John, ed. *Structuralism and Since: From Lévi-Strauss to Derrida*. NY: Oxford University Press 1979.

Special Author: Bakhtin

Bakhtin, Mikhail. *The Dialogic Imagination: Four Essays*. Austin: University of Texas Press 1981.

— *Problems of Dostoevsky's Poetics*. Minneapolis: University of Minnesota Press 1984.

— *Rabelais and His World*. Bloomington: Indiana University Press 1984.

— *Speech Genres and Other Late Essays*. Austin: University of Texas Press 1986.

— *Art and Answerability: Early Philosophical Works*. Austin: University of Texas Press 1990.

Clark, Katerina, and Michael Holquist. *Mikhail Bakhtin*. Cambridge MA: Harvard Univeresity Press 1984.

Medvedev, P. N. *The Formal Method in Literary Scholarship: A Critical Introduction to Sociological Poetics*. Cambridge MA: Harvard Univeristy Press 1985.

Morson, Gary Saul, and Caryl Emerson, edd. *Rethinking Bakhtin: Extensions and Challenges*. Evanston: Northwestern University Press 1989.

Morson, Gary Saul, and Caryl Emerson. *Mikhail Bakhtin: Creation of a Prosaics*. Stanford: Stanford University Press 1990.

Todorov, Tzvetan. *Mikhail Bakhtin: The Dialogical Principle*. Minneapolis: University of Minnesota Press 1984.

Voloshinov, V. N. [Mikhail Bakhtin?] *Marxism and the Philosophy of Language*. Cambridge MA: Harvard University Press 1986.

Special Author: Barthes

[For consultation as needed: Freedman, Sanford, and Carole Anne Taylor. *Roland Barthes: A Bibliographical Reader's Guide*. NY: Garland 1983.]

Barthes, Roland. *A Barthes Reader*. Ed. Susan Sontag. NY: Hill and Wang 1982.

— *Elements of Semiology*. NY: Hill and Wang 1968.

— *The Fashion System*. NY: Hill and Wang 1983.

— *The Grain of the Voice: Interviews 1962–1980*. NY: Hill and Wang 1985.

— *Image–Music–Text*. NY: Hill and Wang 1978.

— *A Lover's Discourse: Fragments*. NY: Hill and Wang 1978,

— *The Pleasure of the Text*. NY: Hill and Wang 1975.

— *The Rustle of Language*. NY: Hill and Wang 1986.

— *S/Z*. NY: Hill and Wang 1974.

— *The Semiotic Challenge*. NY: Hill and Wang 1988.

— *Writing Degree Zero*. NY: Hill and Wang 1968.

Special Author: Foucault

Eribon, Didier. *Michel Foucault*. Cambridge MA: Harvard University Press 1991.

Foucault, Michel. *The Archaeology of Knowledge and The Discourse on Language*. NY: Pantheon 1972.

— *Discipline and Punish: The Birth of the Prison*. NY: Random House 1977.

— *Herculine Barbin, Being the Recently Discovered Memoirs of a Nineteenth Century French Hermaphrodite*. NY: Pantheon 1980.

— *The History of Sexuality*. 3 volumes. NY: Random House 1978–1986. Read volumes 1 and 2, *The History of Sexuality: An Introduction* and *The Use of Pleasure*.

— *Language, Counter-Memory, Practice: Selected Essays and Interviews*. Ithaca NY: Cornell University Press 1977.

— *Madness and Civilization: A History of Insanity in the Age of Reason*. NY: Pantheon 1965.

— *Politics, Philosophy, Culture: Interviews and Other Writings 1977–1984*. NY: Routledge 1988.

— *Power/Knowledge: Selected Interviews and Other Writings 1972–1977*. NY: Pantheon 1980.

Halperin, David M. *Saint Foucault: Towards a Gay Hagiography*. NY: Oxford University Press 1995.

— John T. Kirby

CULTURAL STUDIES

NOTE: Cultural Studies is an unusually wide and extraordinarily rapidly-changing field; and this list is unusually large for one of the four 'modules' of the Purdue M.A. program. For these reasons, *with the approval of her advisor*, the student may delete *one* item from Part I and up to *seven* items from Part II below.

Books (to be read in their entirety).

Anzaldua, Gloria. *Borderlands/La Frontera: The New Mestiza.* San Francisco: Aunt Lute 1987.

Butler, Judith. *Gender Trouble: Feminism and the Subversion of Identity.* NY: Routledge 1990.

Certeau, Michel de. *The Practice of Everyday Life.* Berkeley: University of California Press 1988.

Collins, Patricia Hill. *Black Feminist Thought.* Boston: Unwin Hyman 1990.

Foucault, Michel. *The History of Sexuality.* Vol. 1: An Introduction. NY: Vintage 1978.

Freire, Paulo. *Pedagogy of the Oppressed.* NY: Seabury Press 1970.

Gates, Henry Louis, Jr. *Loose Canons: Notes on the Culture Wars.* NY: Oxford University Press 1992.

hooks, bell. *Teaching to Transgress.* NY: Routledge 1993.

Marx, Karl. *The Eighteenth Brumaire of Louis Bonaparte.* ress: International Publishers 1869, 1981.

Said, Edward W. *Orientalism.* NY: Random House 1978.

Salvidar, Jose David. *The Dialectics of Our America: Genealogy, Cultural Critique, and Literary Histories.* Durham: Duke University Press 1991.

Shorter selections (chapters in single-authored books or essays in edited collections).

Althusser, Louis. *Lenin and Philosophy and Other Essays.* Transl. Ben Brewster. ress: Monthly Review Press 1971. Read 'Ideology and

Ideological State Apparatuses: Notes Towards an Investigation' (127–186).

Anderson, Benedict. *Imagined Communities: Reflections on the Origin and Spread of Nationalism*. London: Verso 1983, 1991. Read 'Introduction,' 'Cultural Roots,' and 'The Origins of National Consciousness' (1–46); 'Census, Map, Museum,' and 'Memory and Forgetting' (163–206).

Baudrillard, Jean. *Selected Writings*. Ed. Mark Poster. Stanford: Stanford University Press 1988. Read 'The System of Objects' and 'Consumer Society' (10–56), and 'Simulacra and Simulations' (166–185).

Benjamin, Walter. *Illuminations: Essays and Reflections*. Ed. Hannah Arendt. Transl. Harry Zohn. NY: Schocken Books 1968. Read 'The Work of Art in the Age of Mechanical Reproduction' (217–252) and 'Theses on the Philosophy of History' (253–264).

Bordo, Susan. *Unbearable Weight: Feminism, Western Culture, and the Body*. Berkeley: University of California Press 1993. Read 'Introduction' (1–44), 'Hunger as Ideology' (99–134), and 'Postmodern Subjects, Postmodern Bodies, Postmodern Resistance' (277–300).

Chow, Rey. *Writing Diaspora: Tactics of Intervention in Contemporary Cultural Studies*. Bloomington: Indiana University Press 1993. Read 'Where Have All the Natives Gone?' and 'Postmodern Automatons' (27–72).

Chow, Rey. *Primitive Passions: Visuality, Sexuality, Ethnography, and Contemporary Chinese Cinema*. NY: Columbia University Press 1995. Read 'Film as Ethnography' (175–202).

Cixous, Hélène, and Catherine Clement. *The Newly Born Woman*. Transl. Betsy Wing. Minneapolis: University of Minnesota Press 1988. Read 'Sorties: Out and Out: Attacks/Ways Out/Forays' (63–134).

Doane, Mary Ann. *Femmes Fatales: Feminism, Film Theory, Psychoanalysis*. NY: Routledge 1991. Read 'Dark Continents: Epistemologies of Racial and Sexual Difference in Psychoanalysis and the Cinema' (209–248).

Fanon, Frantz. *Black Skin/White Masks*. Transl. Charles Lam Markmann. NY: Grove Weidenfeld 1957, 1982. Read 'The Woman of Color and the White Man,' 'The Man of Color and the White Woman' (41–62), and 'The Fact of Blackness' (109–140).

— *The Wretched of the Earth*. Transl. Constance Farrington. NY: Grove Press 1961. Read 'On National Culture' (206–249).

Grossberg, Lawrence, Cary Nelson, and Paula Treichler, edd. *Cultural Studies*. NY: Routledge 1992. Read the essays by Nelson, Triechler, & Grossberg ('Introduction'), Bhabha, Brunt, Chabram-Dernersasian, Clifford, Gilroy, Stuart Hall, hooks, Kipnis, Mani, Radway, Wallace, West, and Wolff.

hooks, bell. *Yearning: Race, Gender, and Cultural Politics*. Boston: South End Press 1990. Read 'The Politics of Radical Black Subjectivity' (15–22), 'Postmodern Blackness' (23–32), and 'Culture to Culture: Ethnography and Cultural Studies as Critical Intervention' (123–134).

Horkheimer, Max and Theodor W. Adorno. *Dialectic of Enlightenment*. Transl. John Cumming. NY: Continuum 1994. Read 'The Concept of Englightenment' (3–43), 'The Culture Industry: Enlightenment as Mass Deception' (120–168), and 'Elements of Anti-Semitism: Limits of Enlightenment' (168–209).

Irigaray, Luce. *This Sex Which is Not One*. Transl. Catherine Porter and Carolyn Burke. Ithaca: Cornell University Press 1985. Read 'The Looking Glass, from the Other Side' (9–22), 'Women on the Market,' 'Commodities Among Themselves' (170–197), and 'When Our Lips Speak Together' (205–218).

Jameson, Fredric. *Postmodernism, Or The Cultural Logic of Late Capitalism*. Durham: Duke University Press 1991. Read 'Conclusion: Secondary Elaborations' (297–418).

Kristeva, Julia. *Strangers to Ourselves*. Transl. Leon S. Roudiez. NY: Columbia University Press 1991. Read 'Toccata and Fugue for the Foreigner' (1–40) and 'Might Not Universality Be … Our Own Foreignness?' (169–192).

Mercer, Kobena. *Welcome to the Jungle*. London: Routledge 1994. Read 'Introduction: Black Britain and the Cultural Politics of Diaspora' (1–32), 'Black Hair/Style Politics' (97–130), and 'Dark & Lovely: Black Gay Image Making' (221–232).

Morton, Donald, ed. *The Material Queer: A LesbiGay Cultural Studies Reader*. Boulder: Westview Press 1996. Read the essays by Donald Morton ('Preface' and 'Changing the Terms'), Chicago Gay Liberation, Freud, Marcuse, Altman, Derrida ('That Dangerous Supplement'), Irigaray ('Female Hom[m]osexuality'), Butler, Wittig, Staples, Watney, D'Emilio, Cherry Smith,

Warner, Cooper, Moraga, Tsang, Halperin, Field, L. A. Research Group, and the 1917 Collective.

Parker, Andrew et al, edd. *Nationalisms and Sexualities.* NY: Routledge, 1992. Read the essays by Parker et al. ('Introduction'), Holland, Patton, Sedgwick, Edelman, Abelove, Heng & Devan, Katrak, and Layoun.

Said, Edward W. *Culture and Imperialism.* NY: Vintage, 1994. Read 'Freedom from Domination in the Future' (282–336).

Spivak, Gayatri Chakravorty. *The Spivak Reader.* Edd. Donna Landry and Gerald MacLean. NY: Routledge, 1996. Read 'Bonding in Difference: Interview' (15–28), 'Subaltern Studies: Deconstructing Historiography' (203–236), 'Translator's Preface and Afterword' (267–286), and 'Subaltern Talk' (287–308).

Stallybrass, Peter, and Allon White. *The Politics and Poetics of Transgression.* Ithaca: Cornell UP, 1986. Read 'Introduction' (1–27), 'The City, the Sewer, the Gaze and the Contaminating Touch,' 'Below Stairs: The Maid and the Family Romance,' and 'Bourgeois Hysteria and the Carnivalesque' (125–202).

Trinh T Minh ha. *Woman, Native, Other: Writing Postcoloniality and Feminism.* Bloomington: Indiana University Press, 1989. Read 'Commitment from the Mirror Writing Box' (5–46) and 'Difference: "A Special Third World Women's Issue"' (79–116).

— *Aparajita Sagar*

FEMINIST HISTORIES AND THEORIES

Beauvoir, Simone de. *The Second Sex*. NY: Knopf 1953.

Belenky, Mary Field. *Women's Ways of Knowing: The Development of Self, Voice, and Mind*. NY: Basic Books 1986.

Brownmiller, Susan. *Against Our Will: Men, Women and Rape*. NY: Simon & Schuster 1976.

Butler, Judith. *Gender Trouble: Feminism and the Subversion of Identity*. NY: Routledge 1990.

Campbell, Karlyn Kohrs. *Man Cannot Speak for Her*. 2 volumes. NY: Praeger 1989. Read *Volume 1: A Critical Study of Early Feminist Rhetoric*.

Chodorow, Nancy J. *Feminism and Psychoanalytic Theory*. New Haven: Yale University Press 1989.

Cixous, Hélène, and Catherine Clement. *The Newly Born Woman*. Minneapolis: University of Minnesota Press 1986.

Daly, Mary. *Gyn/Ecology: The Metaethics of Radical Feminism*. Boston: Beacon Press 1978.

Davis, Angela. *Women, Race, and Class*. NY: Vintage 1981.

Dworkin, Andrea. *Pornography: Men Possessing Women*. NY: Perigee Books 1981.

Faludi, Susan. *Backlash: The Undeclared War against American Women*. NY: Doubleday 1991.

Fraser, Nancy. *Unruly Practices: Power, Discourse, and Gender in Contemporary Social Theory*. Minneapolis: University of Minnesota Press 1989.

Friedan, Betty. *The Feminine Mystique*. NY: Norton 1963.

Gilligan, Carol. *In a Different Voice: Psychological Theory and Women's Development*. Cambridge MA: Harvard University Press 1982.

Hartsock, Nancy. *Money, Sex, and Power: Toward a Feminist Historical Materialism*. NY: Longmans 1983.

hooks, bell. *Feminist Theory: From Margin to Center*. Boston: South End Press 1981.

Irigaray, Luce. *The Irigaray Reader*. Cambridge: Blackwell 1991.

Jardine, Alice, and Paul Smith, edd. *Men in Feminism*. NY: Methuen 1987.

Keller, Evelyn Fox. *Reflections on Gender and Science*. New Haven: Yale University Press 1985.

Kristeva, Julia. *The Portable Kristeva*. Ed. Kelly Oliver. NY: Columbia University Press 1997.

Lauretis, Teresa de. *Alice Doesn't: Feminism, Semiotics, Cinema*. Bloomington: Indiana University Press 1984.

— *Technologies of Gender: Essays on Theory, Film, and Fiction*. Bloomington: Indiana University Press 1987.

MacKinnon, Catherine A. *Feminism Unmodified: Discourses on Life and Law*. Cambridge MA: Harvard University Press 1987.

Millett, Kate. *Sexual Politics*. NY: Avon 1969.

Morgan, Robin, ed. *Sisterhood is Powerful: An Anthology of Writings from the Women's Liberation Movement*. NY: Vintage 1970.

Rich, Adrienne. *Blood, Bread, and Poetry: Selected Prose, 1979–1985*. NY: Norton 1986.

Spivak, Gayatri Chakravorty. *The Spivak Reader*. Edd. Donna Landry and Gerald Maclean. NY: Routledge 1996.

Walker, Alice. *In Search of Our Mothers' Gardens: Womanist Prose*. San Diego: Harcourt Brace Jovanovich 1983.

Wolf, Naomi. *The Beauty Myth: How Images of Beauty Are Used Against Women*. NY: Anchor Books 1991.

Woolf, Virginia. *A Room of One's Own* [1929]. NY: Harcourt Brace Jovanovich 1981.

Young, Iris. *The Thinking Muse*. Bloomington: Indiana University Press 1989.

Reference Works (for consultation as necessary)

Campbell, Karlyn Kohrs. *Women Public Speakers in the United States, 1800–1925: A Bio-critical Sourcebook*. Westport: Greenwood Press 1993.

— *Women Public Speakers in the United States, 1925–1993: A Bio-critical Sourcebook*. Westport: Greenwood Press 1994.

Davidson, Cathy N., et al., edd. *The Oxford Companion to Women's Writing in the United States*. NY: Oxford University Press 1995.

Larrington, Carolyne, ed. *The Woman's Compantion to Mythology*. London: Pandora Press 1992.

Pollack, Sandra, and Denise D. Knight, edd. *Contemporary Lesbian Writers of the United States: A Bio-bibliographical Critical Sourcebook.* Westport: Greenwood Press 1994.

Roses, Lorraine Elena, and Ruth Elizabeth Randolph. *Harlem Renaissance and Beyond: Literary Biographies of 100 Black Women Writers, 1900–1945.* Boston: G.K. Hall 1990.

Shapiro, Ann R., et al., edd. *Jewish American Women Writers: A Bio-bibliographical Critical Sourcebook.* Westport: Greenwood Press 1994.

Showalter, Elaine, et al., edd. *Modern American Women Writers.* NY: Scribner 1991, Collier Books 1993.

— *Edward Schiappa and John T. Kirby*

FIRST NATION NARRATIVE

I. Canada: Native and Inuit

Anthologies and Secondary Sources

Moses, Daniel David, and Terry Goldie, edd. *An Anthology of Canadian Native Literature in English*. Toronto: Oxford University Press 1992.

Nungak, Zebedee, and Eugene Arima, edd. *Inuit Stories: Povungnituk*. Hull, Quebec: Canadian Museum of Civilization (National Museums of Canada) 1988. Contains the English and French texts from *Unikkaatuat sanaugarngnik atyingualiit Purviengniturngmit: Eskimo Stories from Povungnituk, Quebec*. Edd. Zebedee Nungak and Eugene Arima. Bulletin: National Museum of Canada 235; Anthropological Series 90. Ottawa: Musées Nationaux du Canada 1975.

Petrone, Penny, ed. *First People, First Voices*. Toronto: University of Toronto Press 1991.

— *Native Literature in Canada: From the Oral Tradition to the Present*. Toronto: Oxford University Press 1990.

— ed. *Northern Voices: Inuit Writing in English*. Toronto: University of Toronto Press 1988.

Individual Authors

Culleton, Beatrice. *April Raintree*. Winnipeg: Pemmican 1984; Winnipeg: Peguis Publishers 1992.

Slipperjack, Ruby. *Honour the Sun*. Winnipeg: Pemmican Publications 1987.

II. Australia: Aborigine

Anthologies and Secondary Sources

Davis, Jack, et al., edd. *Paperbark: A Collection of Black Australian Writings*. UQP Black Australian Writers. St. Lucia: University of Queensland Press 1990.

Gilbert, Kevin, ed. *Inside Black Australia: An Anthology of Aboriginal Poetry*. Ringwood: Penguin 1988.

Mudrooroo [Narogin] (Colin Johnson). *Writing from the Fringe: A Study of Modern Aboriginal Literature*. South Yarra: Hyland House 1990.

Individual Authors

Morgan, Sally. *My Place*. Fremantle: Fremantle Arts Press 1987; NY: Little Brown [1989].

Mudrooroo [Narogin] (Colin Johnson). *Doctor Wooreddy's Prescription for Enduring the Ending of the World* [1983]. NY: Ballantine 1989.

— *Master of Ghost Dreaming*. Imprint Classics. Pymble, NSW: Angus and Robertson 1991.

— *Wildcat Falling* [1965]. Introduction by Stephen Muecke. Imprint Classics. Pymble, NSW: Angus and Robertson 1992.

— *Wildcat Screaming*. Imprint Classics. Pymble, NSW: Angus and Robertson 1992.

Oodgeroo Nunukul [/Noonuccal] (Kath Walker). *The Dawn is at Hand: Poems*. Introduction by Malcolm Williamson. London and NY: Marion Boyers 1992.

III. New Zealand and Polynesia: Maori and Islander

Anthologies and Secondary Sources

Garrett, Simon, ed. *He Reo Hou: Five Plays by Maori Playwrights*. Wellington: Playmarket 1991.

Ihimaera, Witi, and D.S. Long, edd. *Into the World of Light: An Anthology of Maori Writing*. Auckland: Heinemann 1982.

McGregor, Graham, and Mark Williams, edd. *Dirty Silences: Aspects of Language and Literature in New Zealand. Essays Arising from the University of Waikato Winter Lecture Series of 1990*. Auckland: Oxford University Press 1991.

Subramani. *South Pacific Literature: From Myth to Fabulation*. Revised edition. Suva: Institute of Pacific Studies of the University of the South Pacific 1992.

Wendt, Albert, ed. *Lali: A Pacific Anthology*. Pacific Paperbacks. Auckland: Longman Paul 1980.

— ed. *Nuanua: Pacific Writing in English since 1980*. Talanoa: Contemporary Pacific Literature. Honolulu: University of Hawai'i Press 1995.

Individual Authors

Duff, Alan. *Once Were Warriors*. Talanoa: Contemporary Pacific Literature. Auckland: Tandem Press 1990; Honolulu: University of Hawai'i Press 1994.

— *What Becomes of the Broken-Hearted?* Auckland: Vintage 1996.

Te Awekotuku, Ngahuia. *Tahuri*. Auckland: Women's Press 1989; Toronto: Woman's Press 1993.

Grace, Patricia. *Mutuwhenua: The Moon Sleeps*. Pacific Paperbacks. Auckland: Longman Paul 1978; Auckland: Penguin 1986; London: Women's Press 1987.

— *Potiki*. Talanoa: Contemporary Pacific Literature. Auckland: Penguin 1986; Honolulu: University of Hawai'i Press 1995.

— *Collected Stories*. Auckland: Penguin 1994.

— *Cousins*. Auckland: Penguin 1992; London: Women's Press 1993.

Ihimaera, Witi. *Tangi*. Auckland: Heinemann 1973.

— *Whanau*. Auckland: Heinemann 1974.

— *The Matriarch*. Auckland: Heinemann 1986.

— *Kingfisher Come Home*. Auckland: Secker and Warburg 1995.

— *Nights in the Gardens of Spain*. Auckland: Secker and Warburg 1995.

— *Bulibasha: King of the Gipsies*. Auckland: Penguin 1994.

Figiel, Sia. *The Girl in the Moon Circle*. Suva: Mana Publications 1996.

Hau'ofa, 'Epeli. *Kisses in the Netherends*. Talanoa: Contemporary Pacific Literature. Auckland: Longman Paul 1982; Auckland: Penguin 1987; Honolulu: University of Hawai'i Press 1995.

Wendt, Albert. *Sons for the Return Home*. Pacific Paperbacks. Auckland: Longman Paul 1973.

— *Leaves of the Banyan Tree*. Talanoa: Contemporary Pacific Literature. Auckland: Longman Paul 1979; Honolulu: University of Hawai'i Press 1994.

— *Pouliuli*. Pacific Paperbacks. Auckland: Longman Paul 1977.

Reference Works (for Consultation as Needed) & Optional Further Reading

Bardon, Geoffrey. *Papunya Tula: Art of the Western Desert*. Ringwood: McPhee Gribble/Penguin 1991.

Bell, Leonard. *Colonial Constructs: European Images of the Maori, 1840–1914*. Auckland: Auckland University Press 1995.

Benterrak, Krim, et al. *Reading the Country: An Introduction to Nomadology*. Revised edition. Fremantle: Fremantle Arts Centre Press; Liverpool: Liverpool University Press 1996.

Blythe, Martin. *Naming the Other: Images of the Maori in New Zealand Film and Television*. Metuchen and London: Scarecrow Press 1994.

Caruana, Wally. *Aboriginal Art*. World of Art. London and NY: Thames and Hudson 1993.

Crocombe, Marjorie Tuainekore, et al., edd. *Te Rau Maire: Poems and Stories from the Pacific*. Rarotonga: Tauranga Vananga (Ministry of Cultural Development) 1992.

Culleton, Beatrice. *In Search of April Raintree*. Winnipeg: Pemmican Publications 1987; Winnipeg: Peguis Publishers 1992.

— *Spirit of the White Bison*. Winnipeg: Pemmican Publications 1985; Winnipeg: Peguis Publishers 1992.

Duff, Alan. *One Night Out Stealing*. Talanoa: Contemporary Pacific Literature. Auckland: Tandem Press 1992; Honolulu: University of Hawai'i Press 1995.

— *Maori: The Crisis and the Challenge*. Auckland: HarperCollins 1993.

— *State Ward*. Auckland: Vintage 1994.

Emberley, Julia. *Thresholds of Difference: Feminist Critique, Native Women's Writing, Postcolonial Theory*. Theory/Culture. Toronto: University of Toronto Press 1993.

'Epeli Hau'ofa. *Tales of the Tikongs*. Talanoa: Contemporary Pacific Literature. Auckland: Penguin 1983; Honolulu: University of Hawai'i Press 1994.

Figiel, Sia. *Where We Once Belonged*. Auckland: Pasifika Press 1993.

Fiske, John, et al. *Myths of Oz: Reading Australian Popular Culture*. Media and Popular Culture 2. Boston and London: Allen and Unwin 1987.

Fortescue, Michael, ed. *From the Writings of the Greenlanders. Kalaallit atuakkiaannit*. [Fairbanks]: University of Alaska Press 1990.

Garimara, Nugi. *Caprice — A Stockman's Daughter*. UQP Black Australian Writers. St. Lucia: University of Queensland Press 1991.

Geotzfridt, Nicholas J. *Indigenous Literatures of Oceania: A Survey of Criticism and Interpretation*. Bibliographies and Indexes in World Literature 47. Westport and London: Greenwood Press 1995.

Gibson, Ross. *South of the West: Postcolonialism and the Narrative Construction of Australia*. Art and Politics of the Everyday. Bloomington: Indiana University Press 1992.

Goldie, Terry. *Fear and Temptation: The Image of the Indigene in Canadian, Australian, and New Zealand Literatures*. Kingston and London: McGill/Queen's University Press 1989.

Grace, Patricia. *Dream Sleepers and Other Stories*. Pacific Paperbacks. Auckland: Longman Paul 1980; Auckland: Penguin 1986.

— *Electric City and Other Stories.* Auckland: Penguin 1987, 2nd edition 1989.

— *The Sky People [and Other Stories].* Auckland: Penguin 1994.

— *Waiariki.* Pacific Paperbacks. Auckland: Longman Paul 1975; Auckland: Penguin 1986.

Hamilton, Augustus. *Maori Art.* Wellington: New Zealand Institute, 1896–1901; repr. London: Holland Press 1977; NY: Harmer Johnson 1977.

Hodge, Bob, and Vijay Mishra. *Dark Side of the Dream: Australian Literature and the Postcolonial Mind.* Australian Cultural Studies. North Sydney: Allen & Unwin 1990.

Ihimaera, Witi. *Dear Miss Mansfield: A Tribute to Kathleen Mansfield Beauchamp.* Auckland: Viking 1989.

— *The New Net Goes Fishing.* Auckland: Heinemann 1977.

— *Pounamu, Pounamu.* Auckland: Heinemann 1972. Transl. [into Maori] Jean Wikiriwhi; Auckland: Heinemann 1986.

— ed. *Te Ao Marama: Contemporary Maori Writing.* Volume 1: *Te Whakahuatanga o te Ao: Reflections of Reality.* Volume 2: *He Whakaatanga o te Ao: The Reality.* Volume 3: *Te Puawaitanga o te Korero: The Flowering.* Volume 5: *Te Torino: The Spirit.* Birkenhead: Reed 1992–1996.

— *Vision Aotearoa: Kaupapa New Zealand.* Wellington: Bridget Williams Books 1994.

— *The Whale Rider.* Auckland: Viking 1987.

Isaacs, Jennifer. *Aboriginality: Contemporary Aboriginal Painting and Prints.* St. Lucia: University of Queensland Press 1989, 2nd edition 1992.

— *Australian Aboriginal Painting.* Sydney: Weldon Publishing 1989; NY: Dutton Studio Books/Penguin 1992.

Krupat, Arnold. *Ethno-Criticism: Ethnography, History, Literature.* Berkeley and Oxford: University of California Press 1992.

Leroux, Odette, et al., edd. *Inuit Women Artists: Voices from Cape Dorset* [1995]. NY: Chronicle Books 1996.

Levin, Michael D., ed. *Ethnicity and Aboriginality: Case Studies in Ethnonationalism*. Toronto: University of Toronto Press 1993.

McGrath, Robin. *Canadian Inuit Literature: The Development of a Tradition*. Mercury Series: National Museum of Man: Paper: Canadian Ethnological Service 94. Ottawa: National Museum of Man 1984.

McLaren, John. *New Pacific Literatures: Culture and Environment in the European Pacific*. Garland Reference Library of the Humanities 1054. NY and London: Garland 1993.

Mead, Sidney [Hirini] Moko, ed. *Te Maori: Maori Art from New Zealand Collections*. Revised edition. NY: Abrams and The American Federation of Arts 1985.

Michaels, Eric. *Bad Aboriginal Art: Tradition, Media, and Technological Horizons*. With a foreword by Dick Hebidge. Introduction by Marcia Langdon. Theory out of Bounds 2. Minneapolis: University of Minnesota Press 1994.

Morgan, Sally. *Wanamurraganya: The Story of Jack McPhee*. Fremantle: Fremantle Arts Centre Press 1989.

Mudrooroo [Narogin] (Colin Johnson). *Aboriginal Mythology: An A to Z Spanning the History of Aboriginal Mythology from the Earliest Legends to the Present Day*. London and San Francisco: Aquarian 1994.

— *Doin Wildcat*. South Yarra: Hyland House 1988.

— *The Kwinkan*. Imprint. Pymble, NSW: Angus and Robertson 1993.

— *Us Mob: History, Culture, Struggle: An Introduction to Indigeneous Australia*. Sydney and NY: Angus and Robertson 1995.

Neich, Roger. *Painted Histories: Early Maori Figurative Painting*. Auckland: Auckland University Press 1993.

Ojinmah, Umelo. *Witi Ihimaera: A Changing Vision*. Te Whenua 7. Dunedin: University of Otago Press 1993.

Oodgeroo Nunukul [/Noonuccal] (Kath Walker). *Strathbroke Dreamtime*. Imprint Lives. Pymble, NSW: Angus and Robertson 1992.

— *We Are Going*. Brisbane: Jacaranda Press 1964.

Perreault, Jeanne Martha, and Sylvia Vance, edd. *Writing the Circle: Native Women of Western Canada. An Anthology*. New edition. Edmonton: NeWest 1993.

Pettman, Jan. *Living in the Margins: Racism, Sexism and Feminism in Australia*. North Sydney: Allen and Unwin 1992.

Roman, Trish Fox, ed. *United Under One Sky: Contemporary Native Literature*. Freedom: Crossing Press 1994.

Seidelman, Harold, and James Turner. *The Inuit Imagination: Arctic Myth and Sculpture*. Vancouver: Douglas and McIntyre; NY: Thames and Hudson 1994.

Sharrad, Paul, ed. *Readings in Pacific Literature*. Wollongong: New Literatures Research Centre, University of Wollongong 1993.

Shoemaker, Adam. *Black Words White Pages: Aboriginal Literature 1929–1988*. UQP Studies in Australian Literature. St. Lucia: University of Queensland Press 1989.

Slipperjack, Ruby. *Silent Words*. Saskatoon: Fifth House Publications 1992.

Subramani. *After Narrative: The Pursuit of Reality and Fiction*. Suva: University of the South Pacific 1990.

Swinton, George. *Sculpture of the Inuit*. Toronto: McClelland and Stewart 1972; revised and updated edition 1992.

Te Awekotuku, Ngahuia. *Mana Wahine Maori: Selected Writings on Maori Women's Art, Culture and Politics*. Auckland: New Women's Press 1991.

Thomas, Nicholas. *Oceanic Art*. World of Art. London and NY: Thames and Hudson 1995.

Thompson, Liz, comp. *Aboriginal Voices: Contemporary Aboriginal Artists, Writers and Performers*. Brookvale, NSW: Simon and Schuster 1990.

Walker, Ranginui [J.]. *Ka Whawhai Tonu Matou. Struggle Without End*. Auckland: Penguin 1990.

Wendt, Albert. *Flying Fox in a Freedom Tree*. Pacific Paperbacks. Auckland: Longman Paul 1974.

— *Inside Us the Dead: Poems 1961–1974*. Pacific Paperbacks. Auckland: Longman Paul 1976.

— *Shaman of Visions*. Poems. Auckland: Auckland University Press/ Oxford University Press 1984.

— *The Birth and Death of the Miracle Man: A Collection of Short Stories* [1986]. Auckland: Penguin 1987.

— *Ola*. Auckland: Penguin 1991; Honolulu: University of Hawai'i Press 1995.

— *Black Rainbow*. Auckland: Penguin 1992; Honolulu: University of Hawai'i Press 1995.

— *Photographs. Poems*. Auckland: Auckland University Press 1995.

Williams, Mark. *Post-Colonial Literatures in English: Southeast Asia, New Zealand and the Pacific 1970–1992*. NY: G.K. Hall 1996.

Young, Elspeth. *Third World in the First: Development and Indigenous Peoples*. London and NY: Routledge 1995.

Zinovich, Jordan, et al., edd. *[ka na ki] Canadas*. [=Semiotext(e) #17 (6.2), 1994.] NY: Semiotext(e); Peterborough: Marginal Editions 1994.

— *Shaun F. D. Hughes*

FOLKLORE

NOTE: The realm of folklore is like a whole universe coexisting beside that of written literatures; its bibliography is correspondingly huge. The required list here for the most part excludes studies on particular traditions, although the section of Reference Tools and Sourcebooks does include a few well-known collections of materials from specific cultures.

Reference Tools and Sourcebooks (for consultation as needed)

Azzolina, David S. *Tale Type and Motif Indexes: An Annotated Bibliography*. NY: Garland 1987.

Bonnefoy, Yves, comp. *Mythologies*. 2 volumes. Chicago: University of Chicago Press 1991. (A restructured translation, ed. Wendy Doniger, of *Dictionnaire des mythologies et des religions des sociétés traditionnelles et du monde antique*. Paris: Flammarion 1981.)

Calvino, Italo. *Italian Folktales*. NY: Harcourt Brace Jovanovich 1980.

Campbell, Joseph. *The Hero with a Thousand Faces*. Princeton: Princeton University Press 1972.

— *The Masks of God*. NY: Viking 1959–1968, repr. NY: Penguin 1976. 4 volumes: [1] *Primitive Mythology*; [2] *Oriental Mythology*; [3] *Occidental Mythology*; [4] *Creative Mythology*.

Child, Francis James. *The English and Scottish Popular Ballads*. 5 volumes. Boston: Houghton Mifflin 1882–1898.

Dorson, Richard M., ed. *Peasant Customs and Savage Myths: Selections from the British Folklorists*. 2 volumes. Chicago: University of Chicago Press 1968.

Friedman, Albert B., ed. *The Viking Book of Folk Ballads of the English-Speaking World*. NY: Viking Press 1956, repr. 1963.

Gantz, Timothy. *Early Greek Myth: A Guide to Literary and Artistic Sources*. Baltimore: Johns Hopkins University Press 1993.

Gomme, Alice B. *The Traditional Games of England, Scotland, and Ireland*. 2 vols. London: Folk-Lore Society 1894, 1898, repr. NY: Dover Publications 1964.

Jones, Steven Swann. *Folklore and Literature in the United States: An Annotated Bibliography of Studies of Folklore in American Literature*. NY: Garland 1984.

Laws, G. Malcolm, Jr. *Native American Balladry: A Descriptive Study and a Bibliographical Syllabus*. Philadelphia: Publications of the American Folklore Society, revised edition 1964.

Leach, Maria, ed. *Funk & Wagnalls Standard Dictionary of Folklore, Mythology, and Legend*. 2 volumes. NY: Funk & Wagnalls 1940–1950, repr. Harper & Row 1984.

Newell, William Wells. *Games and Songs of American Children*. NY: Harper & Brothers 1883, repr. NY: Dover Publications 1963.

Opie, Iona, and Moira Tatem. *A Dictionary of Superstitions*. Oxford: Oxford University Press 1989.

Taylor, Archer. *The Proverb and An Index to the Proverb*. Hatboro: Folklore Associates 1962.

Thompson, Stith. *The Types of the Folktale: A Classification and Bibliography*. (A translation and enlargement of Antti Aarne, *Verzeichnis der Märchentypen*.) Helsinki: Academia Scientiarum Fennica 1928, revised 1961, 1973.

— *Motif-Index of Folk-Literature*. 6 volumes. Bloomington: Indiana University Press 1932–1936, revised edition 1955–1958.

Folklore Studies

Bauman, Richard. *Story, Performance, and Event: Contextual Studies of Oral Narrative*. NY: Cambridge University Press 1986.

Ben-Amos, Dan, ed. *Folklore Genres*. Austin: University of Texas Press 1976.

Briggs, Charles, and Amy Shuman, edd. *Theorizing Folklore: Toward New Perspectives on the Politics of Culture*. Special issue of *Western Folklore* 52:2–4 (April, July, October 1993) 109–400.

Clarke, Kenneth and Mary. *Introducing Folklore*. NY: Holt, Rinehart and Winston 1963.

— edd. *A Folklore Reader*. NY: A. S. Barnes 1965.

Dorson, Richard M. *Folklore and Folklife: An Introduction*. Chicago: University of Chicago Press 1972.

Douglas, Mary. *Purity and Danger: An Analysis of the Concepts of Pollution and Taboo*. London: Routledge and Kegan Paul 1966.

Dundes, Alan. *Interpreting Folklore*. Bloomington: Indiana University Press 1980.

— *Folklore Matters*. Knoxville: University of Tennessee Press 1989.

Eliade, Mircea. *The Sacred and the Profane: The Nature of Religion*. NY: Harper & Row 1959.

Georges, Robert A., and Michael Owen Jones. *Folkloristics: An Introduction*. Bloomington: University of Chicago Press 1995.

Goldstein, Kenneth S. *A Guide for Fieldworkers in Folklore*. Hatboro: Folklore Associates 1964.

Goody, Jack. *Literacy in Traditional Societies*. Cambridge: Cambridge University Press 1968, 1993.

Hollis, Susan Tower, et al., edd. *Feminist Theory and the Study of Folklore*. Urbana: University of Illinois Press 1993.

Jackson, Bruce, et al., edd. *Folklore and Folklife*. Washington: American Folklore Society 1984.

Jones, Michael Owen, ed. *Putting Folklore to Use*. Lexington: University Press of Kentucky 1994.

Krappe, Alexander Haggerty. *The Science of Folklore*. NY: Barnes & Noble 1930, repr. NY: Norton 1964.

Krohn, Kaarle. *Folklore Methodology*. Austin: University of Texas Press 1971.

Leach, Edmund R., ed. *The Structural Study of Myth and Totemism*. London: Tavistock 1967.

Lévi-Strauss, Claude. *The Raw and the Cooked*. (Volume 1 of *Mythologiques*, translated as *Introduction to a Science of Mythology*.) NY: Harper & Row 1969, repr. NY: Penguin 1992.

— *The Savage Mind*. Chicago: University of Chicago Press 1966.

Maranda, Pierre, and E. Köngäs Maranda, edd. *Structural Analysis of Oral Tradition*. Philadelphia: University of Pennsylvania Press 1971.

Newall, Venetia J., ed. *Folklore Studies in the Twentieth Century: Proceedings of the Centenary Conference of the Folklore Society*. Totowa: Rowman and Littlefield 1980.

Paredes, Américo, and Richard Bauman, edd. *Toward New Perspectives in Folklore*. Austin: University of Texas Press 1971.

Schechter, Harold. *The Bosom Serpent: Folklore and Popular Art*. Iowa City: Univerity of Iowa Press 1988.

Schoemaker, George H., ed. *The Emergence of Folklore in Everyday Life: A Fieldguide and Sourcebook*. Bloomington: Trickster Press 1990.

Stahl, Sandra Dolby. *Literary Folkloristics and the Personal Narrative.* Bloomington: Indiana University Press 1989.

Sydow, Carl Wilhelm. *Selected Papers on Folklore.* Ed. Laurits Bødker. Copenhagen: Rosenkilde and Bagger 1948.

Thompson, Stith. *The Folktale.* NY: Dryden Press 1946, repr. Berkeley: University of California Press 1977.

Zipes, Jack. *Breaking the Magic Spell: Radical Theories of Folk and Fairy Tales.* Austin: University of Texas Press 1979.

— *Creative Storytelling: Building Community, Changing Lives.* NY: Routledge 1995.

— Myrdene Anderson and John T. Kirby

FRANCOPHONE LITERATURE

Lyric Poetry

Reeve, John, and Clive Wake, edd. *French African Verse*. London: Heinemann 1972.

Brossard, Nicole. *Lovhers*. Montreal: Guernica 1987.

Césaire, Aimé. *Return to My Native Land*. Bilingual edition. Paris: Présence Africaine 1939.

— *Non-vicious Circle: Twenty Poems*. Stanford: Stanford University Press 1984.

Moisan, Clément. *A Poetry of Frontiers*. Toronto: Porcépic 1983.

Senghor, Leopold Sédar. *Collected Poetry*. Charlottesville: University Press of Virginia 1991.

U Tam'si, Tchicaya. *Selected Poems*. London: Heinemann 1970.

Drama

Yacine, Kateb. *Intelligence Powder*. NY: Ubu Repertory Theater Publishers 1959.

Césaire, Aimé. *A Tempest*. NY: Borchardt 1968.

Lab'ou Tansi, Sony. *Parentheses of Blood*. NY: Ubu Repertory Theater Publishers 1981.

Gurik, Robert. *The Trial of Jean-Baptiste M*. Vancouver: Talonbooks 1968.

Tremblay, Michel. *Les Belles-Sœurs*. Vancouver: Talonbooks 1968.

Narrative

Ben Jelloun, Tahar. *Silent Day in Tangiers*. San Diego: Harcourt Brace Jovanovich 1990.

Boudjedra, Rachid. *The Repudiation*. Colorado Springs, Three Continents 1969.

Dib, Mohammed. *Who Remembers the Sea*. Colorado Springs: Three Continents 1962.

Djebar, Assia. *A Sister to Scheherazade*. London: Heinemann 1987.

Dadié, Bernard. *The Black Cloth: A Collection of African Folk Tales*. Amherst: University of Massachusetts Press 1955.

Laye, Camara. *The Dark Child*. NY: Noonday 1953.

Sembène, Ousmane. *God's Bits of Wood*. Garden City: Anchor 1960.

Bâ, Mariama. *So Long a Letter*. London: Virago 1979.

Kourouma, Ahmadou. *Monnew*. San Francisco: Mercury House 1993.

Condé, Maryse. *Tree of Life*. NY: Ballantine 1987.

Glissant, Edouard. *The Ripening*. London: Heinemann 1958.

Vieyra, Myriam Warner. *Juletane*. London: Heinemann 1987.

Roy, Gabrielle. *The Tin Flute*. NY: Reynal and Hitchcock 1945.

Blais, Marie-Claire. *Deaf to the City*. Woodstock NY: Overlook 1965.

Ferron, Jaques. *Tales from the Uncertain Country*. Toronto: Anasi 1972.

Tremblay, Michel. *Making Room*. London: Serpent's Tail 1986.

Stratford, Philip, and Michael Thomas, edd. *Voices from Quebec: An Anthology of Translations*. Toronto: Van Nostrand Reinhold 1977.

Non-Fictional Prose
Fanon, Frantz. *Black Skin, White Masks*. NY: Grove 1952.

— *Thomas F. Broden, Paul Benhamou, and T. Denean Sharpley-Whiting*

FRENCH LITERATURE (Continental)

Lyric Poetry (Except as noted, selections will be taken from *The Penguin Book of French Verse* [4 volumes, NY: Penguin 1958–1961]; the latter will be specified by volume and page-number.)

Villon, François (ca. 1431). *Œuvres*. Paris: Champion 1991. Transl. Anthony Bonner as *Complete Works*. NY: Bantam 1960.

Ronsard, Pierre de (1524–1560) and Joachim du Bellay (1525–ca. 1560), poems in *The Penguin Book of French Verse*, II, 28–77.

Fontaine, Jean de la (1621–1695), selected poems, II, 238–258.

Lamartine, Alphonse de (1790–1869), selected poems, III, 10–18.

Nerval, Gérard de (1808–1855), selected poems, III, 95–108.

Baudelaire, Charles (1821–1867), *Les Fleurs du Mal* [1857]. Paris: Gallimard 1972.

Mallarmé, Stéphane (1842–1898), selected poems, III, 187–208.

Rimbaud, Arthur (1854–1891), *Oeuvres* (1871–1875), Paris: Garnier 1981.

Valéry, Paul (1871–1945), selected poems, IV, 43–76.

Apollinaire, Guillaume (1880–1918), *Alcools* (1913), *Œeuvres*. Paris: Gallimard 1959.

Ponge, Francis (1899–1988), selected poems, IV, 243–263.

Michaux, Henri (1899–1984), selected poems, IV, 254–263.

Char, René (1907–1988), selected poems, IV, 288–294.

Bonnefoy, Yves (1923–), selected poems, IV, 310–316.

Drama (stage-scripts and screenplay)

Corneille, Pierre (1606–1684). *Œuvres*. Paris: Gallimard 1981. Read *Le Cid* [1636] and *Horace* [1640].

Racine, Jean (1639–1699). *Œuvres complètes*. Paris: Gallimard 1980–81. Read *Andromaque* (1667), *Britannicus* (1669), and *Phèdre* (1664).

Molière [Jean Baptiste Poquelin] (1622–1673). *Œuvres*. Paris: Gallimard 1981. Read *Tartuffe* (1664), *Le Misanthrope* (1666), and *Le Bourgeois Gentilhomme* (1670),

Jarry, Alfred (1837–1907). *Œuvres*. Paris: Gallimard 1988. Read *Ubu roi* (1896).

Ionesco, Eugène (1925–1994). *Théâtre complet*. Paris: Gallimard 1991. Read *La cantatrice chauve* (1950).

Beckett, Samuel (1906–1990). *En attendant Godot* (1953). Paris: Editions Minuit 1952.

Duras, Marguerite (1914–1996). *Hiroshima mon Amour* (1959). Paris: Gallimard 1960.

Long Narrative

Anonymous. *La chanson de Roland* [ca. 1080]. Ed. Joseph Bédier. Alfortville: H. Piazza 1974. Transl. Patricia Terry as *The Song of Roland* (Englewood Cliffs: Prentice-Hall 1992).

Béroul and Thomas, *Tristan and Iseut* [ca. 1165]. Paris: Société des anciens textes français 1965. Transll. Janet Hillier Caulkins and Guy R. Mermier as *Tristan and Iseult; a Twelfth Century Poem* (Paris: H. Champion 1967).

Troyes, Chrétien de (12th century). *Perceval le Gallois; ou, Le conte du Graal* [ca. 1177-1181]. NY: Garland 1990. Transl. David Staines in *The Complete Romances of Chrétien de Troyes* (Bloomington: Indiana University Press 1990).

Rabelais, François (ca. 1490–1553). *Gargantua et Pantagruel* [1532]. In *Œuvres complètes*. Paris: Gallimard 1978. Transl. Burton Raffel as *Gargantua and Pantagruel* (NY: Norton 1990). Read books 1–2.

Fayette, Madame Marie de la [Marie-Madeleine Pioche de la Vergne] (1634–1693). *La princesse de Clèves* [1678]. Paris: Imprimerie Nationale 1980.

Voltaire [Arouet, François Marie] (1694–1778). *Candide* [1759]. In *Romans et Contes*. Paris: Flammarion 1964.

Diderot, Denis (1713–1784). *Le neveu de Rameau* [1762]. Paris: Garnier-Flammarion 1967.

Laclos, Choderlos de (1741–1803). *Les liaisons dangereuses* [1782]. Paris: Gallimard 1951, transl. P. W. K. Stone (NY: Penguin 1961).

Stendhal [Marie Henri Beyle] (1783–1842). *Le rouge et le noir* [1831]. Paris: Garnier 1973. Transl. Stirling Haig as *The Red and the Black* (Cambridge: Cambridge University Press 1989).

Balzac, Honoré de (1799–1850). *Le père Goriot* [1834]. In *La comédie humaine*. Paris: Gallimard 1971.

Zola, Emile (1840–1902). *Germinal* [1885]. In *Les Rougon-Macquart*. Paris: Gallimard 1960.

Flaubert, Gustave (1821–1880). *Madame Bovary: Mœurs de province* [1856]. Paris: Gallimard 1954. Transl. Francis Steegmuller as *Madame Bovary: Patterns of Provincial Life* (NY: Modern Library 1957).

Proust, Marcel (1871–1922). *A la recherche du temps perdu* [1913–1927]. Tome 1: *Du côté de chez Swann*. Paris: Gallimard 1954. Transl. C. K. Scott Moncrieff as *Swann's Way* (volume 1 of *Remembrance of Things Past*). NY: Vintage 1970.

Sartre, Jean-Paul (1905–1980). *La nausée* [1938]. In *Œuvres romanesques* (Paris: Gallimard 1981). Transl. Lloyd Alexander as *Nausea* (NY: New Directions 1964).

Camus, Albert (1913–1960). *La peste* [1947]. Paris: Gallimard. Transl. Stuart Gilbert as *The Plague* (NY: Vintage 1991).

Yourcenar, Marguerite [Marguerite Cleenewerck de Crayencour] (1903–1987). *Mémoires d'Hadrien* [1951]. Paris: Gallimard 1982. Transl. Grace Frick as *Memoirs of Hadrian* (NY: Farrar Straus Giroux 1954).

Short Narrative

Navarre, Marguerite de (1492–1549). «Amours d'Amadour et de Floride» (in *Heptaméron*, 1559). Paris: Garnier 1967. Transl. H. P. Clive as 'Love at the Window' in *Tales from the Heptameron*. London: Athlone Press 1970.

Flaubert, Gustave (1821–1880). «Un cœur simple» [1877]. Paris: Garnier 1988. Transl. A. J. Krailsheimer as 'A Simple Heart' in *Gustave Flaubert: Three Tales*. Oxford: Oxford University Press 1991.

Zola, Emile (1840–1902). «Attaque du moulin» [1877]. In *Contes et nouvelles* (Paris: Gallimard 1976). Transl. Belle M. Sherman as 'The Attack on the Mill' in *Emile Zola: The Experimental Novel and Other Essays*. NY: Haskell House 1964.

Maupassant, Guy de (1850–1893). «Boule de suif», «Une ficelle», and «Mademoiselle Fifi». In *Contes et Nouvelles*, tomes I et II (Paris: Gallimard 1979). Transl. as 'Ball of Fat,' 'The Piece of String,' and 'Mademoiselle Fifi,' in *Complete Short Stories*. NY: Hanover House 1955.

Camus, Albert (1913–1960). «L'Hôte». In *L'Exil et le royaume.* Paris: Gallimard 1957. Transl. Justin O'Brien as 'The Guest' in *Exile and the Kingdom.* NY: Vintage 1991.

Non-Fictional Prose

Capellanus, Andreas (12th century). *De Amore* (ca. 1174–1186). Paris: Klincksieck 1974. Transl. John Jay Parry as *The Art of Courtly Love* (NY: Columbia University Press 1990).

Montaigne, Michel de (1533–1592). «Que philosopher c'est apprendre à mourir» [1580]. In *Œuvres complètes.* Paris: Gallimard 1962. Transl. Donald Frame as 'To Philosophize is to Learn to Die' in *The Compete Essays of Montaigne.* Stanford: Stanford University Press 1958.

— «De l'institution des enfants» ('On the Education of Children').

— «De l'amitié» ('On Friendship').

— «Des cannibales» ('On Cannibals').

— «Apologie de Raymond Sebond» ('Apology for Raymond Sebond').

— «Du repentir» ('On Repentance').

— «Sur des vers de Virgile» ('On Some Verse of Vergil').

Descartes, René (1596–1650). *Discours de la méthode* [1637]. Paris: Librairie Philosophique 1967. Transl. George Heffernan as *Discourse on the Method.* Notre Dame: University of Notre Dame Press 1994.

Rousseau, Jean-Jacques (1712–1778). *Confessions* [1782]. In *Œuvres.* Paris: Garnier 1964. Transl. J. M. Cohen as *The Confessions of Jean-Jacques Rousseau.* NY: Penguin 1953. Read books 1 and 5.

Zola, Emile (1840–1902). *Le Roman expérimental* [1880]. Paris: Cercle du Livre 1966. Transl. Belle M. Sherman in *Emile Zola: The Experimental Novel and Other Essays.* NY: Haskell House 1964.

Breton, André (1896–1966). *Manifestes du surréalisme* [1924]. Paris: Gallimard 1963. Transll. Richard Seaver and Helen R. Lane as *Manifestoes of Surrealism.* Ann Arbor: Univeristy of Michigan Press 1969.

Artaud, Antonin (1896–1948). *Le Théâtre et son double* [1938]. Paris: Gallimard 1988. Transl. Mary Caroline Richards as *The Theatre and its Double.* NY: Grove Press 1958.

—Erdmute Wenzel White and Robert S. Freeman

GERMAN LITERATURE

Lyric Poetry

Hamburger, Michael, transl. *German Poetry, 1910–1975: An Anthology*. NY: Dutton 1976.

Welse-Engel, Ingrid, ed. *German Poetry from the Beginnings to 1750*. NY: Continuum 1992.

Vogelweide, Walther von der (1170–1230). 'I saw the world.' In *Sixty Poems from Walther von der Vogelweide*. Westport : Hyperion Press 1978.

Klopstock, Friedrich Gottlieb (1724–1813). 'Frühlingsfeier.' In: *German Poetry from 1750 to 1900*. Ed. Robert Browning. NY: Continuum, 1984.

Goethe, Johann Wolfgang von (1749–1832). *Poems. Selections*. Boston: Insel Publications 1983.

Hölderlin, Friedrich (1770–1843). *Hyperion and Selected Poems*. NY: Continuum 1990.

Novalis [Friedrich Leopold von Hardenberg]. (1772–1801). 'Hymns to the Night.' Pp. 138–159 in *Pollen and Fragments*. Transl. Arthur Versluis. Grand Rapids: Phanes Press 1989.

Droste-Hülshoff, Annette von (1797–1848). *Poems*. Ed. Margaret E. Atkinson. London: Oxford University Press 1964.

Heine, Heinrich (1797–1856). *Germany, a Winter's Tale* [1844]. NY: L. B. Fischer 1944.

Hofmannsthal, Hugo von (1874–1929). *Selected Plays and Libretti*. NY: Pantheon 1963.

Rilke, Rainer Maria (1875–1926). *Between Roots: Selected Poems*. Princeton: Princeton University Press 1986.

Lasker-Schüler, Else (1876–1945). *Concert*. Lincoln: University of Nebraska Press 1994.

Benn, Gottfried (1886–1956). *Prose. Essays. Poems*. NY: Continuum 1986.

Trakl, Georg (1887–1914). *Twenty Poems*. Madison: Sixties Press 1961.

Sachs, Nelly (1891–1917). *O The Chimneys: Selected Poems, including the Verse Play Eli.* NY: Farrar, Straus & Giroux 1967.

Celan, Paul (1920–1970). *Last Poems.* San Francisco: North Point 1986.

Drama

Lessing, Gotthold Ephraim (1729–1781). *Nathan the Wise.* NY: Block Publishing Company 1917.

Schiller, Friedrich (1759–1805). *Wilhelm Tell.* Transl. William F. Mainland. Chicago: University of Chicago Press 1972.

Kleist, Heinrich von (1777–1811).'Penthesilea.' In *Five Plays.* New Haven: Yale University Press 1988.

Goethe, Johann Wolfgang von (1749–1832). *Faust I , Faust II.* Boston: Insel Publications 1984.

Büchner, Georg (1813–1837). *Woyzeck, and Leonce and Lena.* San Francisco: Chandler 1962.

Oskar Kokoschka and other Expressionist Texts. Ed. Mel Gordon. NY: PAJ Publishers 1986. (Includes texts by Georg Kaiser, Gottfried Benn, Walter Hasenclever, and Ernst Toller.)

Brecht, Bertolt (1898–1956). *Galileo.* NY: Grove Press 1966.

Dürrenmatt, Friedrich (1921–)*The Physicists.* Transl. James Kirkup. NY: Grove Press 1967.

Müller, Heiner (1929–). *The Battle: Plays, Prose, Poems.* Ed & transl. Carl Weber. NY: PAJ Publishers 1989.

Narrative: Fiction and Non-Fiction

Blackwell, Jeannine, and Susanne Zantrop edd. *Bitter Healing: German Women Writers 1700–1830. An Anthology.* Lincoln: University of Nebraska Press 1990.

Eschenbach, Wolfram von (12th century). *Parzival.* NY: Continuum 1991.

Brant, Sebastian (1458–1521). *The Ship of Fools.* NY: Columbia University Press 1944.

Luther, Martin (1483–1546) and Erasmus von Rotterdam (1469?–1536). *Free Will and Salvation.* Philadelphia: Westminster Press 1969.

La Roche, Sophie von (1730–1807). 'Two Sisters.' Pp. 149–187 in Blackwell and Zantrop.

Goethe, Johann Wolfgang von (1749–1832). *The Sorrows of Young Werther. The New Melusina. Novelle.* NY: Holt, Rinehart & Winston 1949.

Kant, Immanuel (1724–1804). 'What is Enlightenment?' In *Foundations of Metaphysics of Morals and What is Enlightenment.* NY: Liberal Arts Press 1959.

Schiller, Friedrich (1759–1805). *Essays.* NY: Continuum 1993.

Kleist, Heinrich von (1777–1811). 'On the Marionette Theater.' Transl. Christian-Albrecht Gollup. Pp. 238–244 in *German Romantic Criticism.* Ed. A. Leslie Willson. NY: Continuum 1982.

Varnhagen, Rachel von (1771–1833). 'Selected Letters.' Pp. 403–416 in Blackwell and Zantrop.

Arnim, Bettine von (1785–1859). 'The Queen's Son.' Pp. 443–454 in Blackwell and Zantrop.

Jean Paul [Jean Paul Friedrich Richter] (1763–1825). 'Airshipman Giannozzo's Logbook: Comic Appendix to *Titan.*' Pp. 203–235 in *Jean Paul: A Reader.* Ed. by Timothy J. Casey. Transl. Erika Casey. Baltimore: Johns Hopkins University Press 1992.

Novalis (1772–1801). *Henry of Ofterdingen.* Transl. Palmer Hilty. Prospects Heights: Waveland P, 1990.

Hoffmann, E. T. A. (1776–1822). *The Golden Pot and other Tales.* Oxford: Oxford University Press 1992.

Droste-Hülshoff, Annette von (1797–1848). 'Ledwina.' Pp. 473–526 in Blackwell and Zantrop.

Fontane, Theodor (1819–1898). *Short Novels and Other Writings.* NY: Continuum 1982.

Nietzsche, Friedrich (1844–1900). 'On Truth and Lie in an Extra-Moral Sense.' Pp. 42–47 in *The Portable Nietzsche.* NY: Penguin 1982.

Mann, Thomas (1875–1955). *Death in Venice.* London: Secker & Warburg 1990.

Hesse, Hermann (1877–1962). *Narcissus and Goldmund.* NY: Farrar, Straus & Giroux 1968.

Kafka, Franz (1883–1924). *Metamorphoses.* NY: Schocken Books 1968.

Seghers, Anna (b.1900–) *The Seventh Cross.* Transl. James A. Galston. Boston: Little Brown & Company 1942.

Canetti, Elias (1905–). *The Tongue Set Free: Remembrance of a European Childhood.* NY: Continuum, 1983.

Frisch, Max (1911–). *Andorra.* London: Methuen 1962.

Böll, Heinrich (1917–). *Lost Honor of Katharina Blum: or how violence develops and where it can lead.* NY: McGraw-Hill 1975.

Bachmann, Ingeborg (1926–1973). *Malina.* Transl. Philip Boehm. NY: Holmes & Meier 1990.

Wolf, Christa (1929–). *The Quest For Christa T.* NY: Farrar, Straus & Giroux 1979.

Handke, Peter (1942–) *Absence.* Transl. Ralph Manheim. NY: Farrar, Straus & Giroux 1990.

Kirsch, Sarah (unlisted birth date). *Catlives.* Transll. Marina Roscher and Charles Fischman. Lubbock: Texas Tech University Press 1991.

— *Beate Allert*

GREECE I: Classical Greek Literature in English Translation

NOTES: • This list does not include works in Greek included in the 'Beginnings?' list; it is assumed that the student will read those as well. • For standard critical editions of Greek texts one should consult the *Thesaurus Linguae Graecae Canon of Greek Authors and Works*, edd. Luci Berkowitz et al. (NY: Oxford University Press, 3rd edition 1990).

Reference Works (for consultation as needed) and Abbreviations

Athanassakis = *Hesiod: Theogony, Works and Days, Shield*. Transl. Apostolos Athanassakis. Baltimore: Johns Hopkins University Press 1983.

Boardman, John, et al. edd. *The Oxford History of the Classical World*. Oxford: Clarendon Press 1986.

Cooper = *Plato: Complete Works*. Edd. John M. Cooper and D. S. Hutchinson. Indianapolis: Hackett 1997.

Easterling, P. E., and B. M. W. Knox edd. *Greek Literature*. The Cambridge History of Classical Literature, volume 1. Cambridge: Cambridge University Press 1985.

Fagles/A = *Aeschylus: The Oresteia*. Transl. Robert Fagles. NY: Penguin 1979.

Fagles/S = *Sophocles: The Three Theban Plays*. Transl. Robert Fagles. NY: Penguin 1984.

Fränkel, Hermann. *Early Greek Poetry and Philosophy*. NY: Harcourt Brace Jovanovich 1962.

Hornblower, Simon, and Antony Spawforth edd. *The Oxford Classical Dictionary*. 3nd edition. Oxford: Clarendon Press 1996.

M. C. Howatson ed. *The Oxford Companion to Classical Literature*. 2nd edition. Oxford: Clarendon Press 1989.

Lemprière, J. *Lemprière's Classical Dictionary: Proper Names Cited by the Ancient Authors*. Revised edition London 1865, repr. London: Bracken Books. 1984.

Lesky, Albin. *A History of Greek Literature*. NY: Thomas Y. Crowell 1966, repr. Indianapolis: Hackett 1996.

Reardon = *Collected Ancient Greek Novels*, ed. B. P. Reardon. Berkeley: University of California Press 1989.

Vellacott = *Euripides: Alcestis and Other Plays*. Transl. Philip Vellacott. NY: Penguin 1953.

Melic, Elegiac, and Iambic Poetry

Lyric Poets. Read all the selections in Andrew M. Miller, *Greek Lyric: An Anthology in Translation*. Indianapolis: Hackett 1996.

Pindar (Pindaros, ca. 522–438 BCE). *Pindar's Victory Songs*. Ed. Frank J. Nisetich. Baltimore: Johns Hopkins University Press 1980.

Drama

Aeschylus (Aiskhulos, ca. 525–456 BCE). *Agamemnon*. In Fagles/A.

— *Choephoroe (The Libation Bearers)*. In Fagles/A.

— *Eumenides*. In Fagles/A.

Sophocles (Sophoklês, ca. 496–406 BCE). *Antigone*. In Fagles/S.

— *Oedipus at Colonus*. In Fagles/S.

Euripides (Euripidês, ca. 484–406 BCE). *Alcestis*. In Vellacott.

— *Hippolytus*. In Vellacott.

Aristophanes (Aristophanês, ca. 450–388 BCE). *Frogs*. In *Aristophanes: The Frogs and Other Plays*, transl. David Barrett. NY: Penguin 1964.

— *Clouds*. In *Aristophanes: Lysistrata and Other Plays*, transl. Alan H. Sommerstein. NY: Penguin 1973.

Epic Poetry

Hesiod (Hêsiodos, 8th century BCE). *Theogony*. In Athanassakis.

— *Works and Days*. In Athanassakis.

The Homeric Hymn to Demeter: Translation, Commentary, and Interpretive Essays. Ed. Helene P. Foley. Princeton: Princeton University Press 1994. Read the Hymn and commentary (pp. 2–64).

Apollonius of Rhodes (Apollônios, 3rd century BCE). *Argonautica*. Transl. Richard Hunter as *Jason and the Golden Fleece*. Oxford: Oxford University Press 1995.

History

Herodotus (Hêrodotos, ca. 484–425 BCE). *The Histories*. Transll. Aubrey de Sélincourt and John M. Marincola. NY: Penguin 1996. Read books 1 and 2.

Thucydides (Thoukudidês, † ca 401 BCE). *History of the Peloponnesian War*. Transl. Rex Warner; introduction and notes by M.I. Finley. NY: Penguin 1972. Read books 1–2, 6–7.

Plutarch (L. [?] Mestrius Plutarchus, ca. 49–121 CE). *Lives of the Greeks and Romans*. Read the biographies of Demosthenes and Alexander in *The Age of Alexander*, transl. Ian Scott-Kilvert (NY: Penguin 1973) and those of Caesar and Cicero in *The Fall of the Roman Republic*, transl. Rex Warner (NY: Penguin 1972).

Prose Fiction

Aesop (Aisôpos, attributed author; actual author[s] and date[s] uncertain). *Fables of Aesop*, transl. S. A. Handford. NY: Penguin 1964.

Achilles Tatius (Akhilleus Tatios, 2nd century CE). *Leucippe and Clitophon*. Read the translation by J. J. Winkler in Reardon.

Longus (Loggos, 2nd–3rd century CE). *Daphnis and Chloe*. Read the translation by C. Gill in Reardon.

Philosophy and Rhetoric

Plato (Platôn, ca. 428–348 BCE). *Apology of Socrates*. Transl. G. M. A. Grube. In Cooper.

— *Phaedo*. Transl. G. M. A. Grube. In Cooper.

— *Cratylus*. Transl. C. D. C. Reeve. In Cooper.

Xenophon (Xenophôn, ca. 428–354 BCE). *Conversations of Socrates*, ed. Robin Waterfield. NY: Penguin 1990. Read *Socrates' Defence* and *The Dinner-Party*.

Aristotle (Aristotelês, 384–322 BCE). *On Rhetoric*. Transl. George A. Kennedy. NY: Oxford University Press 1991.

— *Ethics*. Transl. J. A. K. Thomson. NY: Penguin 1976.

Longinus (Logginos, attributed author; actual authorship and date disputed). *On the Sublime*. Read the translation by W. H. Fyfe and D. A. Russell in *Aristotle: Poetics; Longinus: On the Sublime; Demetrius: On Style* (Loeb Classical Library vol. 199, 2nd edition only). Cambridge MA: Harvard University Press 1995.

— John T. Kirby

GREECE II: Late Antique and Byzantine

NOTES: • All dates listed are CE. • Because some of these translations may be unusually difficult to obtain, the student may (with the permission of her advisor in this area) substitute another reputable translation of the same title.

Ammianus Marcellinus († ca. 390). *Roman History*. Transl. J.C. Rolfe. 3 volumes. Cambridge MA: Harvard University Press 1935–1939. Read Book 21 (in volume 2) and *Lineage of the Emperor Constantine* (in volume 3).

Ammonas (4th century). *The Letters of Ammonas, Successor of Saint Anthony*. Transl. D.-J. Chitty. Oxford: Sisters of the Love of God Press, revised edition 1979.

Anonymous. *Life of Pachomius*. Transl. A.N. Athanassakis. Missoula: Scholars Press 1975.

Arethas (Archbishop of Caesarea) (ca. 860–ca. 940). (in) R.J.H. Jenkins et al., 'Nine Orations.' *Byzantinische Zeitschrift* 47 (1954) 1–17.

Athanasius (Athanasios, Saint, Patriarch of Alexandria, † 373). *The Incarnation of the Word of God, being the Treatise of St. Athanasius, De incarnatione verbi Dei*. NY: Macmillan 1946.

— *Life of St. Antony*. In Robert C. Gregg transl., *The Life of Antony and the Letter to Marcellinus*. NY: Paulist Press 1980.

Athanasius I (Athanasios, Patriarch of Constantinople, r. 1289–1293 and 1303–1309). *The Correspondence of Athanasius I Patriarch of Constantinople: Letters to the Emperor Andronicus II, Members of the Imperial Family, and Officials*. Ed. A.-M. Talbot. Washington: Dumbarton Oaks 1975.

Basil the Great (Basilios, Saint, Archbishop of Caesarea, ca. 330–379). *Saint Basil: The Letters.* Ed. Roy J. Deferrari. 4 volumes. London: Heinemann 1926–1934. Read letters 1, 2, 17, 25, 27, 30, 31, 34, 39, 40, 48, 197, 237, 248, 293, and 334-359.

Chrysostom, John (Ioannes Khrusostomos, Saint, Patriarch of Constantinople, † 407). *On the Priesthood.* Transl. Graham Neville. London: SPCK 1964.

Clement of Alexandria (Titus Flauius Clemens Alexandrinus, ca. 150–ca. 212). 'On Spiritual Perfection.' In J.E.L. Oulton and H. Chadwick, transll. *Alexandrian Christianity.* Philadelphia: Westminster Press 1977.

Comnena, Anna (Anna Komnene, 1083–ca. 1150). *The Alexiad of Anna Comnena.* Transl. E.R.A. Sewter. Baltimore: Penguin 1969, 1980.

Constantinus VII Porphyrogenitus (Konstantinos VII Porphyrogenetos 905–959). *De administrando imperio.* Transl. R.J.H. Jenkins. Washington: Dumbarton Oaks 1967.

Constantius II (Flauius Iulius Constantius, Emperor, 317–361). In Swift, L.J., and J.H. Oliver. 'Constantius II on Flavius Philippus.' *American Journal of Philology* 83 (1962) 247–264.

Cyril of Jerusalem (Kyrillos, Saint, Bishop of Jerusalem, ca. 315–ca. 386). *St. Cyril of Jerusalem's Lectures on the Christian Sacraments, the Procatechesis, and the Five Mystagogical Catacheses.* Transl. R.W. Church. London: SPCK 1951.

Digenes Akritas (10th–11th century). Transl. D.B. Hull as *The Two-Blood Border Lord.* Athens: Ohio University Press 1972.

Dio Chrysostom (Dio Cocceianus Chrysostomus, ca. 40–ca. 120). *Works.* Edd. J.W. Cohoon and H. Lamar Crosby. 5 volumes. London: Heinemann 1932–1951. Read Discourses 52–55, 57 (in volume 4) and 70–71 (in volume 5).

Doukas (15th century). *Decline and Fall of Byzantium to the Ottoman Turks.* Transl. H.J. Magoulias. Detroit: Wayne State University Press 1975.

Eunapius (Eunapios, 346–414). *Lives of the Sophists*. In *Philostratus and Eunapius: Lives of the Sophists*. Transl. W.C. Wright. London: Heinemann 1921.

Eusebius of Caesarea (Eusebios, Bishop of Caesarea, ca. 260 – ca. 340). *Ecclesiastical History*. Transll. G.A. Williamson and Andrew Louth as *The History of the Church from Christ to Constantine*. NY: Penguin 1989. Read Book 1.

Eutropios (4th century). *The Breviarium ab urbe condita of Eutropius: The Right Honourable Secretary of State for General Petitions: Dedicated to Lord Valens, Gothicus Maximus and Perpetual Emperor*. Transl. H.W. Bird. Liverpool: Liverpool University Press 1993.

Gregory of Nazianzus (Gregorios Nazianzenos, Saint, 329–389). 'On Saint Basil the Great.' In Leo P. McCauley et al., transll., *Funeral Orations by Saint Gregory Nazianzen and Saint Ambrose*. Washington: Catholic University of America Press 1953.

Gregory of Nyssa (Gregorios, Saint, Bishop of Nyssa, ca. 331–396). 'ΠΕΡΙ ΤΕΛΕΙΟΤΗΤΟΣ — On Perfection.' Transl. Brother Casimir McCambley, O.C.S.O. *Greek Orthodox Theological Review* 32 (1984) 349–379.

Irene Eulogia Choumnaina Palaiologos (Princess, † 1360). *A Woman's Quest for Spiritual Guidance: The Correspondence of Princess Irene Eulogia Choumnaina Palaiologos with Her Spiritual Director*. Ed. Angela C. Hero. Brookline: Hellenic College Press 1986.

John Climacus (Ioannes Klimakos, Saint, † ca. 649). *The Ladder of Divine Ascent*. Transll. C. Luibheid and N. Russell. London: SPCK 1982.

John of Damascus (Ioannes, Saint, ca. 676–749). *On the Divine Images: Three Apologies against Those Who Attack the Holy Images*. Transl. D. Anderson. Crestwood: St. Vladimir's Seminary Press 1980.

Julian the Apostate (Flauius Claudius Iulianus, Emperor, r. 331–363). *The Works of the Emperor Julian*. Ed. Wilmer Cave Wright. 3 volumes. London: Heinemann 1923–1953. Read (in volume

2) the *Misopógón*, and (in volume 3) Letters 36, 58, 58 and *Against the Galileans*.

Justinian I (Petrus Sabbatius Iustinianus, Emperor, r. 527–565). *The Digest of Roman Law: Theft, Rapine, Damage, and Insult*. Transl. C.F. Kolbert. NY: Penguin 1979.

— *Justinian's Institutes*. Transll. Peter Birks and Grant McLeod. Ithaca: Cornell University Press 1987. Read book 1.

Libanius (Libanios, 314–393). *Selected Works*. Ed. A.F. Norman. Cambridge MA: Harvard University Press 1969, 1977. Read (in volume 2) orations 2, 30, 49, and 50.

— *Autobiography and Selected Letters*. Ed. A.F. Norman. 2 volumes. Cambridge MA: Harvard University Press 1992. Read (in volume 1) the *Autobiography*.

Malalas, John (Ioannes Malalas, 6th century). *Chronicle of John Malalas, Books 8–18*. Transll. M. Spinka and G. Downey. Chicago: University of Chicago Press 1940.

Mark the Deacon (Markos Diakonos, fl. 5th century). *The Life of Porphyry Bishop of Gaza*. Oxford: Clarendon Press 1913, or Willits: Eastern Orthodox Books 1977.

Mihailovic, Konstantin (b. ca. 1435). *Memoirs of a Janissary*. Transl. B. Stolz. Ann Arbor: University of Michigan Press 1975.

Nicephorus (Nikêphoros, Patriarch of Constantinople, † 828). (in) P.J. Alexander, *The Patriarch Nicephorus of Constantinople: Ecclesiastical Policy and Image Worship in the Byzantine Empire* (Oxford: Clarendon Press 1958), pp. 242–262. In addition, read P.J. Alexander, 'The Iconoclastic Council of St. Sophia (815),' *Dumbarton Oaks Papers* 7 (1953) 35–66.

Nonnus (Nonnos Panopolitanos, 5th century). *Dionysiaca*. Transl. W.H.D. Rouse. 3 volumes. Cambridge MA: Harvard University Press 1940. Read books 1, 3–5, 7–9, 19, and 45–46.

Otto of Freising († 1158). *The Universal City: A Chronicle of Universal History to the Year 1146 A.D.* Transl. C.C. Mierow. NY: Columbia University Press 1928.

Pachomius (Pakhomios, Saint, 292–346). 'The Rules of Pachomius.' Transl. George H. Schodde. *Presbyterian Review* 6 (1885) 678–689.

Palamas, Gregory (Gregorios Palamas, Saint, Archbishop of Thessalonike, 14th century). *The Decalogue of the Law According to Christ.* In S. Mouselimas, 'Saint Gregory Palamas' "The Decalogue of the Law According to Christ," that is, the New Covenant,' *Greek Orthodox Theological Review* 25 (1980) 297–305.

Photius (Photios, Saint, Patriarch of Constantinople, ca. 820–891). *The Mystagogy of the Holy Spirit.* Transl. J.P.Farrell. Brookline: Holy Cross Orthodox Press 1987.

Procopius (Prokopios of Caesarea, † 565). *The Secret History.* Transl. G.A. Williamson. Baltimore: Penguin 1966.

— *History of the Wars.* Transl. and abridged by Averil Cameron in *History of the Wars, Secret History, and Buildings.* NY: Washington Square Press 1967.

Psellus, Michael (Michael Constantinos Psellos, 1018–1078). *Fourteen Byzantine Rulers: The Chronographia.* Transl. E.R.A. Sewter. Baltimore: Penguin 1966.

Theodoret (Theodoretos, Bishop of Cyprus, † ca. 547). *On Divine Providence.* Transl. Thomas Halton. NY: Newman Press 1988. Read Discourses 1–5.

Theophylact Simocatta (Theophulaktos Simokattes, 7th century). *The History of Theophylact Simocatta.* Transll. Michael and Mary Whitby. Oxford: Clarendon Press 1986.

Zosimus (Zosimos, 5th century). *New History.* Transl. R.T. Ridley. Sydney: Australian Association for Byzantine Studies 1982. Read books 5–6.

Barker, E., transl. *Social and Political Thought in Byzantium from Justinian I to the Last Palaeologus: Passages from Byzantine Writers and Documents.* Oxford: Clarendon Press 1957.

Dawes, E.A.S.,, and N.H. Baynes, transll. *Three Byzantine Saints.* Oxford: Blackwell 1948, repr. Crestwood: St. Vladimir's Seminary Press 1977.

Waddell, Helen. *The Desert Fathers.* Ann Arbor: University of Michigan Press 1957.

Optional Further Reading

Akindunos, Gregorios (ca. 1300–ca.1349). *Letters.* Transl. A.C. Hero. Washington: Dumbarton Oaks 1983.

Anthemius (Anthemios, † ca. 534). *Anthemius of Trales: A Study of Later Greek Geometry.* Transl. G.L. Huxley. Cambridge MA: Harvard University Press 1959.

Arethas (Archbishop of Caesarea) (ca. 860–ca. 940). (in) R.J.H. Jenkins and B. Laourdas, 'Eight Letters of Arethas on the Fourth Marriage of Leo the Wise.' *Hellenika* 14 (1956) 293–307.

Brand, C.M. 'Two Byzantine Treatises on Taxation.' *Traditio* 25 (1969) 35–60.

Choniates, Nicetas (Niketas Khoniates, 12th and early 13th centuries). *O City of Byzantium: Annals of Niketas Choniates.* Transl. H.J. Magoulias. Detroit: Wayne State University Press 1984.

Chronicles of Morea. Transl. H.E. Lurier. NY: Columbia University Press 1964.

Chrysostom, John (Ioannes Khrusostomos, Saint, Patriarch of Constantinople, † 407). *Six Books on the Priesthood.* Transl. G. Neville. Crestwood: St. Vladimir's Seminary Press 1977.

Dennis, G.T. 'Three Reports from Crete on the Situation in Romania, 1401–1402.' *Studi Veneziani* 12 (1970) 243–265.

Germanus (Germanos, Patriarch of Constantinople, r. 715–730). *On the Divine Liturgy.* Transl. P. Meyendorff. Crestwood: St. Vladimir's Seminary Press 1984.

Jones, J.R.M., transl. *The Siege of Constantinople 1453: Seven Contemporary Accounts.* Amsterdam: Hakkert 1972.

Maximus the Confessor (Maximos, Saint, ca. 580–662). *The Church, the Liturgy, and the Soul of Man: The Mystagogia of St. Maximus the Confessor.* Transl. Dom J. Stead OSB. Still River: St. Bede's Publications 1982.

Runciman, Sir Steven. *The Great Church in Captivity: A Study of the Patriarchate of Constantinople from the Eve of the Turkish Conquest to the Greek War of Independence.* London: Cambridge University Press 1968.

Talbot, Alice-Mary. *Holy Women of Byzantium: Byzantine Saints' Lives in Translation.* Washington: Dumbarton Oaks 1996.

For Reference

Farrar, Clarissa P., and A.P. Evans. *English Translations from Medieval Sources.* NY: Columbia University Press 1946.

Ferguson, Mary Ann Heyward. *Bibliography of English Translations from Medieval Sources, 1943–1967.* NY: Columbia University Press 1974.

Hanawalt, Emily Albu. *An Annotated Bibliography of Byzantine Sources in English Translation.* Brookline: Hellenic College Press 1988.

Kazhdan, Alexander, et al., edd. *The Oxford Dictionary of Byzantium.* NY: Oxford University Press 1991.

Kennedy, George A. *Greek Rhetoric under Christian Emperors.* Princeton: Princeton University Press 1983.

Mango, Cyril. *The Art of the Byzantine Empire, 312–1453: Sources and Documents.* Englewood Cliffs: Prentice-Hall 1972.

— *Byzantium: The Empire of New Rome.* NY: Scribner 1980.

Ostrogorsky, George. *History of the Byzantine State.* Transl. Joan Hussey. New Brunswick: Rutgers University Press 1969.

Photius (Photios, Saint, Patriarch of Constantinople, ca. 820–891). *The Library of Photius.* Transl. J.H. Freese. NY: Macmillan 1920.

Rees, B.R. *Papyri from Hermopolis and Other Documents of the Byzantine Period.* London: Egypt Exploration Society 1964.

Treadgold, Warren. *A History of the Byzantine State and Society.* Stanford: Stanford University Press 1997.

Wellesz, E. *A History of Byzantine Music and Hymnography.* Oxford: Clarendon Press, 2nd edition 1961.

The student should also consult Paul Halsall's invaluable 'Internet Medieval Sourcebook' on the World Wide Web (http://www.fordham.edu/halsall/sbook.html) which includes significant material on things Byzantine.

— *John T. Kirby*

GREECE III: Modern Greek Literature in English Translation

Reference Works (for consultation as needed) and Abbreviations

Barnstone = Barnstone, Willis, ed. *Eighteen Texts: Writings by Contemporary Greek Authors*. Cambridge MA: Harvard University Press 1972.

Beaton, Roderick. *An Introduction to Modern Greek Literature*. Oxford: Clarendon Press 1994.

Dalven = Dalven, Rae, ed. and transl. *Daughters of Sappho: Contemporary Greek Women Poets*. Rutherford: Fairleigh Dickinson University Press 1994.

Decavalles = Decavalles, Andonis, et al. *The Voice of Cyprus: An Anthology of Cypriot Literature*. NY: October House 1965.

Dimaras, C. Th. *A History of Modern Greek Literature*. Transl. Mary P. Gianos. Albany: State University of New York Press 1972.

Friar = Friar, Kimon, ed. *Modern Greek Poetry*. NY: Simon & Schuster 1973.

Gianos = Gianos, Mary, ed. *Introduction to Modern Greek Literature: An Anthology of Fiction, Drama, and Poetry*. NY: Twayne 1969.

Holton, David, ed. *Literature and Society in Renaissance Crete*. Cambridge: Cambridge University Press 1991.

Keeley, Edmund, and Philip Sherrard, edd. *Six Poets of Modern Greece*. NY: Knopf 1961.

Politis, Linos. *A History of Modern Greek Literature*. Oxford: Clarendon Press 1973.

Watts, Niki. *The Greek Folk Songs*. Bristol: Bristol Classical Press 1988.

Fiction

Cicellis, Kay. 'Brief Dialogue.' Barnstone 5–10.

Doxas, Takis. 'The Traffic Officer of Phigalia.' Gianos 229–239.

Durrell, Lawrence. *The Alexandria Quartet: Justine*. NY: Dutton 1958.

Fakinos, Aris. *The Marked Men*. Transl. Jacqueline Lapidus. NY: Liveright 1971.

Fakinou, Eugenia. *The Seventh Garment*. Transl. Ed Emery. London: Serpent's Tail 1991.

Galanaki, Rhea. *The Life of Ismail Ferik Pasha*. Transl. Kay Cicellis. London: Peter Owen 1996.

Hadzopoulos, Konstantinos. 'Clara's Dream.' Gianos 187–191.

Ioannides, Panos. 'Gregory.' Decavalles 184–187.

Karkavitsas, Andreas. 'The Sea.' Gianos 172–186.

Kazantzakis, Nikos. *Zorba the Greek*. Transl. Carl Wildman. NY: Simon & Schuster 1953.

— *The Last Temptation of Christ*. Transl. P.A. Bien. NY: Simon & Schuster 1960.

Lazaridis, Markos. 'Fear.' In Gianos.

Manglis, Yiannis. 'The Wedding.' In Gianos.

Panayotopoulos, I.M. 'Humble Life.' Gianos 34–118.

Papadiamantis, Alexandros. *Tales from a Greek Island*. Transl. Elizabeth Constantinides. Baltimore: Johns Hopkins University Press 1987.

Papageorghio. 'Douros the Turkomerite.' Decavalles 164–183.

Politis, Kosmas. 'A Double.' Gianos 215–221.

Prevelakis, Pandelis. *The Sun of Death*. Transl. Rick Abbott. NY: Simon & Schuster 1964.

Taktis, Costas. *The Third Wedding*. NY: Red Dust 1971.

Theotokis, Konstantinos. 'Village Life.' Gianos 160–171.

Venezias, Ilias. *Beyond the Aegean*. Transl. E.D. Scott-Kilvert. NY: Vanguard Press n.d.

Vizyenos, Gergios. *My Mother's Sin and Other Stories*. Transl. William F. Wyatt Jr. Hanover: University Press of New England 1988. Read 'My Mother's Sin,' 'The Only Journey of His Life.'

Yiakos, Demetrios. 'The Path of Dawn.' Gianos 275.

Poetry

Alithersis, Glafkos. Decavalles 23–25.

Cavafy, Constantine. *Complete Poems*. Transl. Rae Dalven. NY: Harcourt & Brace 1961.

Chrysanthis, Kypros. Decavalles 37–38.

Elytis, Odysseus. *Maria Nephele: A Poem in Two Voices*. Transl. Athan Anagnostopoulos. Boston: Houghton Mifflin 1981.

— (in) Keeley 147–164.

Embiricos, Andreas. Friar 346–360.

Gatsos, Nikos. Keeley 167–171.

Karelli, Zoe. Dalven 38–52.

Kazantzakis, Nikos. *The Odyssey: A Modern Sequel.* Transl. Kimon Friar. NY: Simon & Schuster 1958.

Kralis, Manos. Decavalles 32–35.

Krandiotes, Nikos. Decavalles 28–30.

Lipertis, Demetrios. Decavalles 18–21.

Liasides, Pavlos. Decavalles 25–27.

Mastoraki, Jenny. Dalven 216–222.

Melissanthi. Dalven 80–90.

Montis, Kostas. Decavalles 30–32.

Nikolaides, Nikos. Decavalles 21–23.

Ouranis, Kostas. Friar 240–248.

Panayotopoulos, I.M. Friar 362–375.

Papadopoulos, Yiannis K. Decavalles 38–39.

Papatsonis, Takis. Friar 249–279.

Pappa, Rita Boumi. Dalven 53–64.

Ristos, Yannis. Friar 488–518.

Seferis, George. Keeley 101–137.

Sikhelianos, Anghelos. Keeley 67–98.

Thelemis, George. Friar 313–329.

Theodhorou, Victoria. Dalven 117–122.

Varnalis, Nikos. Decavalles 35–36.

Zevgholi-Ghlezou, Dhialehti. Dalven 65–73.

Drama

Akritas, Loukis. *Hostages.* Gianos 418–474.

Prevelakis, Pandelis. *The Last Tournament.* Gianos 368–417.

Theotokas, George. *The Game of Folly vs. Wisdom.* Gianos 319–367.

Xenopoulos, Gregorios. *Divine Dream.* Gianos 289–318.

Nonfiction

Anagnostakis, Nora. 'A Testimony.' Barnstone 63–68.

Kasdaglis, Nikos. 'Athos. Barnstone 135–152.

Seferis, George. *A Poet's Journal: Days of 1945–1951.* Transl. Athan Anagnostopoulos. Cambridge MA: Belknap Press of Harvard University Press 1974.

Stavour, Theo. 'Letter from Cyprus.' Decavalles 188–190.

— *Carol Poster*

HUNGARIAN LITERATURE in English Translation

Novels

Aczél, Tamás. *Illuminations*. NY: Pantheon 1981.

Esterházy, Péter. *The Book of Hrabal*. Transl. Judith Szollosy. Evanston: Northwestern University Press 1994.

— *A Little Hungarian Pornography*. Transl. Judith Szollosy. Evanston: Northwestern University Press 1995.

Faludy, George. *My Happy Days in Hell*. Transl. Kathleen Szasz. NY: William Morrow & Co. 1962.

Füst, Milán. *The Story of My Wife*. Transl. Ivan Sanders. NY: PAJ Publications 1987.

Hargitai, Péter. *Attila: A Barbarian Bedtime Story*. NY: Puski-Corvin 1994.

Kertész, Imre. *Fateless*. Transll. Christopher and Katharine Wilson. Evanston: Northwestern University Press 1992.

Konrád, George. *The Caseworker*. Transl. Paul Aston. NY: Harcourt Brace Jovanovich 1974; repr. NY: Bantam 1976.

— *The Loser*. Transl. Ivan Sanders. NY: Harcourt Brace Jovanovich 1980.

Kosztolányi, Dezsö. *Skylark*. Transl. Richard Aczel. Budapest, London, NY: Central European University Press 1993.

Krúdy, Gyula. *The Adventures of Sinbad*. Transl. George Szirtes. Budapest/London/NY: Central European University Press 1997.

Lengyel, Péter. *Cobblestone: A Philosophical Mystery for the Millennium*. Transl. John Bátki. London: Readers International 1988.

Móritz, Zsigmond. *Be Faithful unto Death*. Transl. Stephen Vizinczey. Budapest/London/NY: Central European University Press 1995.

Nádas, Péter. *A Book of Memories*. Transl. Ivan Sanders. NY: Farrar Straus & Giroux 1997.

Németh, László. *Guilt*. London: Peter Owen 1966.

Örkény, István. *The Flower Show and The Toth Family*. Transll. Michael Heim and Clara Györgyey. NY: New Directions 1982.

Ottlik, Géza. *School at the Frontier*. Transl. Kathleen Szasz. NY: Harcourt Brace & World 1966.

Szabó, Magda. *The Door*. Transl. Stefan Draughon. Boulder: East European Monographs 1994.

Szerb, Antal. *The Traveler*. Transl. Péter Hargitai. NY: Puski-Corvin 1996.

Short Stories

Csáth, Géza. *The Magician's Garden and Other Stories*. Transl. Jascha Kessler. NY: Columbia University Press 1980.

Váradi, Paul, ed. *Hungarian Short Stories*. Toronto: Exile Editions 1983.

Szakolczay, Lajos, ed. *Give or Take a Day: Contemporary Hungarian Short Stories*. Budapest: Corvina 1997.

Essays, Biographies, Memoirs

Basa, Enikő Molnár. *Sándor Petőfi: Biography*. Boston: Twayne Publishers 1980.

Györgyey, Clara. *Ferenc Molnár: Biography*. Boston: Twayne Publishers 1980.

Hay, Julius. *Born 1900: A Memoir*. Transl. J.A. Underwood. London: Hutchison 1974.

Karinthy, Frigyes. *A Journey Round My Skull*. Transl. Vernon D. Barker. Budapest: Corvina 1992.

Kopácsi, Sándor. *In the Name of the Working Class: The Inside Story of the Hungarian Revolution*. Transll. Daniel and Judy Stoffman. Toronto: Lester/Orpen/Dennys 1986.

Márai, Sándor. *Memoir of Hungary, 1944–1948*. Transl. Albert Tezla. Budapest: Corvina 1996.

Scheer, Steven C. *Kálmán Mikszáth: Biography*. Boston: Twayne Publishers 1977.

Szász, Béla. *Volunteers for the Gallows: Anatomy of a Show Trial*. Transl. Kathleen Szasz. NY: W. W. Norton 1971.

Poetry

Madách, Imre. *The Tragedy of Man*. Transl. George Szirtes. NY: Puski-Corvin 1988.

Makkai, Adam, sel. and transl. *In Quest of the 'Miracle Stag': The Poetry of Hungary*. Volume 1 (of 2). Budapest: Corvina 1996.

Radnóti, Miklós. *Foamy Sky*. Transll. Zsuzsanna Ozsváth and Frederick Turner. Princeton: Princeton University Press 1992.

Tandori, Dezső. *Birds and Other Relations: Selected Poetry*. Transl. Bruce Berlind. Princeton: Princeton University Press 1986.

Vajda, Miklós, ed. *Modern Hungarian Poetry*. NY: Columbia University Press 1977.

Drama

Brogyányi, Jenő, ed. and transl. *New Hungarian Drama*. Budapest: Corvina 1991.

Göncz, Árpád. *Plays and Other Writings*. Transll. Christopher and Katharina Wilson. NY: Garland 1990.

Györgyey, Clara, ed. and transl. *A Mirror to the Cage: Contemporary Hungarian Plays*. Fayetteville: University of Arkansas Press 1993.

Upor, László, sel. and introd. *Hungarian Plays: Five New Dramas from Hungary*. London: Nick Hern Books 1996.

— *Clara Györgyey*

INDIA: Literatures of the Subcontinent
In English or in English Translation

NOTES: • This list includes some writers of Pakistan and Sri Lanka, some writers of Indian descent, and some works about India. • It is assumed that the student will also have read the selections from the *Bhagavad-Gita* and the *Ramayana* listed in 'Beginnings?.'

Traditional Texts

Dhammapada: The Sayings of the Buddha [1st century BCE?]. Transl. Thomas Byrom. Boston: Shambhala 1993.

The Pancatantra. Transl. Chandra Rajan. NY: Penguin 1993.

The Principal Upanishads. Transl. S. Radhakrishnan. NY: Harper 1953. Read the *Brhad-âranyaka Upanishad.*

Shantideva. *The Bodhicaryâvatâra* [8th century CE?]. Transll. Kate Crosby and Andrew Skilton. Oxford: Oxford University Press 1995.

Modern Texts

Ahmad, Aijaz. '"Indian Literature": Notes towards the Definition of a Category.' Chapter 7 in Ahmad, *In Theory: Classes, Nations, Literatures.* London: Verso 1992.

Anand, Mulk Raj. *Untouchable* [1935]. London: Wishart Books.

Appachana, Anjana. *Listening Now.* NY: Random House 1998.

Banerjee, Bibhutibhushan [Bibhutibhushana Bandyopadhyaya]. *Pather Panchali: Song of the Road: A Bengali Novel.* Transll. T. W. Clark and Tarapada Mukherjee. Bloomington: Indiana University Press 1968.

Chandra, Vikram. *Love and Longing in Bombay: Stories*. Boston: Little, Brown 1997.

Chatterjee, Bankim Chandra. *Krishnakanta's Will*. Norfolk: New Directions 1962.

Coomaraswamy, Ananda Kentish. *The Dance of Siva: Fourteen Indian Essays*. NY: Gordon Press 1975.

Desai, Anita. *In Custody*. London: Heinemann 1984.

Desani, G. V. *All about Mr. Hatterr: A Gesture*. London: Aldor 1951, revised as *All About H. Hatterr: A Novel*. London: The Bodley Head 1970.

Divakaruni, Chitra Banerjee. *The Mistress of Spices*. NY: Anchor 1997.

Gandhi, Mohandas K. *Gandhi's Autobiography: The Story of My Experiments with Truth* [1927–1929]. Transl. Mahadev Desai. Washington: Public Affairs Press 1948. Read Parts I and V.

Jhabvala, Ruth Prawer. *Heat and Dust*. London: Murray 1975.

Kipling, Rudyard. *Kim* [1901]. Ed. Edward W. Said. NY: Penguin 1989.

Mehta, Gita. *Snakes and Ladders*. NY: Nan A. Talese 1997.

Mehta, Ved. *Vedi*. NY: Oxford University Press 1982.

Mistry, Rohinton. *Such a Long Journey*. NY: Random House 1991.

Mukherjee, Bharati. *Wife*. Boston: Houghton Mifflin 1975.

Naipaul, V.S. *India: A Million Mutinies Now*. London: Heinemann 1990.

Narayan, R. K. *The Guide* [1958]. NY: New American Library 1966.

Nehru, Jawaharlal. *Toward Freedom: The Autobiography of Jawaharlal Nehru*. NY: John Day 1941. Read chapters 1–16, 36, 40–53, the Epilogue, and the Appendices.

Ondaatje, Michael [Sri Lankan]. *The English Patient*. NY: Alfred A. Knopf 1992.

Paz, Octavio. *In Light of India*. NY: Harcourt Brace 1997.

Premchand [Premacanda]. *The Gift of a Cow*. Bloomington: Indiana University Press 1968.

Radhakrishnan, S. *An Idealist View of Life*. NY: Barnes & Noble 1961.

Rao, Narasimha. *A Little Lamp and Other Short Stories from Telugu*. Hyderabad: Navya Sahiti Samiti 1996.

Rao, Raja. *Kanthapura* [1938]. NY: New Directions 1963.

Ray, Satyajit. *Stories*. London: Secker & Warburg 1987.

Roy, Arundhati. *The God of Small Things*. NY: Random House 1997.

Rushdie, Salman. *The Satanic Verses*. London: Viking 1988.

Seth, Vikram. *A Suitable Boy*. NY: HarperCollins 1993.

Sidhwa, Bapsi [Pakistani]. *Cracking India: A Novel*. Minneapolis: Milkweed Editions 1991.

Suleri, Sara [Pakistani]. *Meatless Days*. Chicago: University of Chicago Press 1989.

Tagore, Rabindranath. *Gitanjali (Song Offerings)*. Transl. by the author. London: Macmillan [1913] second edition 1952.

Verghese, Abraham. *My Own Country: A Doctor's Story*. NY: Simon & Schuster 1994.

Vijayan, O. V. *The Saga of Dharmapuri*. NY: Penguin 1987.

Optional: Further Reading

Hindu Myths: A Sourcebook. Transl. Wendy Doniger O'Flaherty. NY: Penguin 1975.

Rig Veda: A Metrically Restored Text with an Introduction and Notes. Edd. Baren A. Van Nooten and Gary B. Holland. Cambridge MA: Harvard University Press 1994.

The Rig Veda. An Anthology. One Hundred and Eight Hymns. Transl. Wendy Doniger O'Flaherty. NY: Penguin 1981.

Anand, Mulk Rag. *Coolie*. NY: Penguin 1994.

Ananthamurthy, U. R. *A Rite for a Dead Man*. Transl. A.K. Ramanujan. NY: Oxford University Press 1978.

Chatterjee, Bankim Chandra. *Kamalakanta: A Collection of Satirical Essays and Reflections*. Calcutta: Rupa & Co. 1992.

Chatterjee, Upamanyu. *English August: An Indian Story*. London: Faber 1988.

Chaudhuri, Amit. *A Strange and Sublime Address*. London: Minerva 1992.

Chaudhuri, Nirad C. *The Autobiography of an Unknown Indian*. London: Macmillan 1951.

Desai, Anita. *Clear Light of Day*. London: Heinemann 1980.

Deussen, Paul. *The System of the Vedânta according to Bâdarâyana's Brahma-Sûtras and Çankara's Commenting Thereon*. Chicago: Open Court 1912.

Gandhi, Mahatma. *All Men Are Brothers: Life and Thoughts of Mahatma Gandhi as Told in His Own Words*. Paris: UNESCO 1958, 2nd edition 1969.

Ghosh, Amitav. *In an Antique Land*. NY: Alfred A. Knopf 1993.

Gunesekera, Romesh. *Monkfish Moon*. London: Granta Books 1992.

Hariharan, Githa. *The Art of Dying and Other Stories*. NY: Penguin 1993.

Hyder, Qurratulain. *Fireflies in the Mist: A Novel*. New Delhi: Sterling Publishers 1994.

Joshi, Suresh. *Janantike: Intimate Asides. Selected Essays*. Transl. V.Y. Kantak. New Delhi: Sahitya Akademi 1995.

Kolatkar, Aruna. *Jejuri*. Bombay: Clearing House 1976.

Macdonell, Arthur A. *Vedic Mythology* [1897]. NY: Gordon Press 1974.

— *India's Past: A Survey of Her Literatures, Religions, Languages, and Antiquities*. Oxford: Clarendon Press 1927, repr. Westport: Hyperion Press 1979.

Manto, Sa'adat Hasan. *The Best of Manto: A Collection of His Short Stories*. New Delhi: Sterling Publishers 1989.

Mukherjee, Bharati. *Jasmine*. NY: Grove Weidenfeld 1989.

Müller, Friedrich Max. *A History of Ancient Sanskrit Literature So Far as It Illustrates the Primitive Religion of the Brahmans* [1860]. Thoroughly revised and edited with several appendices and indices by Surendra Nath Sastri. Varanasi: Chowkhamba Sanskrit Series Office 1968.

— *The Six Systems of Indian Philosophy*. NY: Longmans, Green & Company 1899.

— *Râmakrishna: His Life and Sayings*. London: Longmans, Green & Company 1901.

Naipaul, V. S. *An Area of Darkness*. London: A. Deutsch 1964.

— *India: A Wounded Civilization*. NY: Alfred A. Knopf 1977.

Narayan, R.K. *The Painter of Signs* [1976]. NY: Penguin 1982.

Nehru, Jawaharlal. *India's Freedom: Essays, Letters and Speeches* [1936]. NY: Barnes & Noble 1962

Perera, Padma. *Dr. Salaam & Other Stories of India*. Santa Barbara: Capra Press 1978.

Rushdie, Salman. *Midnight's Children*. NY: Alfred A. Knopf 1980.

Tagore, Rabindranath. *Selected Short Stories*. Transl. William Radice. NY: Penguin 1994.

— *Later Poems of Rabindranath Tagore*. Transl. Aurobindo Bose. NY: Funk & Wagnalls 1974.

Vakil Ardashir. *Beach Boy*. London: Hamish Hamilton 1997.

Verma, Nirmal. *Maya Darpan and Other Stories*. NY: Oxford University Press 1986.

Vijayan, O. V. *After the Hanging and Other Stories*. NY: Penguin 1989.

Zimmer, Heinrich. *Myths and Symbols in Indian Art and Civilization*. Princeton University Press 1992.

— *Philosophies of India*. Princeton: Princeton University Press 1951.

— *John T. Kirby*

ITALIAN LITERATURE

Basic Reference Works (for consultation as needed)
Bondanella, Peter, et al., edd. *Dictionary of Italian Literature*. Westport:
Greenwood Press, 2nd edition 1996.
Brand, Peter, and Lino Pertile, edd. *The Cambridge History of Italian
Literature*. Cambridge: Cambridge University Press 1996.
Donadoni, Eugenio, et al., edd. *History of Italian Literature*. 2 volumes.
NY: New York University Press 1969.

Lyric Poetry. Selections will be taken from the following anthologies:
Allen, Beverly, et al., edd. *Italian Poetry from the Middle Ages to the
Present: A Bilingual Anthology*. NY: Feminist Press 1986.
Gioia, D., and W. Smith, transll. *Poems from Italy*. St. Paul: New
Rivers Press 1985.
Kay, George, ed. *The Penguin Book of Italian Verse*. Baltimore:
Penguin 1965.

Francesco Petrarca (1304–1374). *Selections from the Canzoniere and
Other Works*, transl. Mark Musa. Oxford: Oxford University
Press 1985.
Lorenzo de' Medici (1449–92). 'Triumph of Bacchus and Ariadne,'
in Gioia.
Colonna, Vittoria (1490–1547). All the poems in Allen and in Gioia.
Stampa, Gaspara (1523–54). All the poems in Allen and in Gioia.
Foscolo, Ugo (1778–1827). 'Self Portrait,' 'My Father's Death,' 'To
The Evening,' 'To Zacinto,' 'To Himself,' and 'My Brother
Giovanni's Death,' in Kay and Gioia.
Leopardi, Giacomo (1798–1837). 'The Solitary Sparrow,' 'The Infi-
nite,' 'To Sylvia,' 'Village Saturday,' 'To Himself,' and 'The
Broom,' in *Leopardi: Poems and Prose*, ed. Angel Flores. Bloom-
ington: Indiana University Press 1966.
Carducci, Giosue (1835–1907). All the poems in Kay and Gioia.
Pascoli, Giovanni (1855–1912). All the poems in Kay and Gioia.

D'Annunzio, Gabriele (1863–1938). All the poems in Kay and Gioia.

Marinetti, Filippo Tommaso (1876–1944). All the poems in *The Blue Moustache*. Transl. Felix Stefanile (New Rochelle: Elizabeth Press 1981) and in Gioia.

Palazzeschi, Aldo (1885–1974). All poems in *The Blue Moustache* and in Gioia.

Ungaretti, Giuseppe (1888–1970). All the poems in Kay and Gioia.

Saba, Umberto (1883–1957). All poems in *Umberto Saba, 31 Poems*. Transl. Felix Stefanile. New Rochelle: Elizabeth Press 1978.

Quasimodo, Salvatore (1901–1968). All the poems in Kay and Gioia.

Montale, Eugenio (1896–1981). All the poems in Kay and Gioia.

Theatre

Machiavelli, Niccolò (1469–1527). *The Mandrake Root* (1520).

Aretino, Pietro (1492–1556). *The Stablemaster* (1533).

Goldoni, Carlo (1707–1793). *La Locandiera* (1751). Transl. Frederick Davies in *Goldoni: Four Comedies*. NY: Penguin 1968.

Pirandello, Luigi (1867–1936). *Six Characters in Search of an Author* (1921). In Pirandello, *Naked Masks: Five Plays*. Ed. Eric Bentley. NY: Dutton 1952.

Long Narrative: Verse

Alighieri, Dante (1265–1321). *Divine Comedy* (1307–21). Use a translation by John Ciardi, Allen Mandelbaum, Mark Musa, or Dorothy L. Sayers.

Ariosto, Ludovico (1474–1533). *Orlando Furioso* (1532). Read cantos 1–4, 19, 23, 29–30, 32, 34–36, 39, 46.

Tasso, Torquato (1544–1595). *Gerusalemme liberata* (1575), transl. Joseph Tusiani as *Jerusalem Delivered* (Rutherford: Fairleigh Dickinson University Press 1970). Read cantos 1, 3–4, 6, 7, 12, 20.

Long Narrative: Prose

Manzoni, Alessandro (1785–1873). *I promessi sposi* (1842). Transl. A. Colquhoun as *The Betrothed, 'I promessi sposi'; A Tale of XVII Century Milan*. NY: Dutton 1956.

Verga, Giovanni (1840–1922). *Malavoglia* (1880). Transl. Raymond Rosenthal as *The House by the Medlar Tree*. Berkeley: University of California Press 1983.

Aleramo, Sibilla (1876–1960). *A Woman* (1906: University of California Press).

Palazzeschi, Aldo (1885–1974). *Man of Smoke* (1911). NY: Italica Press 1992.

Svevo, Italo (1861–1928). *La coscienza di Zeno* (1923). Transl. B. de Zoete as *The Confessions of Zeno*. NY: Vintage 1958.

Vittorini, Elio (1908–1966). *Conversazione in Sicilia* (1941). Transl. Wilfrid David as *In Sicily*. NY: New Directions 1949.

Levi, Carlo (1902–1975). *Cristo si è fermato a Eboli* (1945). Transl. Frances Frenaye as *Christ Stopped at Eboli*. NY: Farrar Straus & Giroux 1947.

Calvino, Italo (1923–1985). *Se una notte d'inverno un viaggiatore* (1979). Transl. William Weaver as *If on a winter's night a traveler*. NY: Harcourt Brace Jovanovich 1981.

Pavese, Cesare (1908–1950). *The Moon and the Bonfire* (1950). London: J. Lehmann 1952.

Pasolini, Pier Paolo (1922–1975). *The Ragazzi* (1956). NY: Grove Press 1968.

Bassani, Giorgio (1908–). *The Garden of the Finzi-Continis* (1962). NY: Athenaeum 1965.

Maraini, Dacia (1939–). *Woman at War*. NY: Italica Press 1988.

Short Narrative

Boccaccio, Giovanni (1313–1375). *Decamerone* (1354). Transll. Mark Musa and Peter Bondanella as *The Decameron*. NY: Norton 1982. Read the 1st, 4th–7th, and 10th days.

Calvino, Italo (1923–1985). *Le cosmicomiche* (1966). Transl. William Weaver as *Cosmicomics*. NY: Harcourt Brace & World 1968.

Moravia, Alberto (1907– 1990). *La cosa e altri racconti* (1981). Transl. Tim Parks as *Erotic Tales*. NY: Farrar, Straus & Giroux 1986.

Pirandello, Luigi (1867–1936). *Novelle per un anno* (1920s). Read the selections transll. Arthur and Henrie Mayne in *The Naked Truth and Eleven Other Stories*. NY: Dutton 1934.

Non-Fictional Prose

Alighieri, Dante (1265–1321). 'Letter to Can Grande della Scala.' (Epistola X: 1318?).

Petrarca, Francesco (1304–1374). 'The Ascent of Mount Ventoux' (1336) and 'Letter to Posterity.' In *Selections from the Canzoniere and Other Works*, transl. Mark Musa. Oxford: Oxford University Press 1985.

Pico della Mirandola, Gianfrancesco (1470–1533). 'Oration of the Dignity of Man.' Edd. E. Cassirer et al. in *The Renaissance Philosophy of Man*. Chicago: University of Chicago Press 1965.

Machiavelli, Niccolò (1469–1527). *The Prince* (1513).

Castiglione, Baldassare (1478–1529). *The Book of the Courtier* (1528).

Vico, Giambattista (1668–1744). *La Scienza Nuova* (3rd edition 1744). Transl. and abridged by Thomas Goddard Bergin and Max Harold Fisch as *The New Science of Giambattista Vico*. Ithaca: Cornell University Press 1979.

Leopardi, Giacomo (1798–1837). From the *Operette morali*: 'The History of Mankind,' 'Dialogue between Nature and an Icelander,' 'Dialogue between an Almanac Peddler and a Passer-by.' In *Leopardi: Poems and Prose*, ed. Angel Flores. Bloomington: Indiana University Press 1966.

Marinetti, Filippo Tommaso (1876–1944). 'The Founding and the Manifesto of Futurism.' In *Marinetti: Selected Writings*. Ed. W. R. Flint. NY: Farrar, Straus and Giroux 1972.

Gramsci, Antonio (1891–1937). *The Southern Question*. Transl. Pasquale Verdicchio. West Lafayette: Bordighera 1995.

— *Anthony Julian Tamburri and Ben Lawton*

ITALIAN/AMERICAN STUDIES

Prose Fiction

Ardizzone, Tony. *Taking It Home*. Champaign-Urbana: University of Illinois Press 1996.

Barolini, Helen. *Umbertina*. NY: Seaview Books 1979.

Bryant, Dorothy. *Miss Giardino*. Berkeley: ATA Books 1978.

DeLillo, Don. *Underworld*. NY: Scribner's 1997.

DeRosa, Tina. *Paper Fish* [1980]. NY: The Feminist Press 1996.

Di Donato, Pietro. *Christ in Concrete* [1939]. NY: Signet 1993.

Fante, John. *Dago Red* [1940]. In *The Wine and Youth*. Santa Barbara: Black Sparrow Press 1986.

— *Wait until Spring Bandini* [1938]. Santa Barbara: Black Sparrow Press 1983.

Guido deVries, Rachel. *Tender Warriors*. Ithaca: Firebrand 1986.

Maso, Carol. *Ghost Dance* [1986]. NY: Echo Press 1994.

Misurella, Fred. *Short Time*. West Lafayette: Bordighera 1996.

Puzo, Mario. *The Fortunate Pilgrim*. NY: Atheneum 1964.

— *The Godfather*. NY: Putnam 1969.

Rimanelli, Giose. *Benedetta in Guysterland*. Montréal: Guernica 1993.

Tomasi, Mari. *Like Lesser Gods* [1942]. Shelburne: The New England Press 1993.

Viscusi, Robert. *Astoria*. Toronto: Guernica 1995.

Wachtel, Chuck. *Joe The Engineer* [1986]. NY: Viking 1994.

Poetry

Di Prima, Diane. *Pieces of a Song*. NY: City Lights 1990.

Gillan, Maria. *Where I Come From: New and Selected Poems*. Toronto: Guernica 1994.

Gioia, Dana. *Daily Horoscope*. St. Paul: Graywolf 1986.

Gioseffi, Daniela. *Word Wounds and Water Flowers*. West Lafayette: Bordighera 1995.

Patriarca, Gianna. *Italian Women and Other Tragedies*. Toronto: Guernica 1996.

Romano, Rose. *The Wop Factor*. Brooklyn/Palermo: malafemmina 1994.

Stefanile, Felix. *The Dance at Saint Gabriel's*. Brownsville: Story Line Press 1995.

Anthologies

Bona, Mary Jo, ed. *The Voices We Carry: Recent Italian/American Women's Fiction*. Montréal: Guernica 1994.

Barolini, Helen, ed. *The Dream Book: An Anthology of Writings by Italian American Women*. NY: Schocken 1985.

Tamburri, Anthony Julian, Paolo A. Giordano, and Fred L. Gardaphé, edd. *From the Margin: Writings in Italian Americana*. West Lafayette: Purdue University Press 1991.

Critical Studies

Barolini, Helen. *Chiaroscuro: Essays of Identity*. West Lafayette: Bordighera 1997.

Basile Green, Rose. *The Italian-American Novel: Documentation of an Interaction between Two Cultures*. Madison: Fairleigh Dickinson University Press 1974.

Boelhower, William. *Immigrant Autobiography in the United States: Four Versions of the Italian American Self*. Verona: Essedue Edizioni 1982.

— *Through a Glass Darkly: Ethnic Semiosis in American Literature*. NY: Oxford University Press 1987.

Giordano, Paolo, and Anthony Julian Tamburri. *Beyond the Margin: Readings in Italian Americana*. Madison: Fairleigh-Dickinson University Press 1997.

Gardaphé, Fred L. *Italian Signs, American Streets: The Evolution of Italian American Narrative*. Durham: Duke University Press 1996.

— *Dagoes Read: Tradition and the Italian/American Writer*. Toronto: Guernica 1996.

Tamburri, Anthony Julian. *To Hyphenate or Not to Hyphenate: The Italian/American Writer as Other American*. Montréal: Guernica 1991.

— *A Semiotic of Ethnicity: In (Re)cognition of the Italian/American Writer*. Albany: SUNY Press 1998.

— ed. *Fuori: Essays by Italian/American Lesbians and Gays*. West Lafayette: Bordighera 1996.

Verdicchio, Pasquale. *Bound by Distance: Rethinking Nationalism through the Italian Diaspora*. Madison: Fairleigh Dickinson University Press 1997.

Films
Cimino, Michael. *The Deer Hunter*. (1978)
Coppola, Francis Ford. *The Cotton Club*. (1984)
— *The Godfather*. (1972)
— *The Godfather II*. (1974)
— *The Godfather III*. (1991)
Decerchio, Tom. *Nunzio's Second Cousin*. (1994, 16 min.)
DeNiro, Robert. *A Bronx Tale*. (1993)
Dymtryk, Edward. *Give Us This Day*. (1951)
Greco, Joseph. *Lena's Spaghetti*. (1994, 23 min.)
Savoca, Nancy. *Household Saints*. (1993)
Savoca, Nancy. *True Love*. (1989)
Scorsese, Martin. *Italianamericans*. (1974)
— *Mean Streets*. (1973)
— *Raging Bull*. (1980)
— *Taxi Driver*. (1976)
— *Who's That Knocking at My Door?* (1968)
Turturro, John. *Mac*. (1992)

— *Anthony Julian Tamburri*

JAPANESE LITERATURE in English Translation

Classical Texts

Kojiki. Tokyo: University of Tokyo Press 1968.

The Man'yôshû. Tokyo: Hokuseido Press 1967. Read books 1–6 (pp. 1–90) and books 17–19 (pp. 289–324), with special attention to the following poets: Hitomaro, Nukatano Okimi, Akahito, Tabito, Okura, and Yakamochi.

Kokinshû: A Collection of Poems Ancient and Modern. Princeton: Princeton University Press 1984. Read Kanajo (pp. 35–47), books 1–6 (pp. 49–144), and books 11–15 (pp. 183–286), with special attention to the following poets: Onono komachi, Narihira, Tsurayuki, Tomonori, and Mitsune.

Lady Murasaki. *The Tale of Genji.* 2 volumes. NY: Knopf 1976.

Sei Shônagon. *The Pillow Book of Sei Shonagon.* NY: Columbia University Press 1967.

Mediaeval Texts

The Tale of the Heike. Stanford: Stanford University Press 1988.

Yoshida Kenkô. *Essays in Idleness.* Tokyo: Tuttle 1981.

Nippon Gakujutsu Shinkôkai, ed. *Japanese Noh Drama: Ten Plays Selected and Translated from the Japanese.* Tokyo: Nippon Gakujutsu Shinkôkai 1955. Read 'Izutsu' (pp. 91–105) and 'Sumidagawa' (pp. 143–159).

Premodern Texts

Matsuo Bashô. *A Haiku Journey: Basho's Narrow Road to a Far Province.* Tokyo: Kodansha International 1980.

Chikamatsu Monzaemon. *Major Plays of Chikamatsu.* NY: Columbia University Press 1961. Read 'The Battle of Coxinga' (pp. 202–269) and 'The Love Suicide at Amijima' (pp. 387–425).

Ihara Saikaku. *Five Women Who Loved Love.* Tokyo: Tuttle 1956.

Modern Texts

Natsume Sôseki. *Kokoro, a Novel and Selected Essays*. Lanham: Madison Books 1992.

Yosano Akiko. *Tangled Hair*. West Lafayette: Purdue University Studies 1971.

Hagiwara Sakutarô. *Howling at the Moon*. Tokyo: University of Tokyo Press 1978.

Shiga Naoya. *The Paper Door and Other Stories*. San Francisco: North Point Press 1987. Read 'Han's Crime' (pp. 46–56) and 'At Kinosaki' (pp. 57–64).

Kawabata Yasunari. *Snow Country*. NY: Knopf 1956.

Tanizaki Jun'ichirô. *The Makioka Sisters*. NY: Knopf 1957.

Enchi Fumiko. *The Waiting Years*. Tokyo: Kodansha International 1971.

Mishima Yukio. *Five Modern No Plays*. NY: Knopf 1957.

Abe Kôbô. *The Woman in the Dunes*. NY: Knopf 1964.

Oe Kenzaburô. *The Silent Cry*. Tokyo: Kodansha International 1974.

Hibbett, Howard, ed. *Contemporary Japanese Literature: An Anthology of Fiction, Film, and Other Writing Since 1945*. NY: Knopf 1977. Read Ozu Yasujirô, 'Tokyo Story,' and Furui Yoshikichi, 'Wedlock.'

Gessel, Van C., and Tomone Matsumoto, edd. *The Showa Anthology*. Tokyo: Kodansha International 1985. Read Tsushima Yûko, 'The Silent Traders,' and Nakagami Kenji, 'The Immortal.'

Critical Studies

Karatani Kôjin. *Origins of Modern Japanese Literature*. Durham: Duke University Press 1993. Read 'Landscape' and 'Interiority.'

Kawamoto Kôji. 'The Poetics of Short Poems: Haiku and Imagist Poetry.' In R. Thomas, ed., *Poetics of Japanese Literature* (Proceedings of the 1992 Midwest Seminar on the Teaching of Japanese Literature). West Lafayette: Purdue University 1993.

Mizuta Noriko. 'Watakushikatari and monogatari: Women's Self-Expression and the Tradition of Monogatari in Modern Japanese Literature.' In E. Sekine, ed., *The Desire for Monogatari* (Proceedings of the Second Midwest Research/Pedagogy Seminar on Japanese Litearture, 1993). West Lafayette: Purdue University 1994.

Takahashi Tôru. 'Space/Time of Monogatari and Psycho-Perspective.' In E. Sekine, ed., *Revisionism in Japanese Literary*

Studies (Proceedings of the Midwest Association for Japanese Literary Studies, volume 2). West Lafayette: Purdue University 1996.

— *Eiji Sekine*

LATIN LITERATURE (Classical)
in English Translation

NOTES: • This list does not include works in Latin included in the 'Beginnings?' list; it is assumed that the student will read those as well. • For standard critical editions of Latin texts one should consult the 'Authors and Works' section of the *Oxford Latin Dictionary*, ed. P. G. W. Glare (Oxford: Clarendon Press 1982).

Literary Histories (for consultation as needed; see also the 'Basic Reference Works' listed under GREECE I: Classical Greek Literature in English Translation.)
Conte, Gian Biagio. *Latin Literature: A History.* Baltimore: Johns Hopkins University Pres 1994.
Kenney, E. J., and W. V. Clausen edd. *Latin Literature.* The Cambridge History of Classical Literature, volume 2. Cambridge: Cambridge University Press 1982.

Hexameter Verse
Lucretius (Titus Lucretius Carus, ca. 96–55 BCE). *De rerum natura.* Read book 1 in *On the Nature of Things*, transl. Cyril Bailey (Oxford: Clarendon Press 1921) or in *On the Nature of the Universe*, transl. R. E. Latham (NY: Penguin 1951).
Vergil (Publius Vergilius Maro, 70–19 BCE). *Eclogues.* Transl. Guy Lee. NY: Penguin 1980.
— *Georgics.* Transl. L. P. Wilkinson. NY: Penguin 1982. Read book 4.
Horace (Quintus Horatius Flaccus, 65–8 BCE). *Satires* and *Epistles*. In *Horace: Satires and Epistles; Persius: Satires.* Transl. Niall Rudd. NY: Penguin 1979. Satires: read book 1, nos. 1, 4, 6, 9, 10; book 2, nos. 1, 5–7. Epistles: read book 1, nos. 2, 16; book 2, nos. 1 and 3 (the *Ars poetica*).

Lucan (Marcus Annaeus Lucanus, 39–65 CE). *Pharsalia*. Transl. Jane Wilson Joyce. Ithaca: Cornell University Press 1993. Read book 7.

Juvenal (Decimus Iunius Iuuenalis, ca. 60–127 CE). *Satires*. Read Satires 1, 6, and 10 in *Juvenal: The Sixteen Satires*, transl. Peter Green. NY: Penguin 1974.

Elegy

Propertius (Sextus Propertius, ca. 50–15 BCE). *Elegies*. Read book 1 (entire); book 2, nos. 8, 10, 12, 13b, 15, and 26a; book 3, nos. 1–3; and book 4, nos. 2, 7, 9, and 11, in *Propertius: The Poems*, transl. W. G. Shepherd (NY: Penguin 1985), or in *Propertius: The Poems*, transl. Guy Lee (Oxford: Oxford University Press 1994).

Ovid (Publius Ouidius Naso, 43 BCE–?17 CE). *The Art of Love*. Read book 1. In *Ovid: The Love Poems*, transl. A. D. Melville. Oxford: Oxford University Press 1990.

— *The Cures for Love*. In *Ovid: The Love Poems*, transl. A. D. Melville. Oxford: Oxford University Press 1990.

— *Heroides*. Transl. Harold Isbell. NY: Penguin 1990. Read nos. 1, 3, 4, 7, 9, 10, 12, 15, and 16.

Drama

Plautus (Titus Macchius Plautus, ca. 254–184 BCE). *The Brothers Menaechmus (Menaechmi)*. Transl. Palmer Bovie. In *Plautus: The Comedies, Volume IV*. Edd. David R. Slavitt and Palmer Bovie. Baltimore: Johns Hopkins University Press 1995.

— *Stichus*. Transl. Carol Poster. In *Plautus: The Comedies, Volume IV*. Edd. David R. Slavitt and Palmer Bovie. Baltimore: Johns Hopkins University Press 1995.

Terence (Publius Terentius Afer, ca. 186–159 BCE). *Adelphoe*. In *Terence: The Comedies*, transl. Betty Radice. NY: Penguin 1976.

Seneca (Lucius Annaeus Seneca [the younger], ca. 4 BCE–65 CE). *Phaedra*. In *Seneca: Four Tragedies and Octavia*. Transl. E. F. Watling. NY: Penguin 1966.

— *Oedipus*. In *Seneca: Four Tragedies and Octavia*. Transl. E. F. Watling. NY: Penguin 1966.

Oratory, Rhetoric, and Philosophy

Cicero (Marcus Tullius Cicero, 106–43 BCE). *Against Lucius Sergius Catilina* 1–4. In *Selected Political Speeches of Cicero*, transl. Michael Grant. NY: Penguin 1973.

— *The First Philippic against Marcus Antonius*. In *Selected Political Speeches of Cicero*, transl. Michael Grant. NY: Penguin 1973.

— *On the Republic*. Read the 'Dream of Scipio' in *Cicero: On the Good Life*, transl. Michael Grant. NY: Penguin 1971.

Quintilian (Marcus Quintilianus, ca 35–100 CE). *Education of the Orator*. Read book 10, chapter 1, in volume 4 of *The Institutio oratoria of Quintilian*, transl. H. E. Butler. Cambridge MA: Harvard University Press 1922.

Augustine (Aurelius Augustinus, 354–430 CE). *Confessions*. Transl. R. S. Pine-Coffin. NY: Penguin 1961. Read books 1–3 and 8.

History

Caesar (Gaius Iulius Caesar, 100–44 BCE). *The Civil War*, transl. Jane F. Gardner. NY: Penguin 1967. Read book 3.

Sallust (Gaius Sallustius Crispus, ca 86–35 BCE). *Catilina*. Read the translation by S. A. Handford in *Sallust: The Jugurthine War and The Conspiracy of Catiline*. NY: Penguin 1963.

Livy (Titus Liuius, ca. 59 BCE–17 CE). *Ab urbe condita*. Read book 1 in *The Early History of Rome*, transl. Aubrey de Sélincourt. NY: Penguin 1971.

Tacitus (Publius [?] Cornelius Tacitus, ca. 56–120 CE). *Annales*. Read books 1–6 in *The Annals of Imperial Rome*, transl. Michael Grant. NY: Penguin 1989.

Suetonius. *The Twelve Caesars*, transl. Robert Graves. NY: Penguin 1979. Read the biographies of Julius Caesar, Augustus, Caligula, and Nero.

Fictional Narrative

Petronius Arbiter (Titus [?] Petronius Niger [?], † 66 CE). *Satyrica*. Read the translation by J. P. Sullivan in *Petronius: The Satyricon; Seneca: The Apocolocyntosis*. NY: Penguin 1977.

Apuleius (Lucius Apuleius, ca 125–170 CE). *The Golden Ass*. Transl. Jack Lindsay. Bloomington: Indiana University Press 1962. Read at least the Cupid and Psyche narrative (pp. 105–142).

— *John T. Kirby*

LUSO-BRAZILIAN LITERATURE

Lyric Poetry

Alves, Castro (Brazil, 19th century). Read 'Voice of Africa' and 'Tragedy at Sea: The Slave Ship' in *The Major Abolitionist Poems*, transl. Amy A. Peterson. NY: Garland 1990.

Pessoa, Fernando (Portugal, early 20th century). *Selected Poems*, transl. Peter Rickard. Austin: University of Texas Press 1971.

Bandeira, Manuel (Brazil, 20th century). *Libertinism*, in *This Earth, That Sky*, transl. Candace Slater. Berkeley: University of California Press 1989.

Drummond de Andrade, Carlos (Brazil, 20th century). *The Minus Sign*, transl. Virginia de Araújo. Redding Ridge: Black Swan 1980.

Pignatari, Décio (Brazil, 1927–). Concrete poetry in *Brazilian Poetry (1950-1980)*.

Campos, Haroldo de (Brazil, 1929–). Concrete poetry in: *Brazilian Poetry (1950-1980)*, edd. E. Brasil and W. J. Smith (Middletown: Wesleyan University Press, 1983).

Drama

Suassuna, Ariano (Brazil, 20th century). *The Rogue's Trial*, transl. Dillwyn R. Ratcliff. Berkeley: University of California Press 1963.

Rodrigues, Nélson (Brazil, 20th century). *The Wedding Dress*, transl. Fred Clark. Chapel Hill: Albatros 1980.

Long Narrative, Prose and Verse

Camões, Luís de (Portugal, 1524–1580). *The Lusiads* [1572]. Transl. Richard Fanshawe. London: Centaur 1963.

Queirós, Eça de (Portugal, 1845–1900). *Cousin Bazilio* [1878]. Transl. Roy Campbell. New York: Noonday 1953.

Machado de Assis (Brazil, 1839–1908). *Dom Casmurro* [1900]. Transl. Helen Caldwell. NY: Noonday 1953.

Ribeiro, Aquilino (Portugal, 1885–1963). *When the Wolves Howl*. Transl. Patricia McGowan Pinheiro. NY: Macmillan 1963.

Ramos, Graciliano (Brazil, 1892–1953). *Barren Lives*. Transl. Ralph Dimmick. Austin: University of Texas Press 1965.

Queiroz, Rachel de (Brazil, 1910–). *The Three Marias*. Transl. Fred Ellison. Austin: University of Texas Press 1963.

Amado, Jorge (Brazil, 1912–). *Gabriela: Clove and Cinnamon*. Transll. J. Taylor and W. Grossman. NY: Knopf 1972.

Guimarães Rosa, João (Brazil, 1908–1967). *The Devil to Pay in the Backlands*. Transll. J. Taylor and H. de Onís. NY: Knopf 1963.

Lispector, Clarice (Brazil, 1925–1977). *The Passion According to G. H.* Transl. Ronald Sousa. Minneapolis: University of Minnesota Press 1988.

Short Narrative

Machado de Assis (Brazil, 1839–1908). *'The Devil's Church' and other Stories*. Transll. J. Schmitt and L. Ishimatsu. Manchester: Carcanet 1985.

Honwana, Luís Bernardo (Mozambique, 20th century). *We Killed Mangy Dog*. Transl. Dorothy Guedes. London: Heinemann 1969.

Trevisan, Dalton (Brazil, 20th century). *The Vampire of Curitiba*. Transl. Gregory Rabassa. NY: Knopf 1972.

— *Paul Dixon*

MIDDLE EASTERN STUDIES

NOTE: In keeping with current scholarly trends, the term 'Middle Eastern' has been adopted to refer to the various Arab countries in Asia and Africa, as well as Israel, Turkey and Iran. This designation therefore encompasses a wide geographic as well as ethnic and linguistic distribution. It is assumed that the student working in this area will have read the selections from the Bible (Hebrew and Christian scriptures) as well as from *The Qur'an* and from *The Arabian Nights* that are listed in 'Beginnings.'

Poetry Anthologies

Khouri, Mounah A., and Hamid Algar, edd. *An Anthology of Modern Arabic Poetry*. Berkeley: University of California Press 1974.

Tuetey, Charles Greville, transl. *Classical Arabic Poetry: 162 Poems from Imrulkais to Ma'arri*. Boston: Routledge 1985.

Islamic Thinkers

al-Ghazali (Abû Hamid Muhammad al-Ghaz[z]âlî, 1058–1111; name also westernized as 'Algazel'). *The Faith and Practice of al-Ghazali*. Transl. and ed. M. Montgomery Watt. London: George Allen and Unwin Ltd. 1963 (includes a full translation of al-Ghazali's *The Incoherence of Philosophy*).

ibn Rushd (1126–1198; name also westernized as 'Averroës'). *The Incoherence of Incoherence*. London: Luzac 1954.

ibn Tufayl (Muhammad ibn 'Abd al-Malik ibn Tufayl, d. 1185). *Ibn Tufayl's Hayy ibn Yaqzan: A Philosophical Tale*. Transl. Lenn Evan Goodman. NY: Twayne 1972.

Francophone Maghrebian Literature

Ben Jalloun, Tahar. *Sand Child*. Transl. Alan Sheridan. San Diego: Harcourt Brace Jovanovich 1987.

Charef, Mehdi. *Tea in the Harem*. Transl. Ed Emery. London: Serpent's Tail 1989.

Djebar, Assia. *Fantasia: An Algerian Cavalcade*. Transl. Dorothy Blair. Portsmouth: Heinemann 1993.

— *A Sister To Sheherazade*. Transl. Dorothy Blair. Portsmouth: Heinemann 1987.

Khatibi, Abdelkebir. *Love in Two Languages*. Transl. Richard Howard. Minneapolis: University of Minnesota Press 1990.

Yacine, Kateb. *Nedjma*. NY: George Braziller 1961.

Arabic Literature (The Levant, Egypt, the Sudan, and the Arabian Gulf)

Adnan, Etel. *Sitt Marie Rose*. Sausalito: Post-Apollo Press 1982.

Adonis [Ali Ahmed Said; also westernized as 'Adunis']. *The Pages of Day and Night*. Transl. Samuel Hazo. Marlboro: Marlboro Press 1994.

al-Hakim, Tawfik. *Fate of a Cockroach and Other Plays*. Transl. Denys Johnson-Davies. Washington: Three Continents Press 1994.

al-Salih, Tayyeb. *Season of Migration to the North*. Transl. Denys Johnson-Davies. Portsmouth: Heinemann African Writers Series 1969.

al-Shaykh, Hanan. *The Story of Zahra*. Transl. Peter Ford. NY: Anchor Books 1994.

Barakat, Halim. *Days of Dust*. Transl. Trevor Legassick. Washington: Three Continents Press 1983.

Bogary, Hamza. *The Sheltered Quarter: A Tale of Boyhood in Mecca*. Transl. Olive Kenny. Austin: University of Texas Center for Middle Eastern Studies 1991.

Kanafani, Ghassan. *Palestine's Children*. Transl. Barbara Harlow. London: Heinemann 1984.

Khoury, Elias. *Little Mountain*. Transl. Maia Tabet. Minneapolis: University of Minnesota Press 1989.

Maalouf, Amin. *Samarkand*. Transl. Russell Harris. London: Abacus 1994; NY: Interlink 1996.

Mahfouz, Naguib. *Midaq Alley*. Transl. Trevor Le Gassick. Washington: Three Continents Press 1981.

— *Palace Walk*. Transl. Olive Kenny. NY: Doubleday 1989.

Mina, Hanna. *Fragments of Memory: A Story of a Syrian Family*. Transll. Olive Kenny and Lorne Kenny. Austin: University of Texas Center for Middle Eastern Studies 1993.

Qabbani, Nizar. *On Entering the Sea: The Erotic and Other Poetry of Nizar Qabbani*. NY: Interlink 1996.

Saadawi, Nawal. *Woman at Point Zero*. Transl. Sherif Hetata. London: Zed 1983.

— *The Fall of the Imam*. Transl. Sherif Hetata. London: Minerva 1989.

Iran

Pezeshkzad, Iraj. *My Uncle Napoleon*. Transl. Dick Davis. Washington: Mage 1996.

Sullivan, Soraya Paknazar, transl. *Stories by Iranian Women Since the Revolution*. Austin: University of Texas Center for Middle Eastern Studies 1991.

Yalfani, Mehri. *Parastoo*. Toronto: Women's Press 1995.

Turkey

Oren, Aras. *Please, No Police*. Transl. Teoman Sipahigil. Austin: University of Texas Press 1992.

Wilson, Epiphanius, transl. *Turkish Literature: Comprising Fables, Belles-Lettres, and Sacred Traditions*. Freeport: Books for Libraries Press 1970.

Israel

Appelfeld, Aharon. *Katerina*. Transl. Jeffrey Green. NY: Random House 1992.

Hareven, Shulamit. *Twilight and Other Stories*. Transll. Hillel Halkin et al. San Francisco: Mercury House 1992.

Oz, Amos. *The Slopes of Lebanon*. NY: Harcourt Brace Jovanovich 1989.

Reference Works (for consultation as needed) and Optional Further Reading

Adonis. *An Introduction to Arab Poetics*. Austin: University of Texas Press 1990.

Allen, Roger. *The Arabic Novel: An Historical and Critical Introduction*. Syracuse: Syracuse University Press 1982, 2nd edition 1995.

— *Modern Arabic Literature*. NY: Frederick Ungar 1987.

Alloula, Malek. *The Colonial Harem*. Transll. Myrna Godzich and Wlad Godzich. Minneapolis: University of Minnesota Press 1986.

Badawi, M.M. *A Short History of Modern Arabic Literature*. Oxford: Clarendon Press 1993.

Badran, Margot, and Miriam Cooke, edd. *Opening the Gates: A Century of Arab Feminist Writing*. Bloomington: Indiana University Press 1990.

Fernea, Elizabeth Warnock, and Basima Qattan Bezirgan, edd. *Middle Eastern Muslim Women Speak*. Austin: University of Texas Press 1977.

Gibb, E.J.W. *A History of Ottoman Poetry*. 6 volumes. London: Luzac 1958.

Hargreaves, Alec. *Voices from the North African Immigrant Community in France: Immigration and Identity in Beur Fiction*. NY: St. Martin's Press 1991.

Hourani, Albert. *A History of the Arab Peoples*. Cambridge: Harvard University Press 1991.

Kabbani, Rima. *Europe's Myths of Orient*. Bloomington: Indiana University Press 1986.

Kadi, Joanna, ed. *Food for Our Grandmothers: Writings by Arab-American and Arab-Canadian Feminists*. Boston: South End Press 1994.

Lyons, M.C. *The Arabic Epic: Heroic and Oral Story-Telling.* 3 volumes. Cambridge: Cambridge University Press 1995.

Mernissi, Fatima. *Beyond the Veil: Male-Female Dynamics in Modern Muslim Society.* Bloomington: Indiana University Press 1987.

— *The Veil and the Male Elite: A Feminist Interpretation of Women's Rights in Islam.* Transl. Mary Jo Lakeland. Reading: Addison-Wesley 1991.

Mostyn, Trevor, and Albert Hourani, edd. *The Cambridge Encyclopedia of the Middle East and North Africa.* Cambridge: Cambridge University Press 1988.

Said, Edward W. *Orientalism.* NY: Vintage 1978.

— *The Question of Palestine.* NY: Vintage 1979.

Smith, Estella, et al., edd. *Anthology of Contemporary Kurdish Poetry.* London: Kurdish Solidarity Committee 1994.

Tuqan, Fadwa. *A Mountainous Journey: A Poet's Autobiography.* Transll. Olive Kenny and Naomi Shihab Nye. London: Graywolf 1990.

Woodhull, Winifred. *Transfigurations of the Maghreb: Feminism, Decolonization, and Literatures.* Minneapolis: University of Minnesota Press 1993.

— *Nada Elia*

NATIVE AMERICAN STUDIES

Oral Texts (Songs, Narratives, Ceremonies)

Bierhorst, John, ed. *Four Masterworks of American Indian Literature.* Tucson: University of Arizona Press 1984. Read 'The [Navajo] Night Chant.'

Bright, William, ed. *A Coyote Reader.* Berkeley: University of California Press 1993.

Evers, Larry, and Felipe Molina. *Yaqui Deer Songs/Maso Bwikam: A Native American Poetry.* Tucson: University of Arizona Press 1987.

Tedlock, Dennis. *Finding the Center: Narrative Poetry of the Zuni Indians.* NY: Dial Press 1972.

Autobiography

Apes[s], William. 'A Son of the Forest' (1829). Pp. 1–97 in Barry O'Connell, ed., *On Our Own Ground: The Complete Writings of William Apess, a Pequot.* Amherst: University of Massachusetts Press 1992. Also read O'Connell's introduction, pp. xiii–lxxvii.

Black Elk and John G. Neihardt. *Black Elk Speaks* [1932]. Lincoln: University of Nebraska Press, revised edition 1979. Also read Raymond DeMallie's introductory essay, 'Nicholas Black Elk and John G. Neihardt: An Introduction,' pp. 1–74 in DeMallie, ed., *The Sixth Grandfather: Black Elk's Teachings Given to John G. Neihardt.* Lincoln: University of Nebraska Press 1984.

Eastman, Charles Alexander. *From the Deep Woods to Civilization: Chapters in the Autobiography of an Indian* [1916]. Lincoln: University of Nebraska Press 1977.

Glancy, Diane. *Claiming Breath*. Lincoln: University of Nebraska Press 1992.

Momaday, N. Scott. *The Way to Rainy Mountain*. Albuquerque: University of New Mexico Press 1969. Also read 'The Man Made of Words,' pp. 162–173 in Geary Hobson, ed., *The Remembered Earth: An Anthology of Contemporary Native American Literature*. Albuquerque: University of New Mexico Press 1980.

Silko, Leslie Marmon. *Storyteller*. NY: Seaver Books 1981.

Zitkala-Ša [Gertrude Simmons Bonnin]. *American Indian Stories* [1921]. Lincoln: University of Nebraska Press 1985.

Fiction

Alexie, Sherman. *The Lone Ranger and Tonto Fistfight in Heaven*. NY: Atlantic Monthly Press 1993.

— *Reservation Blues*. NY: Atlantic Monthly Press 1995.

Erdrich, Louise. *Love Medicine* [1984]. NY: HarperCollins, revised edition 1993.

— *Tracks*. NY: Henry Holt 1988.

McNickle, D'Arcy. *The Surrounded* [1936]. Albuquerque: University of New Mexico Press 1978.

Momaday, N. Scott. *House Made of Dawn*. NY: Harper and Row 1968.

Silko, Leslie Marmon. *Ceremony* [1977]. NY: Penguin 1986.

Vizenor, Gerald. *The Heirs of Columbus*. Hanover: University Press of New England/Wesleyan University Press 1991.

Welch, James. *The Death of Jim Loney*. NY: Harper and Row 1979.

— *Fools Crow*. NY: Viking Penguin 1986.

Poetry

Allen, Paula Gunn. *Skins and Bones: Poems 1979–87*. Albuquerque: West End Press 1988.

Harjo, Joy. *In Mad Love and War*. Hanover: University Press of New England/Wesleyan University Press 1990.

Niatum, Duane, ed. *Harper's Anthology of 20th Century Native American Poetry*. San Francisco: HarperSanFranciso 1988.

Ortiz, Simon. *Woven Stone*. Tucson: University of Arizona Press 1992.

Rose, Wendy. *Bone Dance: New and Selected Poems, 1965–1993*. Tucson: University of Arizona Press 1994.

Critical and Theoretical Studies

Allen, Paula Gunn. *The Sacred Hoop: Recovering the Feminine in American Indian Traditions*. Boston: Beacon Press, revised edition 1992.

Bruchac, Joseph, ed. *Survival This Way: Interviews with American Indian Poets*. Tucson: University of Arizona Press 1987.

Brumble, H. David. *American Indian Autobiography*. Berkeley: University of California Press 1988.

Krupat, Arnold. *Ethnocriticism: Ethnography, History, Literature*. Berkeley: University of California Press 1992.

— 'On the Translation of Native American Song and Story: A Theorized History.' Pp. 3–32 in Brian Swann, ed., *On the Translation of Native American Literatures*. Washington: Smithsonian Institution Press 1992.

Lincoln, Kenneth. *Native American Renaissance*. Berkeley: University of California Press 1983.

Owens, Louis. *Other Destinies: Understanding the American Indian Novel*. Norman: University of Oklahoma Press 1992.

Tedlock, Dennis. 'On the Translation of Style in Oral Narrative.' Pp. 31–61 in Tedlock, *The Spoken Word and the Work of Interpretation*. Philadelphia: University of Pennsylvania Press 1983.

Vizenor, Gerald. 'A Postmodern Introduction' and 'Trickster Discourse: Comic Holotropes and Language Games.' Pp. 3–16 and 187–211 in Gerald Vizenor, ed., *Narrative Chance: Postmodern Discourse on Native American Indian Literatures*. Norman: University of Oklahoma Press 1989, 1993.

Wiget, Andrew. *Native American Literature*. Boston: Twayne 1985.

Reference Works (for consultation as needed)

Bataille, Gretchen, and Kathleen M. Sands. *American Indian Women: Telling Their Lives*. Lincoln: University of Nebraska Press 1984.

— *American Indian Women: A Guide to Research*. NY: Garland 1991.

Brumble, H. David. *An Annotated Bibliography of American Indian and Eskimo Autobiographies*. Lincoln: University of Nebraska Press 1981.

Davis, Mary B., ed. *Native America in the Twentieth Century*. NY: Garland 1994.

Krupat, Arnold, ed. *Native American Autobiography: An Anthology*. Madison: University of Wisconsin Press 1994.

Ruoff, A. LaVonne Brown. *American Indian Literatures: An Introduction, Bibliographic Review, and Selected Bibliography*. NY: Modern Language Association 1990.

Wiget, Andrew, ed. *Dictionary of Native American Literature* NY: Garland 1994.

Witalec, Janet, et al, edd. *Native North American Literature*. NY: Gale 1994.

— *Nancy J. Peterson*

PHILOSOPHY OF AESTHETICS

Reference Works (for consultation as needed) and Abbreviations

Audi, Robert, ed. *The Cambridge Dictionary of Philosophy*. Cambridge: Cambridge University Press 1995.

Cooper = Cooper, John M., and D. S. Hutchinson, edd. *Plato: Complete Works*. Indianapolis: Hackett 1997.

Edwards, Paul, ed. *Encyclopedia of Philosophy*. 8 volumes. NY: Macmillan 1967.

Embree, Lester, et al., edd. *Encyclopedia of Phenomenology*. Dordrecht: Kluwer 1997.

Honderich, Ted, ed. *The Oxford Companion to Philosophy*. Oxford: Oxford University Press 1995.

Sesonske = Alexander Sesonske, ed. *What is Art? Aesthetic Theory from Plato to Today*. NY: Oxford University Press 1965.

Ancient and Mediaeval (The selection of ancient texts in this module presupposes that the student will also read those required in the 'Beginnings?' module)

Presocratic Philosophers. *A Presocratics Reader: Selected Fragments and Testimonia*. Ed. Patricia Curd, with translations by Richard D. McKirahan, Jr. Indianapolis: Hackett 1996. Read entire.

Sophists. *The Older Sophists*. Ed. Rosamund Kent Sprague. Columbia: University of South Carolina Press 1972, 2nd edition 1990. Read the fragments of Progatoras and Gorgias, the *Anonymus Iamblichi*, and the *Dissoi Logoi*.

Plato (ca. 427–ca. 327 BCE). *Hippias Major* or *Greater Hippias* (authorship contested). Read the translation by Paul Woodruff in Cooper.

— *Ion*. Read the translation by Paul Woodruff in Cooper.

— *Theaetetus*. Read the translation by Levett and Burnyeat in Cooper.

Aristotle (384–322 BCE). *Categories* and *On Interpretation*. Read the translations by J. L. Ackrill in *Aristotle: Categories and De interpretatione*. Oxford: Clarendon Press 1963.

— *On Rhetoric*. Transl. George A. Kennedy. NY: Oxford University Press 1991.

Aquinas, Thomas (1225?–1274). Read 'The Theory of Art' Umberto Eco, *The Aesthetics of Thomas Aquinas*. Transl. Hugh Bredin. Cambridge MA: Harvard University Press 1988.[1]

Augustine (Aurelius Augustinus, 354–430). *Confessions*. Transl. R. S. Pine-Coffin. NY: Penguin 1961. Read books 1–3 and 8.

Early Modern (Through Nineteenth Century)

Alison, Archibald (1757–1839). *Essays on the Nature and Principles of Taste* [1790]. Read the selections reprinted in Sesonske.

Burke, Edmund (1729–1797). *A Philosophical Enquiry into the Origin of Our Ideas of the Sublime and Beautiful* [1757, sixth edition 1770]. NY: Garland 1971. Read 'Introduction: On Taste'; Part One, §§ vii, x, xv–xvi; Part Two, §§i–iii, v; Part Four, §§1–vi; Part Five (entire).

Hegel, Georg Wilhelm Friedrich (1770–1831). *Introductory Lectures on Aesthetics*. Transl. Bernard Bosanquet. NY: Penguin 1993.

Hume, David (1711–1776). 'Of the Standard of Taste.' In Hume, *Of the Standard of Taste and Other Essays*. Indianapolis: Bobbs-Merrill 1965.

Kant, Immanuel (1724–1804). *Critique of Judgment*. Use the translation by Werner S. Pluhar (Indianapolis: Hackett 1987) or else that by James Creed Meredith (Oxford: Clarendon Press 1978).

---

[1] This essay constitutes the singular exception to our provision of primary sources for a history of the philosophy of aesthetics in the western tradition. In the case of Aquinas, it would be exceedingly difficult to gather primary sources that would give a clear and adequate sense of Thomist aesthetics, while not also overwhelming the student with a massive reading-assignment.

— *Observations on the Feeling of the Beautiful and Sublime.* Transl. John T. Goldthwait. Berkeley: University of California Press 1960, 1991.

Kierkegaard, Søren (1813–1855). *Either/Or.* 2 parts (= volumes iii–iv of Kierkegaard's writings). Transll. Howard V. Hong and Edna H. Hong. Princeton: Princeton University Press 1987. Read 'Dipsalmata' and 'The Tragic in Ancient Drama Reflected in the Tragic in Modern Drama' in volume 1.

Nietzsche, Friedrich Wilhelm (1844–1900). *The Birth of Tragedy.* In *The Birth of Tragedy and The Case of Wagner,* transl. Walter Kaufmann. NY: Vintage Books 1967.

Schiller, Johann Christoph Friedrich von (1759–1805). 'Naive and Sentimental Poetry.' In *Naive and Sentimental Poetry, and On the Sublime: Two Essays.* Transl. Julius A. Elias. NY: F. Ungar 1967

— 'On the Sublime.' In *Naive and Sentimental Poetry, and On the Sublime: Two Essays.* Transl. Julius A. Elias. NY: F. Ungar 1967.

Schopenhauer, Arthur (1788–1860). *The World as Will and Representation.* Transl. E. F. J. Payne. 2 volumes. NY: Dover 1969. Read Book 3 (i.e. §§30–52) and Supplement xxxvii, 'On the Aesthetics of Poetry.'

— 'On Aesthetics.' In Schopenhauer, *Essays and Aphorisms,* transl. R. J. Hollingdale. NY: Penguin 1970.

Tolstoy, Leo (Lev Nikolaevich Tolstoi, 1828–1910). *What is Art?* Transl. A. Maude. London: Bristol Classical Press 1994.

Vico, Giambattista (1668–1744). *The New Science* [1725, 3rd edition 1744]. Transll. Thomas G. Bergin and Max H. Fisch. Ithaca NY: Cornell University Press 1948, repr. 1984. Read books 2–3.

Twentieth Century

Arendt, Hannah. *The Life of the Mind.* San Diego: Harcourt Brace & Co. 1978. Read 'Metaphor and the Ineffable' and 'The Pre-philosophic Assumptions of Greek Philosophy.'

Bakhtin, Mikhail Mikhailovich (1895–1975). *The Dialogic Imagination: Four Essays*. Austin: University of Texas Press 1981. Read 'Discourse in the Novel.'

Camus, Albert. 'The Myth of Sisyphus.' In *The Myth of Sisyphus, and Other Essays*. Transl. Justin O'Brien. NY: Vintage 1991.

Collingwood, R. G. *The Principles of Art*. Oxford: Oxford University Press 1958.. Read chapters 1–2, 11–12.

Croce, Benedetto. *The Aesthetic as the Science of Expression and of the Linguistic in General*. Transl. Colin Lyas. Cambridge: Cambridge University Press 1992. Read chapters 3, 6, 9–10, and 17–18.

Danto, Arthur C. *The Transfiguration of the Commonplace: A Philosophy of Art*. Cambridge MA: Harvard University Press 1981. Read 'Philosophy and Art' and 'Aesthetics and the Work of Art.'

Derrida, Jacques. *Of Grammatology*. Transl. Gayatri Chakravorty Spivak. Baltimore: Johns Hopkins University Press 1976. Read the introduction by Spivak.

— *Margins of Philosophy*. Transl. Alan Bass. Chicago: University of Chicago Press 1982. Read 'White Mythology.'

Dewey, John. *Art as Experience*. NY: Minton, Balch 1934.

Gadamer, Hans-Georg. *Truth and Method*. 2nd revised edition, transll. Joel Weinsheimer and Donald G. Marshall. NY: Crossroad 1989. Read 'First Part: The Question of Truth as It Emerges in the Experience of Art.'

— *Philosophical Hermeneutics*. Transl. David E. Linge. Berkeley: University of California Press 1976. Read 'Part I: The Scope of Hermeneutical Reflection.'

Goodman, Nelson. *Languages of Art*. Indianapolis: Bobbs-Merrill 1968. Read I, 'Reality Remade'; II, 'The Sound of Pictures'; and VI, 'Art and the Understanding.'

Heidegger, Martin. *Poetry, Language, Thought*. Transl. Albert Hofstadter. NY: Harper & Row 1975.

Kristeva, Julia. *Revolution in Poetic Language*. NY: Columbia University Press 1984.

Langer, Susanne K. *Feeling and Form: A Theory of Art. Developed from Philosophy in a New Key*. NY: Scribner 1953. Read chapters 1–4, 13, 20–21.

Ricœur, Paul. *The Rule of Metaphor*. Transll. Robert Czerny et al. Toronto: University of Toronto Press 1977. Read chapters 1–4.

Rorty, Richard. *Philosophy and the Mirror of Nature*. Princeton: Princeton University Press 1979. Read 'Part Three: Philosophy.'

Santayana, George. *The Sense of Beauty. Being the Outline of Aesthetic Theory*. NY: Collier 1961. Read 'Part 1: The Nature of Beauty.'

Sartre, Jean-Paul. 'What is Literature?' In Sartre, *What is Literature? and Other Essays*. Cambridge MA: Harvard University Press 1988.

— *Calvin O. Schrag and John T. Kirby*

POLISH LITERATURE in English Translation

Lyric Poetry: Anthologies

Barańczak, Stanisław, and Clare Cavanagh, transll. *Polish Poetry of the Last Two Decades of Communist Rule: Spoiling Cannibals' Fun.* Evanston: Northwestern University Press 1991.

Carpenter, Bogdana, ed. *Monumenta Polonica: The First Four Centuries of Polish Poetry.* Ann Arbor: Michigan Slavic Publications 1989.

Miłosz, Czesław, ed. *Postwar Polish Poetry: An Anthology.* Berkeley: University of California Press 1983.

Lyric Poetry: Individual Authors

Herbert, Zbigniew. *Mister Cogito.* Transll. John and Bogdana Carpenter. NY: Ecco Press 1985.

— *Report from the Besieged City and Other Poems.* Transll. John and Bogdana Carpenter. NY: Ecco Press 1985.

Kochanowski, Jan. *Laments.* Transll. Stanisław Barańczak and Seamus Heaney. NY: Farrar, Straus & Giroux 1995.

Miłosz, Czesław. *The Collected Poems, 1931–1987.* NY: Ecco Press 1988.

— *Facing the River: New Poems.* Transll. Czesław Miłosz and Robert Hass. Hopewell: Ecco Press 1995.

Różewicz, Tadeusz. *Conversations with Prince and Other Poems.* Transl. Adam Czerniawski. London: Anvil Press Poetry 1982.

Szymborska, Wisława. *View with a Grain of Sand. Selected Poems.* Transll. Stanisław Barańczak and Clare Cavanagh. NY: Harcourt Brace & Co. 1995.

Wat, Aleksander. *Mediterranean Poems.* Transl. Czesław Miłosz. Ann Arbor: Ardis 1977.

Zagajewski, Adam. *Canvas*. Transll. Renata Gorczynski et al. NY: Farrar, Straus & Giroux 1985.

Epic Poetry

Mickiewicz, Adam. *Pan Tadeusz, or The Last Foray into Lithuania*. Transl. Kenneth R. Mackenzie. London: Polish Cultural Foundation 1986.

Drama

Gombrowicz, Witold. *The Marriage*. Transl. Louis Iribarne. NY: Grove Press 1969.

Mrożek, Sławomir. *The Emigrants*. Transl. Henry Beissel. NY: Grove Press 1984.

Różewicz, Tadeusz. *The Card Index and Other Plays*. Transl. Adam Czerniawski. NY: Grove Press 1970.

Segel, Harold B., ed. *Polish Romantic Drama: Three Plays in English Translation*. Ithaca: Cornell University Press 1977.

Long Narrative

Białoszewski, Miron. *A Memoir of the Warsaw Uprising*. Transl. Madeleine G. Levine. Ann Arbor: Ardis 1977.

Gombrowicz, Witold. *Ferdydurke*. Transl. Eric Mosbacher. London: Penguin 1986.

— *Trans-Atalantyk*. Transll. Carolyn French and Nina Karsov. New Haven: Yale University Press 1994.

Konwicki, Tadeusz. *The Polish Complex*. Transl. Richard Lourie. NY: Farrar, Straus & Giroux 1981.

Lem, Stanislaw. *Solaris*. Transll. Joanna Kilmartin and Steve Cox. NY: Walker & Co. 1970.

Short Narrative

Herling-Grudziński, Gustaw. *The Island: Three Tales*. Transl. Ronald Storm. London: Owen 1990.

Schulz, Bruno. *The Complete Fiction of Bruno Schulz*. Transl. Celina Wieniewska. NY: Walker & Co. 1989.

Sienkiewicz, Henryk. *The Charcoal Sketches and Other Tales*. Transl. Adam Zamoyski. London: Angel Books 1990.

Non-Fictional Prose

Gombrowicz, Witold. *Diary*. Transl. Lilian Vallee. Evanston: Northwestern University Press 1988–1993.

Miłosz, Czesław. *The Captive Mind*. Transl. Jane Zielonko. NY: Knopf 1953.

Wat, Aleksander. *My Century: The Odyssey of a Polish Intellectual*. Transl. Richard Lourie. Berkeley: University of California Press 1988.

Reference Works and Studies of Specific Authors (for consultation as needed)

Barańczak, Stanisław. *A Fugitive from Utopia: The Poetry of Zbigniew Herbert*. Cambridge MA: Harvard University Press 1987.

Filipowicz, Halina. *A Laboratory of Impure Forms: The Plays of Tadeusz Różewicz*. NY: Greenwood Press 1991.

Fiut, Aleksander. *The Eternal Moment: The Poetry of Czeslaw Milosz*. Transl. Theodosia Robertson. Berkeley: University of California Press 1990.

Krżyzanowski, Julian. *A History of Polish Literature*. Transl. Doris Ronowicz. Warszawa: Polish Scientific Publishers 1978.

Miłosz, Czesław. *The History of Polish Literature*. Berkeley: University of California Press 1983.

Weintraub, Wiktor. *The Poetry by Adam Mickiewicz*. The Hague: Mouton & Co. 1954.

— *Bożena Shallcross*

POSTCOLONIAL LITERATURES
in English or in English Translation

Poetry

Brathwaite, Kamau (Edward). *The Arrivants: A New World Trilogy*. Oxford: Oxford University Press 1973.

Collins, Merle, and Rhonda Cobham edd. *Watchers and Seekers*. Cambridge: Cambridge University Press 1990.

Nichols, Grace. *The Fat Black Woman's Poems*. London: Virago 1984.

p'Bitek, Okot. *Song of Lawino and Song of Ocole*. London: Heinemann 1984.

Walcott, Derek. *The Arkansas Testament*. NY: Farrar, Straus and Giroux 1987.

Drama (including Screenplay)

Aidoo, Ama Ata. *The Dilemma of a Ghost*. NY: Collier 1971.

Kureishi, Hanif. *My Beautiful Laundrette*. In Kureishi's *My Beautiful Laundrette and The Rainbow Sign*. London: Faber and Faber 1986.

Matura, Mustapha. *Play Mas*. In Matura's *Six Plays*. London: Methuen 1992.

Thiong'o, Ngugi wa. *The Trial of Dedan Kimathi*. London: Heinemann 1976.

Soyinka, Wole. *Death and the King's Horseman*. London: Eyre Methuen 1975.

Walcott, Derek. *Dream on Monkey Mountain*. NY: Farrar Straus and Giroux 1970.

Prose Narrative

Achebe, Chinua. *Things Fall Apart*. London: Heinemann 1986.

Aidoo, Ama Ata. *Changes: A Love Story*. NY: The Feminist Press at CUNY 1993.

Cliff, Michelle. *Abeng*. NY: Dutton 1984.

Coetzee, J. M. *Foe*. NY: Viking 1987.

Collins, Merle. *Angel*. Seattle: Seal Press 1988.

Dangarembga, Tsitsi. *Nervous Conditions*. Seattle: Seal Press 1989.

Desai, Anita. *Baumgartner's Bombay*. NY: Knopf 1988.

Djebar, Assia. *Fantasia: An Algerian Cavalcade*. Portsmouth: Heinemann 1985.

Emecheta, Buchi. *The Joys of Motherhood*. NY: Braziller 1989.

Head, Bessie. *A Question of Power*. London: Heinemann 1974.

Kincaid, Jamaica. *Annie John*. NY: Farrar, Straus and Giroux 1985.

Lamming, George. *In the Castle of My Skin*. NY: Scocke 1983.

Devi, Mahasweta. *Imaginary Maps*. NY: Routledge 1993.

Okri, Ben. *The Famished Road*. NY: Talese 1991.

Thiong'o, Ngugi wa. *Devil on the Cross*. London: Heinemann 1982.

Rhys, Jean. *Wide Sargasso Sea*. NY: Norton 1989.

Rushdie, Salman. *Midnight's Children*. NY: Knopf 1981.

el-Sa'adawi, Nawal. *God Dies by the Nile*. London: Zed Books 1985.

Salih, Tayeb. *Season of Migration to the North*. London: Heinemann 1969.

Nonfiction Prose

Fanon, Frantz. *The Wretched of the Earth*. NY: Grove Weidenfeld 1963, 1991.

— *Black Skin/White Masks*. NY: Grove Weidenfeld 1967, 1991.

Head, Bessie. *Serowe, Village of the Rainwind*. London: Heinemann 1981.

Kincaid, Jamaica. *A Small Place*. NY: Farrar, Straus and Giroux 1988.

Prince, Mary. *The History of Mary Prince, A West Indian Slave*. Ann Arbor: University of Michigan Press 1993.

Trinh T. Minh ha. *Woman, Native, Other: Writing Postcoloniality and Feminism*. Bloomington: Indiana University Press 1989.

— *Aparajita Sagar*

PSYCHOANALYSIS

Basic Reference Works (for consultation as needed)

Freud, Sigmund. *The Standard Edition of the Complete Psychological Works of Sigmund Freud*. Ed. James Strachey, with Anna Freud et al. 24 volumes. London: Hogarth Press 1953–1974.

Holland, Norman H. *Holland's Guide to Psychoanalytic Psychology and Literature-and-Psychology*. NY: Oxford University Press 1990.

IPSA (Institute for the Psychological Study of the Arts) has a World Wide Web site that includes several years of bibliography on literature and psychology; the URL is <www.clas.ufl.edu/ipsa/ipsabib.htm>.

Jung, Carl Gustav. *The Collected Works of C. J. Jung*. Edd. Herbert Read et al. 20 (and 2 supplementary) volumes. NY: Pantheon Books, and Princeton: Princeton University Press 1954–1992.

Kiell, Norman, ed. *Psychoanalysis, Psychology, and Literature: A Bibliography*. 2 volumes. Metuchen: Scarecrow Press, 2nd edition 1982.

Laplanche, Jean, and J.-B. Pontalis. *The Language of Psychoanalysis*. NY: Norton 1974.

Natoli, Joseph P., and Frederik L. Rusch, comp. *Psychocriticism: An Annotated Bibliography*. Westport: Greenwood Press 1984.

Van Meurs, Jos. *Jungian Literary Criticism, 1920–1980: An Annotated Bibliography of Works in English (with a Selection of Titles after 1980)*. Metuchen: Scarecrow Press 1988.

Psychoanalytic Theory and Criticism

Bettelheim, Bruno. *The Uses of Enchantment: The Meaning and Importance of Fairy Tales*. NY: Random House1981.

Bloom, Harold. *The Anxiety of Influence: A Theory of Poetry*. NY: Oxford University Press 1973.

Caldwell, Richard. *The Origin of the Gods: A Psychoanalytic Study of Greek Theogonic Myth*. NY: Oxford University Press 1989.

Coen, Stanley J. *Between Author and Reader: A Psychoanalytic Approach to Writing and Reading.* NY: Columbia University Press 1994.

Chodorow, Nancy J. *Feminism and Psychoanalytic Theory.* New Haven: Yale University Press 1989.

Elliott, Anthony. *Psychoanalytic Theory: An Introduction.* Oxford: Blackwell 1994.

Felman, Shoshana. *Literature and Psychoanalysis.* Baltimore 1982.

Flax, Jane. *Thinking Fragments: Psychoanalysis, Feminism, and Post-modernism in the Contemporary West.* Berkeley: University of California Press 1991.

Freud, Sigmund. *An Outline of Psycho-Analysis.* NY: Norton 1949.

— *Three Essays on the Theory of Sexuality.* NY: Basic Books 1962.

— *New Introductory Lectures on Psychoanalysis.* NY: Norton 1964.

Girard, René. *Violence and the Sacred.* Baltimore: Johns Hopkins University Press 1977. Read chapters 1–3.

Gordon, David J. *Literary Art and the Unconscious.* Baton Rouge: Louisiana State University Press 1976.

Gunn, Daniel. *Psychoanalysis and Fiction.* Cambridge: Cambridge University Press 1988.

Hall, Calvin S. *A Primer of Freudian Psychology.* NY: World Publishing Company 1954, revised edition NY: New American Library 1979.

Hall, Calvin S., and Vernon J. Nordby. *A Primer of Jungian Psychology.* NY: New American Library 1973.

Hartman, Geoffrey H., ed. *Psychoanalysis and the Question of the Text.* Baltimore: Johns Hopkins University Press 1978.

Jung, Carl. *Man and His Symbols.* NY: Doubleday 1964.

— *The Spirit in Man, Art, and Literature.* Princeton: Princeton University Press 1966.

Knapp, Bettina L. *A Jungian Approach to Literature.* Carbondale: Southern Illinois University Press 1984.

Lacan, Jacques. *Ecrits: A Selection.* NY: Norton 1977.

— 'Seminar on "The Purloined Letter."' *Yale French Studies* 48 (1972) 39–72.

Lemaire, Anika. *Jacques Lacan.* NY: Routledge 1977.

Lesser, Simon O. *Fiction and the Unconscious.* Boston: Beacon Press 1957.

MacCannell, Juliet Flower. *Figuring Lacan: Criticism and the Cultural Unconscious.* Lincoln: University of Nebraska Press 1986.

Mitchell, Juliet. *Psychoanalysis and Feminism.* NY: Pantheon 1974.

Muller, John, and William Richardson edd. *The Purloined Poe: Lacan, Derrida, and Psychoanalytic Reading*. Baltimore: Johns Hopkins University Press 1988.

Ragland-Sullivan, Ellie. *Jacques Lacan and the Philosophy of Psychoanalysis*. Urbana: University of Illinois Press 1986.

Skura, Meredith. *The Literary Use of the Psychoanalytic Process*. New Haven: Yale University Press 1981.

Wright, Elizabeth. *Psychoanalytic Criticism: Theory in Practice*. London: Methuen 1984.

— *John T. Kirby*

QUEER STUDIES

Abelove, Henry, Michèle Aina Barale, and David M. Halperin, edd. *The Lesbian and Gay Studies Reader*. NY: Routledge 1993. (Hereafter abbreviated as 'Abelove.')

Bad Object Choices, edd. *How Do I Look? Queer Film and Video*. Seattle: Bay Press 1991.

Beemyn, Brett, and Mickey Eliason, edd. *Queer Studies: A Lesbian, Gay, Bisexual, and Transgender Anthology*. NY: New York University Press 1996.

Bell, Alan P., and Martin S. Weinberg. *Homosexualities: A Study of Diversity among Men and Women*. NY: Simon & Schuster 1978.

Berlant, Lauren, and Michael Warner. 'What does Queer Theory Teach Us about X?' *PMLA* 110.3 (May 1995) 343–349.

Bersani, Leo. *Homos*. Cambridge MA: Harvard University Press 1995.

Butler, Judith. *Gender Trouble: Feminism and the Subversion of Identity*. NY: Routledge 1990.

— *Bodies That Matter: On the Discursive Limits of "Sex."* NY: Routledge 1993.

Califia, Pat. *Sex Changes: The Politics of Transgenderism*. San Francisco: Cleis Press 1997.

Chauncey, George. *Gay New York: Gender, Urban Culture, and the Making of the Gay Male World 1890–1940*. NY: Basic Books 1994.

Crimp, Douglas S., ed. *AIDS: Cultural Analysis, Cultural Activism*. Cambridge MA: MIT Press 1988.

Dollimore, Jonathan. 'Different Desires: Subjectivity and Transgression in Wilde and Gide.' In *Sexual Dissidence: Augustine to Wilde, Freud to Foucault*. Oxford: Clarendon 1991. Anthologized in Abelove.

Duggan, Lisa. 'The Discipline Problem: Queer Theory Meets Lesbian and Gay History.' *GLQ* 2 (1995) 179–191.

Dyer, Richard, ed. *Now You See It: Studies on Lesbian and Gay Film*. NY: Routledge 1990.

Edelman, Lee. 'Tearooms and Sympathy, or, The Epistemology of the Water Closet.' In *Homographesis: Essays in Gay Literary and Cultural Theory*. NY: Routledge 1994. Anthologized in Abelove.

Ekins, Richard. *Male Femaling: A Grounded Theory Approach to Cross-Dressing and Sex-Changing*. NY: Routledge 1997.

Foucault, Michel. *The History of Sexuality*. Volume 1: An Introduction. NY: Random House 1978.

— *The Use of Pleasure*. (The History of Sexuality, volume 2.) NY: Random House 1985.

Fuss, Diana, ed. *Inside/Out: Lesbian Theories, Gay Theories*. NY: Routledge 1994.

Garber, Marjorie. *Vice Versa: Bisexuality and the Eroticism of Everyday Life*. NY: Simon and Schuster 1995.

Halperin, David M. 'Is There a History of Sexuality?' In *One Hundred Years of Homosexuality and Other Essays on Greek Love*. NY: Routledge 1990. Anthologized in Abelove.

— *Saint Foucault: Towards a Gay Hagiography*. NY: Oxford University Press 1995.

Hocquenghem, Guy. *Homosexual Desire*. London: Allison and Busby 1978.

Hollibaugh, Amber, and Cherrie Moraga. 'What We're Rollin' Around in Bed With: Sexual Silences in Feminism.' Pp. 394–405 in Ann Snitow et al., edd., *Powers of Desire: The Politics of Sexuality*. NY: Monthly Review Press 1983.

Katz, Jonathan Ned. *Gay American History*. NY: Meridian 1992.

— *The Invention of Heterosexuality*. NY: Dutton 1995.

Lauretis, Teresa de. 'Queer Theory: Lesbian and Gay Sexualities. An Introduction.' *differences* 3.2 (1991) iii–xviii.

Lewes, Kenneth. *The Psychoanalytic Theory of Male Homosexuality*. NY: Simon and Schuster 1988.

Martin, Biddy. 'Lesbian Identity and Autobiographical Difference[s].' In Bella Brodzki and Celeste Schenck, edd., *Life/Lines: Theorizing Women's Autobiography*. Ithaca: Cornell University Press 1988. Anthologized in Abelove.

Mohr, Richard D. *Gay Ideas: Outing and Other Controversies*. Boston: Beacon Press 1992.

Patton, Cindy. 'From Nation to Family: Containing African AIDS.' In Patton, *Inventing AIDS*. NY: Routledge 1990. Anthologized in Abelove.

Plummer, Kenneth, ed. *The Making of the Modern Homosexual.* Totowa: Barnes & Noble 1981.

Russo, Vito. *The Celluloid Closet: Homosexuality in the Movies.* NY: Harper & Row 1981.

Sedgwick, Eve Kosofsky. 'Epistemology of the Closet.' In *Epistemology of the Closet.* Berkeley: U of CA Press 1990. Anthologized in Abelove.

— *Tendencies.* Durham: Duke U Press 1993.

Seidman, Steven, ed. *Queer Theory/Sociology.* Oxford: Blackwell 1996.

Signorile, Michelangelo. *Queer in America: Sex, the Media, and the Closets of Power.* NY: Doubleday 1993, 2nd edition 1994.

Stein, Edward, ed. *Forms of Desire: Sexual Orientation and the Social Constructionist Controversy.* NY: Garland 1990.

Sullivan, Andrew. *Virtually Normal: An Argument about Homosexuality.* NY: Random House 1995.

Tripp, C. A. *The Homosexual Matrix.* NY: New American Library 1975, 2nd edition 1987.

Vaid, Urvashi. *Virtual Equality: The Mainstreaming of Gay and Lesbian Liberation.* NY: Doubleday 1995.

Warner, Michael, ed. *Fear of a Queer Planet: Queer Politics and Social Theory.* Minneapolis: U of MN Press 1993.

Weeks, Jeffrey. *Coming Out: Homosexual Politics in Britain from the Nineteenth Century to the Present.* London: Quartet 1977, 2nd edition 1990.

White, Edmund. *The Burning Library: Essays.* NY: Random House 1994.

Winkler, John J. 'Double Consciousness in Sappho's Lyrics.' In *The Constraints of Desire: The Anthropology of Sex and Gender in Ancient Greece.* NY: Routledge 1990. Anthologized in Abelove.

Winterson, Jeanette. 'The Semiotics of Sex.' Pp. 103–118 in *Art Objects: Essays on Ecstasy and Effrontery.* NY: Random House 1995.

Wittig, Monique. 'One Is Not Born a Woman.' In *The Straight Mind.* Boston: Beacon Press 1992. Anthologized in Abelove.

Reference Works and Optional Further Reading

Balderston, Daniel, and Donna J. Guy, edd. *Sex and Sexuality in Latin America.* NY: New York University Press 1997.

Blasius, Mark, and Shane Phelan, edd. *We Are Everywhere: A Historical Sourcebook of Gay and Lesbian Politics.* NY: Routledge 1997.

Burg, B.R. *Sodomy and the Pirate Tradition: English Sea Rovers in the Seventeenth-Century Caribbean.* NY: New York University Press 1983, 2nd edition 1995.

Carrier, Joseph. *De los Otros: Intimacy and Homosexuality among Mexican Men.* NY: Columbia University Press 1995.

Conner, Randy P., et al. *Cassell's Encyclopedia of Queer Myth, Symbol, and Spirit: Gay, Lesbian, Bisexual, and Transgender Lore.* London: Cassell 1997.

Devor, Holly. *FTM: Female-to-Male Transsexuals in Society.* Bloomington: Indiana University Press 1997.

Dowsett, Gary W. *Practicing Desire: Homosexual Sex in the Era of AIDS.* Stanford: Stanford University Press 1996. [On Australia.]

Duberman, Martin, ed. *A Queer World: The Center for Lesbian and Gay Studies Reader.* NY: New York University Press 1997.

Fellows, Will. *Farm Boys: Lives of Gay Men from the Rural Midwest.* Madison: University of Wisconsin Press 1996.

Gevisser, Mark, and Edwin Cameron, edd. *Defiant Desire: Gay and Lesbian Lives in South Africa.* NY: Routledge 1995.

Gill, John. *Queer Noises: Male and Female Homosexuality in Twentieth-Century Music.* Minneapolis: University of Minnesota Press 1995.

Hawkeswood, William G. *One of the Children: Gay Black Men in Harlem.* Berkeley: University of California Press 1996.

Herdt, Gilbert, ed. *Third Sex, Third Gender: Beyond Sexual Dimorphism in Culture and History.* NY: Zone Books 1996.

Hightower, Jamake. *The Mythology of Transgression: Homosexuality as Metaphor.* NY: Oxford University Press 1997.

Hinsch, Bret. *Passions of the Cut Sleeve: The Male Homosexual Tradition in China.* Berkeley: University of California Press 1990.

Kinsman, Gary. *The Regulation of Desire: Sexuality in Canada.* Montreal: Black Rose Books 1987.

Leap, William L. *Word's Out: Gay Men's English.* Minneapolis: University of Minnesota Press 1996.

Lemke, Jürgen, et al. *Gay Voices from East Germany.* Bloomington: Indiana University Press 1991.

Leong, Russell, ed. *Asian American Sexualities: Dimensions of the Gay and Lesbian Experience.* NY: Routledge 1996.

Leupp, Gary P. *Male Colors: The Construction of Homosexuality in Tokugawa Japan.* Berkeley: University of California Press 1995.

Lim-Hing, Sharon, ed. *The Very Inside: An Anthology of Writing by Asian and Pacific Islander Lesbian and Bisexual Women.* Toronto: Sister Vision Press 1994.

Mendès-Leite, Rommel, and Pierre-Olivier de Busscher, ed. *Gay Studies from the French Cultures: Voices from France, Belgium, Brazil, Canada and the Netherlands.* NY: Harrington Park Press 1993.

Moore, Tracy, ed. *Lesbiôt: Israeli Lesbians Talk about Sexuality, Feminism, Judaism and Their Lives.* London: Cassell 1995.

Murray, Raymond. *Images in the Dark: An Encyclopedia of Gay and Lesbian Film and Video.* Philadelphia: TLA Publications 1994.

Murray, Stephen O. *Latin American Male Homosexualities.* Albuquerque: University of New Mexico Press 1995.

— and Will Roscoe. *Islamic Homosexualities: Culture, History, and Literature.* NY: New York University Press 1997.

Naerssen, A.X. van, ed. *Gay Life in Dutch Society.* NY: Harrington Park Press 1987.

National Museum and Archive of Lesbian and Gay History, comp. *The Gay Almanac.* NY: Berkeley Books 1996.

— *The Lesbian Almanac.* NY: Berkeley Books 1996.

O'Carroll, Íde, and Eoin Collins, edd. *Lesbian and Gay Visions of Ireland: Towards the Twenty-First Century.* London: Cassell 1995.

Ramos, Juanita, ed. *Compañeras: Latina Lesbians. An Anthology.* NY: Routledge 1994.

Roscoe, Will. *The Zuni Man-Woman.* Albuquerque: University of New Mexico Press 1991.

Schmitt, Arno, and Jehoeda Sofer, edd. *Sexuality and Eroticism among Males in Moslem Societies.* NY: Harrington Park Press 1992.

Singco-Holmes, Margarita Go. *A Different Love: Being Gay in the Philippines.* Manila: Anvil Publishing 1993.

Stewart, William, and Emily Hamer. *Cassell's Queer Companion: A Dictionary of Lesbian and Gay Life and Culture.* London: Cassell 1995.

Stone, Sharon Dale, ed. *Lesbians in Canada.* Toronto: Between the Lines 1990.

Summers, Claude J. *The Gay and Lesbian Literary Heritage: A Reader's Companion to the Writers and Their Works, from Antiquity to the Present.* NY: Henry Holt 1995.

Thadani, Giti. *Sakhiyani: Lesbian Desire in Ancient and Modern India.* London: Cassell 1996.

Tuller, David. *Cracks in the Iron Closet: Travels in Gay and Lesbian Russia*. Boston: Faber & Faber 1996.

Wright, J.W., Jr., and Everett K. Rowson. *Homoeroticism in Classical Arabic Literature*. NY: Columbia University Press 1997.

— *Denis Bullock*

RHETORIC I:
5th Century BCE to 3rd Century CE

Basic Reference Works (for consultation as needed)

Enos, Theresa, ed. *The Enclopedia of Rhetoric and Composition: Communication from Ancient Times to the Information Age.* NY: Garland 1996.

Kennedy, George A. *The Art of Persuasion in Greece.* Princeton: Princeton University Press 1963.

— *The Art of Rhetoric in the Roman World.* Princeton: Princeton University Press 1972.

— *Greek Rhetoric under Christian Emperors.* Princeton: Princeton University Press 1983.

Lausberg, Heinrich. *Handbuch der literarischen Rhetorik.* 2 volumes. München: M. Heubner 1960.

Martin, Josef. *Antike Rhetorik: Theorie und Methode.* München: Beck 1974.

Volkmann, Richard. *Die Rhetorik der Griechen und Römer in systematischer Übersicht* [2nd edition 1885]. Hildesheim: Georg Olms Verlag 1987.

Ancient Authors (It is assumed that the student will also have read the following texts from the 'Beginnings?' module: Plato's *Republic, Symposium,* and *Phaedrus,* and Aristotle's *Poetics*)

Protagoras (Prôtagoras, ca. 490–ca. 420 BCE). Read the fragments by and about Protagoras collected in Rosamund Kent Sprague ed., *The Older Sophists.* 2nd edition. Columbia: University of South Carolina Press 1990.

Gorgias (Gorgias, ca. 480–ca. 380 BCE). Read the fragments by and about Gorgias collected in Rosamund Kent Sprague ed., *The Older Sophists.* 2nd edition. Columbia: University of South Carolina Press 1990.

Isocrates (Isokratês, 436–388 BCE). *Kata tôn sophistôn* [*Against the Sophists*]. In *Isocrates: On the Peace; Areopagiticus; Against the*

Sophists; Antidosis; Panathenaicus, transl. George Norlin (Loeb Classical Library, vol. 229). Cambridge MA: Harvard University Press 1929.

— *Peri antidoseôs* [*On the Challenge*]. In *Isocrates: On the Peace; Areopagiticus; Against the Sophists; Antidosis; Panathenaicus*, transl. George Norlin (Loeb Classical Library, vol. 229). Cambridge MA: Harvard University Press 1929.

Plato (Platôn, ca. 427–ca. 347 BCE). *Gorgias*. Transl. Robin Waterfield. Oxford: Oxford University Press 1994.

— *Menexenos* [*Menexenus*]. Transl. P. Ryan. In John M. Cooper and D. S. Hutchinson, edd., *Plato: Complete Works*. Indianapolis: Hackett 1997.

— *Prôtagoras* [*Protagoras*]. Transl. R. E. Allen in *Ion, Hippias Minor, Laches, Protagoras: The Dialogues of Plato, Volume III* (New Haven: Yale University Press 1996), or transll. S. Lombardo and K. Bell in John M. Cooper and D. S. Hutchinson, edd., *Plato: Complete Works*. Indianapolis: Hackett 1997.

Aristotle (Aristotelês, 384–322 BCE). *Tekhnê rhêtorikê* [Lat. *Ars rhetorica*; *Rhetorical Art*]. Transl. George A. Kennedy as *Aristotle on Rhetoric: A Theory of Civic Discourse*. NY: Oxford University Press 1991.

Anaximenes (?) (Anaximenês, 4th century BCE; formerly attributed to Aristotle). *Rhêtorikê pros Alexandron* [Lat. *Rhetorica ad Alexandrum*; *Rhetorical Handbook for Alexander (the Great)*]. Transl. H. Rackham in *Aristotle: Problems II; Rhetorica ad Alexandrum* (Loeb Classical Library, vol. 317). Revised edition. Cambridge MA: Harvard University Press 1957.

Anonymous (1st century BCE; formerly attributed to Cicero). *Rhetorica ad Herennium* [*Rhetorical Handbook for Herennius*]. Transl. Harry Caplan. (Loeb Classical Library vol. 403). Cambridge MA: Harvard University Press 1954.

Cicero (Marcus Tullius Cicero, 106–43 BCE). *De inuentione* [*On Invention*]. Transl. H. M. Hubbell. (Loeb Classical Library, vol. 386.) Cambridge MA: Harvard University Press 1949.

— *Brutus*. In *Cicero: Brutus and Orator*, transll. G. L. Hendrickson and H. M. Hubbell. (Loeb Classical Library, vol. 342.) Cambridge MA: Harvard University Press 1962.

— *Orator* [*The Orator*]. In *Cicero: Brutus and Orator*, transll. G. L. Hendrickson and H. M. Hubbell. (Loeb Classical Library, vol. 342.) Cambridge MA: Harvard University Press 1962.

Longinus (?) (perhaps 1st century CE; formerly attributed to Cassius Longinus, 3rd century CE). *Peri hupseôs* [Lat. *De sublimitate*; *On the Sublime*]. Read the translation by W. H. Fyfe and D. A. Russell in *Aristotle: Poetics; Longinus: On the Sublime; Demetrius: On Style* (Loeb Classical Library vol. 199, 2nd edition only). Cambridge MA: Harvard University Press 1995.

Demetrius (?) (authorship and date disputed; perhaps 1st or 2nd century CE; formerly attributed to Demetrius of Phaleron, b. ca. 350 BCE). *Peri Hermêneias* [Lat. *De elocutione*; *On Style*]. Use the translation by Doreen C. Innes (thoroughly revising that of W. Rhys Roberts) in *Aristotle: Poetics; Longinus: On the Sublime; Demetrius: On Style* (Loeb Classical Library vol. 199, 2nd edition only). Cambridge MA: Harvard University Press 1995. Also acceptable is that by G. M. A. Grube in *A Greek Critic: Demetrius on Style* (Toronto: University of Toronto Press 1961).

Quintilian (Marcus Fabius Quintilianus, ca. 35–100 CE). *Institutio oratoria* [*Oratorical Education*]. Transl. H. E. Butler. 4 volumes. (Loeb Classical Library, vols. 124–127.) Cambridge MA: Harvard University Press 1920–1922. Read books 1, 10, 12.

Dionysius of Halicarnassus (Dionusios, 1st century CE). *Peri suntheseôs onomatôn* [Lat. *De compositione uerborum*; *On the Arrangement of Words*]. Transl. S. Usher in volume 2 of *Dionysius of Halicarnassus: The Critical Essays* (Loeb Classical Library vol. 466). Cambridge MA: Harvard University Press 1985.

Tacitus (Publius [?] Cornelius Tacitus, ca. 56–120 CE). *Dialogus de oratoribus* [*Dialogue on Orators*]. Transl. M. Winterbottom in Russell, D. A., and M. Winterbottom edd., *Ancient Literary Criticism: The Principal Texts in New Translations* (Oxford: Clarendon Press 1972).

Suetonius (Gaius Suetonius Tranquillus, b. ca. 70 CE). *De grammaticis et rhetoribus* [*On Teachers of Grammar and Rhetoric*]. Transl. Robert A. Kaster. Oxford: Clarendon Press 1995.

Hermogenes (Hermogenês, b. ca. 161 CE). *Peri staseôn* [*On Stases*]. Use the translation by Malcolm Heath in *Hermogenes on Issues: Strategies of Argument in Later Greek Rhetoric* (Oxford: Clarendon Press 1995), or by Ray Nadeau, 'Hermogenes *On Stases*: A Translation with an Introduction and Notes,' *Speech Monographs* 31 (1964) 361–424.

— *Peri ideón* [*On Forms*]. Transl. Cecil W. Wooten as *Hermogenes On Types of Style*. Chapel Hill: University of North Carolina Press 1987.

Modern Scholarship
Barthes, Roland. 'The Old Rhetoric: An Aide-Mémoire.' In Barthes, *The Semiotic Challenge*. NY: Farrar, Straus and Giroux 1988.
Kennedy, George A. *Classical Rhetoric and its Christian and Secular Tradition from Ancient to Modern Times*. Chapel Hill: University of North Carolina Press 1980.
— *A New History of Classical Rhetoric*. Princeton: Princeton University Press 1994.
Kirby, John T. 'Greek Rhetoric.' In Theresa Enos ed., *The Enclopedia of Rhetoric and Composition: Communication from Ancient Times to the Information Age*. NY: Garland 1996.
— 'The Second Sophistic.' In Theresa Enos ed., *The Enclopedia of Rhetoric and Composition: Communication from Ancient Times to the Information Age*. NY: Garland 1996.

— *John T. Kirby*

Reference Works (for consultation as needed) and Abbreviations

Baldwin, Charles Sears. *Medieval Rhetoric and Poetic (to 1400) Interpreted from Representative Works*. NY: Macmillan 1928.

— *Renaissance Literary Theory and Practice: Classicism in the Rhetoric and Poetic of Italy, France, and England, 1400–1600*. Ed. Donald Lemen Clark. NY: Columbia University Press 1939.

Clark, Donald Lemen. *Rhetoric and Poetry in the Renaissance: A Study of Rhetorical Terms in English Renaissance Literary Criticism*. NY: Columbia University Press 1922, repr. NY: Russell & Russell 1963.

Curtius, Ernst. *European Literature and the Latin Middle Ages*. NY: Harper and Row 1963.

Howell, Wilbur Samuel. *Logic and Rhetoric in England, 1500–1700*. Princeton: Princeton University Press 1956, repr. Russell & Russell 1961.

Kennedy, George A. *Classical Rhetoric and Its Christian and Secular Tradition from Ancient to Modern Times*. Chapel Hill: University of North Carolina Press 1980.

Lanham, Richard A. *The Motives of Eloquence: Literary Rhetoric in the Renaissance*. New Haven: Yale University Press 1976.

McKeon, Richard. 'Rhetoric in the Middle Ages.' *Speculum* 17 (1942) 1–42, repr. in R. S. Crane ed., *Critics and Criticism: Ancient and Modern*. Chicago: University of Chicago Press 1952.

— 'Poetry and Philosophy in the Twelfth Century: The Renaissance of Rhetoric.' *Modern Philology* 43 (1946) 217–234, repr. in Richard McKeon, *Rhetoric: Essays in Invention and Discovery*, ed. Mark Backman (Woodbridge: Ox Bow Press 1987).

Miller = Miller, Joseph M., et al. edd., *Readings in Medieval Rhetoric*. Bloomington: Indiana University Press 1973.

Minnis, A. J., and A. B. Scott edd. *Medieval Literary Theory and Criticism, c. 1100–c. 1375: The Commentary Tradition*. Revised edition. Oxford: Clarendon Press 1991.

Murphy, James J. *Rhetoric in the Middle Ages: A History of Rhetorical Theory from St. Augustine to the Renaissance.* Berkeley: University of California Press 1974.

— ed. *Medieval Eloquence: Studies in the Theory and Practice of Medieval Rhetoric.* Berkeley: University of California Press 1974.

— *Medieval Rhetoric: A Select Bibliography.* Toronto: University of Toronto Press 1989.

Ong, Walter J., S.J. *Ramus, Method, and the Decay of Dialogue: From the Art of Discourse to the Art of Reason.* Cambridge MA: Harvard University Press 1983.

Quinn, Arthur. *Figures of Speech: Sixty Ways to Turn a Phrase.* Salt Lake City: G.M. Smith 1982.

Seigel, Jerrold. *Rhetoric and Philosophy in Renaissance Humanism: The Union of Eloquence and Wisdom, Petrarch to Valla.* Princeton: Princeton University Press 1968.

Vickers, Brian. *In Defence of Rhetoric.* Revised edition. Oxford: Clarendon Press 1989.

Mediaeval and Renaissance Theorists

Alain de Lille (Alanus de Insulis, ca. 1128–ca. 1203). *Summa de arte praedicatoria* [*Compendium on the Art of Preaching*] [?1199]. Partial translation by Joseph M. Miller in Miller.

Alberic of Monte Cassino (Albericus Casinensis, 11th century). *Flores rhetorici* [*Rhetorical Flowers*] or *Dictaminum radii* [*Basics of Letter-Writing*] [ca. 1087]. Transl. Joseph M. Miller in Miller.

Alcuin (Alcuinus, also known as Albinus Flaccus or Albinus Magister, ca. 732–804). *Disputatio de rhetorica et de uirtutibus sapientissimi Regis Karli et Albini Magistri* [*Dialogue between the Most Wise King Charles and Master Albinus on Rhetoric and the Virtues*] [794]. Transl. Wilbur Samuel Howell in *The Rhetoric of Alcuin and Charlemagne.* Princeton: Princeton University Press 1941, repr. NY: Russell and Russell 1961.

Aphthonius of Antioch (Aphthonios, early 5th century). *Progymnasmata* [*Preliminary Exercises*]. Transl. Ray Nadeau in 'The Progymnasmata of Aphthonius in Translation,' *Speech Monographs* 19 (1952) 264–285.

Augustine (Aurelius Augustinus, 354–430 CE). *De doctrina christiana* [*On Christian Doctrine*]. Transl. D. W. Robertson Jr. Indianapolis: Bobbs-Merrill 1958. Read book 4.

Bacon, Francis (1565–1621). *De dignitate et augmentis scientiarum* [*On the Dignity and Advancements of Learning*] [1623]. Translation in John M. Robertson ed., *The Philosophical Works of Francis Bacon* (London: Routledge and Sons 1905). Read book 2, chapter 18.

Bede, The Venerable (Beda [or Baeda] Venerabilis, ca. 672–735). *De schematibus et tropis* [*On Figures and Tropes*] [?700]. Transl. Gussie Hecht Tannenhaus in Miller.

Boethius (Anicius Manlius Seuerinus Boethius, ca. 480–524). *Speculatio de cognatione rhetoricae* [*Overview of the Structure of Rhetoric*]. Transl. Joseph M. Miller in Miller.

— *De topicis differentiis* [*On Topical Differences*]. Transl. Eleonore Stump as *Boethius's De Topicis Differentiis*. Ithaca: Cornell University Press 1978. Read book 4.

Cassiodorus (Flauius Magnus Cassiodorus, ca. 490–ca. 583). *Institutiones diuinarum et saecularium litterarum* [*Teachings on Sacred and Secular Texts*]. Transl. Leslie Webber Jones in *An Introduction to Divine and Human Readings* (NY: Columbia University Press 1946).

Dante Alighieri (1265–1321). *De uulgari eloquentia* [*On Vernacular Eloquence*]. Transl. by Marianne Shapiro as *De vulgari eloquentia: Dante's Book of Exile*. Lincoln : University of Nebraska Press 1990

Erasmus of Rotterdam (Geert Geerts, Lat. Desiderius Erasmus, 1466?–1536). *Ciceronianus* [*The Ciceronian*] [1528]. Transl. Izora Scott in *Controversies over the Imitation of Cicero in the Renaissance*. Davis: Hermagoras Press 1991.

Fortunatianus (Gaius Chirius Fortunatianus, fl. ca. 450). *Ars rhetorica* [*Rhetorical Art*]. Partial translation by Joseph M. Miller in Miller.

Geoffrey of Vinsauf (early 13th century). *Poetria noua* [*New Poetics*] [ca. 1208–1213]. Transl. Jane Baltzell Kopp in James J. Murphy ed., *Three Medieval Rhetorical Arts* (Berkeley: University of California Press 1971).

Harvey, Gabriel. (1550?–1631). *Ciceronianus* [1584]. Transll. Harold S. Wilson and Clarence A. Forbes in *Gabriel Harvey's Ciceronianus*. Lincoln: University of Nebraska Press 1945.

Hugh of St. Victor (ca. 1096–1141). *Didascalicon* [*Teaching Manual*] or *Eruditio didascalica* [*Lore of Teaching*]. Transl. Jerome Taylor in *The Didascalicon of Hugh of St. Victor: A Medieval Guide to the Arts*. NY: Columbia University Press 1961.

Isidore of Seville (ca. 560–636). *Etymologiae* [*Etymologies*] or *Origines* [*Origins*]. Read book 2.1-15 (transl. Dorothy V. Cerino in Miller).

John of Garland (Johannes de Garlandia, ca. 1195–1272). *De arte prosayca, metrica, et rithmica* [*On the Art of Prose-writing, Metrics, and Rhythm*; known as the *Poetria*]. Transl. Traugott Lawler as *The Parisiana poetria of John of Garland* (New Haven: Yale University Press 1974).

John of Salisbury (ca. 1115–1180). *Metalogicon* [ca. 1159]. Transl. Daniel D. McGarry as *The Metalogicon of John of Salisbury*. Berkeley: University of California Press 1971.

Llull, Ramón (1232?–1316). *Rhetorica noua.* In *New Rhetoric: Text and Translation of Llull's 'Rhetorica Nova.'* Davis: Hermagoras Press 1996.

Martianus Capella (Martianus Minneus Felix Capella, fl. 410–429). *De nuptiis Philologiae et Mercurii* [410–427]. Transll. W. H. Stahl et al. as *On the Marriage of Philology and Mercury* in volume 2 of *Martianus Capella and the Seven Liberal Arts*. NY: Columbia University Press 1971–1977. Read book 5, 'Rhetoric.'

Matthew of Vendôme (late 12th century). *Ars uersificatoria* [*The Art of Making Verses*] [ca. 1175]. Transl. Ernest Gallo in 'Matthew of Vendôme: Introductory Treatise on the Art of Poetry,' *Proceedings of the American Philosophical Society* 118 (1974) 51–92.

Peacham, Henry (1546–1634). *The Garden of Eloquence* [1577, 2nd edition 1593]. Facsimile edition by William G. Crane. Gainesville: Scholars' Facsimiles & Reprints 1951.

Peter of Blois [fl. 1190]. *Compilacio de arte dictandi.* Transl. Martin Camargo in *Medieval Rhetorics of Prose Composition: Five English Artes Dictandi and Their Tradition*. Binghamton: Medieval and Renaissance Texts and Studies 1995.

Priscian (Priscianus grammaticus, fl. ca. 500). *Praeexercitamina* [*Progymnasmata*, i.e. *Preliminary Exercises*]. Partial translation by Joseph M. Miller in Miller.

Puttenham, George (?) (1520?–1590). *The Arte of English Poesie* [1589]. Edd. G. Willcock and A. Walker. Cambridge: Cambridge University Press 1936, repr. 1970.

Rabanus Maurus (Rabanus or Hrabanus Maurus Magnentius, ca. 780–856). *De clericorum institutione* [*On the Training of Clerics*]. Partial translation by Joseph M. Miller in Miller.

Ramus, Peter (Pierre de la Ramée, Lat. Petrus Ramus, 1515–1572). *Rhetoricae distinctiones in Quintilianum* [1549]. Transll. Carole Newlands and James J. Murphy as *Arguments in Rhetoric against Quintilian*. DeKalb: Northern Illinois University Press 1986. Read pp. 83–133.

Robert of Basevorn (early 14th century). *Forma praedicandi* [*The Form of Preaching*] [ca. 1322]. Transl. Leopold Krul, OSB, in James J. Murphy ed., *Three Medieval Rhetorical Arts* (Berkeley: University of California Press 1971).

Scaliger, Julius Caesar. *Poetices libri septem* [*Seven Books on Poetics*] [1561]. Partial translation in F. M. Padelford, *Select Translations from Scaliger's Poetics*. NY: Henry Holt 1905.

Sidney, Philip (1554–1586). *An Apology for Poetry* [1595] ed. G. K. Shepherd. London: Nelson 1965.

Valla, Lorenzo (1406–1457). *De uero falsoque bono* [*On True and False Good*] or *De uoluptate* [*On Pleasure*] [1431–1433]. Transll. Maristella Lorch and A. K. Hieatt as *De Voluptate*. NY: Abaris Books 1977.

Vico, Giambattista (1668–1744). *La nuova scienza* [*The New Learning*] [1725, 3rd edition 1744]. Transll. Thomas G. Bergin and Max H. Fisch as *The New Science of Giambattista Vico* (Ithaca NY: Cornell University Press 1948, repr. 1984). Read the selections from books 2 and 3 of the 3rd edition that are included in *Vico: Selected Writings*, ed. Leon Pompa. Cambridge: Cambridge University Press 1982.

Vives, Juan Luis (1492–1540). *De tradendis disciplinis* [*On Handing Down Teachings*] or *De institutione christiana* [*On Christian Teaching*] [1531]. Translated by Foster Watson as *Vives on Education*. Cambridge: Cambridge University Press 1913, repr. Totowa: Rowman & Littlefield 1971. Read book 3, chapters 5–9; book 4, chapters 1–4; and chapters 1–3 of the Appendix.

Wilson, Thomas (1525–1581). *The Arte of Rhetorique* [1553]. Ed. Peter E. Medine as *The Art of Rhetoric*. University Park PA: Pennsylvania State University Press 1994.

— *John T. Kirby*

RHETORIC III: 17th to 20th Centuries CE

Basic Reference Works (for consultation as needed)

Barilli, Renato. *Rhetoric*. Minneapolis: University of Minnesota Press 1989.

Enos, Theresa, ed. *The Encyclopedia of Rhetoric and Composition: Communication from Ancient Times to the Information Age*. NY: Garland 1996.

Foss, Sonja K., et al., edd. *Contemporary Perspectives on Rhetoric*. Prospect Heights: Waveland Press 1985.

Kennedy, George A. *Classical Rhetoric and Its Christian and Secular Tradition from Ancient to Modern Times*. Chapel Hill: University of North Carolina Press 1980.

Lanham, Richard A., ed. *A Handlist of Rhetorical Terms: A Guide for Students of English Literature*. Berkeley: University of California Press, 2nd edition 1991. (Revised in digital format as *A Hypertext Handlist of Rhetorical Term: For Macintosh Computers*. Berkeley: University of California Press 1996).

17th–19th Centuries

Arnauld, Antoine (1612–1694), and Pierre Nicole (1625–1695). *La logique, ou l'art de penser* [1662; the 'Port-Royal Logic']. Transll. James Dickoff and Patricia James as *The Art of Thinking*. Indianapolis: Bobbs-Merrill 1964.

Austin, Gilbert (1753–1837). *Chironomia, or, A Treatise on Rhetorical Delivery* [1806]. Carbondale: Southern Illinois University Press 1966.

Bentham, Jeremy (1748–1832). *Bentham's Theory of Fictions*. Ed. C. K. Ogden. London: Kegan Paul 1932.

Blair, Hugh (1718–1800). *Lectures on Rhetoric and Belles Lettres* [1783]. Ed. Harold F. Harding. Carbondale: Southern Illinois University Press 1965.

Campbell, George (1719–1796). *Philosophy of Rhetoric* [1776]. Ed. Lloyd Bitzer. Carbondale: Southern Illinois University Press 1988. Read book 1.

Fénelon, François de Salignac de la Mothe (1651–1715). *Dialogues sur l'éloquence en général, et sur celle de la chaire en particulier* [1717]. Transl. Wilbur Samuel Howell as *Fénelon's Dialogues on Eloquence*. Princeton: Princeton University Press 1951.

Hume, David (1711–1776). 'Of Eloquence' [1743]. Part I, Essay XIII, in T. H. Green and T. H. Grose edd., *David Hume: Essays Moral, Political, and Literary*. London: Longmans, Green 1882, repr. Aalen: Scientia Verlag 1992.

Locke, John (1632–1704). *An Essay Concerning Human Understanding* [1690]. Ed. Peter H. Nidditch. Oxford: Clarendon Press 1975. Read 1.1; 2.9–12, 19; 3.1–3, 6–7, 10; 4.6, 14–15, 17, 21.

Nietzsche, Friedrich (1844–1900). *Friedrich Nietzsche on Rhetoric and Language*. Edd. Sander Gilman et al. NY: Oxford University Press 1989. Read 'On the Origin of Language,' 'History of Greek Eloquence,' and 'On Truth and Lying in an Extra-Moral Sense.'

Whately, Richard (1787–1863). *Elements of Rhetoric* [1828, 7th edition 1846]. Ed. Douglas Ehninger. Carbondale: Southern Illinois University Press 1963.

20th Century

Barthes, Roland. *Image, Music, Text*. NY: Hill & Wang 1977.

Bitzer, Lloyd, and Edwin Black, edd. *The Prospect of Rhetoric; Report of the National Developmental Project, Sponsored by Speech Communication Association*. Englewood Cliffs: Prentice-Hall 1971. Read chapters 1–11.

Black, Edwin. *Rhetorical Criticism: A Study in Method*. Madison: University of Wisconsin Press 1978.

Booth, Wayne. *The Rhetoric of Fiction*. 2nd edition. Chicago: University of Chicago Press 1983. Read chapter 6.

Burke, Kenneth. *On Symbols and Society*. Ed. Joseph R. Gusfield. Chicago: University of Chicago Press 1989.

Cohen, David. 'Classical Rhetoric and Modern Theories.' In Ian Worthington, ed., *Persuasion: Greek Rhetoric in Action*. London: Routledge 1994.

Derrida, Jacques. 'White Mythology.' In Derrida, *Margins of Philosophy*. Chicago: University of Chicago Press 1982.

Dubois, J., et al. (Group μ). *A General Rhetoric.* Baltimore: Johns Hopkins University Press 1981. Read pp. 1–45.

Foss, Sonja K., et al., edd. *Contemporary Perspectives on Rhetoric.* Prospect Heights: Waveland Press 1985, second edition 1991. Read chapters 4 (Toulmin), 6 (Grassi), and 8 (Foucault).

Foucault, Michel. 'The Discourse on Language.' In Foucault, *The Archaeology of Knowledge and The Discourse on Language.* NY: Pantheon Books 1982.

Genette, Gérard. *Figures of Literary Discourse.* NY: Columbia University Press 1982. Read chapter 6, 'Rhetoric Restrained.'

Grassi, Ernesto. *Rhetoric as Philosophy: The Humanist Tradition.* University Park: Pennsylvania State University Press 1980.

Gross, Alan G., and William G. Keith, edd. *Rhetorical Hermeneutics: Invention and Interpretation in the Age of Science.* Albany: State University of New York Press 1997. Read the essays by Michael Leff and Deirdre McCloskey.

Ijsseling, Samuel. *Rhetoric and Philosophy in Conflict: An Historical Survey.* The Hague: Martinus Nijhoff 1976.

Leff, Michael. 'In Search of Ariadne's Thread: A Review of the Recent Literature on Rhetorical Theory.' *Central States Speech Journal* 29 (1978) 73–91.

Lyotard, Jean François. *The Differend: Phrases in Dispute.* Minneapolis: University of Minnesota Press 1988. Read chapter 1.

Man, Paul de. *Allegories of Reading: Figural Language in Rousseau, Nietzsche, Rilke, and Proust.* New Haven: Yale University Press 1979. Read 'Semiology and Rhetoric.'

McKeon, Richard. *Rhetoric: Essays in Invention and Delivery.* Woodbridge: Ox Bow Press 1987. Read 'The Uses of Rhetoric in a Technological Age: Architectonic Productive Arts.'

Perelman, Chaim, and Lucie Olbrechts-Tyteca. *The New Rhetoric: A Treatise on Argumentation.* Notre Dame: University of Notre Dame Press 1957. Read §§1–21, 41, 72–73, 87.

Richards, I. A. *The Philosophy of Rhetoric.* NY: Oxford University Press 1936.

Ricœur, Paul. *The Rule of Metaphor: Multi-disciplinary Studies of the Creation of Meaning in Language.* Toronto: University of Toronto Press 1977.

Schrag, Calvin O. *Communicative Praxis and the Space of Subjectivity.* Bloomington: Indiana University Press 1986. Read chapter 1, 'Figures of Discourse.'

Toulmin, Stephen. *The Uses of Argument*. Cambridge: Cambridge University Press 1958.

Valesio, Paolo. *Novantiqua: Rhetorics as a Contemporary Theory*. Bloomington: Indiana University Press 1980. Read chapter 1.

Weaver Richard M. *The Ethics of Rhetoric*. Davis: Hermagoras Press 1985.

White, Hayden. *Metahistory: The Historical Imagination in Nineteenth-Century Europe*. Baltimore: Johns Hopkins University Press 1973. Read Part One (i.e. chapters 1 and 2).

— John T. Kirby

RUSSIAN LITERATURE

Reference Works (for consultation as needed)

Bristol, Evelyn. *A History of Russian Poetry*. Oxford: Oxford University Press 1991.

Mirsky, Dimitry P. *A History of Russian Literature from its Beginnings to 1900*. NY: Vintage 1958.

Terras, Victor. *A History of Russian Literature*. New Haven: Yale University Press 1992.

Lyric Poetry. Selections will be taken from the following anthologies:
- Markov, Vl., and M. Sparks, edd. *Modern Russian Poetry*. Indianapolis: Bobbs-Merrill 1967.
- Obolensky, D., ed. *The Heritage of Russian Verse*. Bloomington: Indiana University Press 1976.

Lomonosov, Mikhail (1711–1765). 'Vechernee razmyshlenie,' in Obolensky.

Derzhavin, Gavril (1743–1816). 'Vlastiteliam i sudiiam' and 'Pamiatnik,' in Obolensky.

Pushkin, Aleksandr (1799–1837). 'K★★★'; 'Zimnii vecher'; Prorok'; 'Poet'; 'Talisman'; 'Anchar'; 'Besy'; 'Dlia beregov'; 'Osen''; and 'Pora, moi drug, pora!' in Obolensky.

Tiutchev, Fedor (1803–1873). 'Videnie'; 'Vesenniaia groza'; 'Son na more'; 'Tsitseron'; 'Silentium'; 'Liubliu glaza tvoi'; 'Eti bednye selen'ia'; and 'Pevuchest' est' v morskikh volnakh' in Obolensky.

Pavlova, Karolina (1809–1893). 'O bylom, o pogibshem' and 'Rim' in Obolensky.

Lermontov, Mikhail (1814–1841). 'Angel'; 'Kogda volnuetsia'; 'Pervoe ianvaria'; 'Kazach'ia kolybel'naia pesnia'; 'I skuchno i grustno'; 'Otchizna'; 'Son'; and 'Vykhozhu odin ia na dorogu' in Obolensky.

Solov'ev, Vladimir (1853–1900). 'U tsaritsy moei' in Obolensky.

Annenskii, Innokentii (1853–1909). 'Sentiabr''; 'Smychok i struny'; 'Stal'naia tsikada'; 'Posle kontserta'; and 'Toska mirazha' in Obolensky.

Gippius, Zinaida (1869–1945). 'Pyl'; 'P'iavki'; 'Ona'; 'Petersburg'; 'Voznia'; and 'Banal'nostiam' in Markov and Sparks.

Blok, Aleksandr (1880–1921). 'Devushka pela'; 'Neznakomka'; 'Na pole Kulikovom'; 'Noch', ulitsa, fonar', apteka'' in Markov and Sparks. 'Ravenna'; 'Khudozhnik'; and 'Rozhdennye v goda glukhie' in Obolensky.

Akhmatova, Anna (1889–1960). 'Pushkin'; 'Muze'; 'Uedinenie'; 'Teper' nikto ne stanet slushat''; and 'Mne ni k chemu odicheskie rati' in Markov and Sparks; 'Zvenela muzyka v sadu'; 'Iul', 1914'; 'Vse raskhishcheno, predano, prodano'; and 'Bezhetsk' in Obolensky.

Pasternak, Boris (1890–1960). 'Marburg'; 'Pamiati demona'; 'Uroki angliiskogo'; 'Avgust'; 'Vo vsem mne khochetsia ...' ; and 'Byt' znamenitym — nekrasivo' in Markov and Sparks; 'Step'; 'Gamlet'; 'Gefsimanskii sad'; and 'Veter' in Obolensky.

Mandel'shtam, Osip (1891–1938). 'Dano mne telo'; 'Notre Dame'; 'Amerikanka'; 'Bessonitsa. Gomer'; 'Tristia'; 'Proslavim, brat'ia'; 'Vek'; and 'Ariost' in Markov and Sparks; 'Hagia Sophia' in Obolensky.

Tsvetaeva, Marina (1892–1941). 'Don'; 'Andre Chenier'; 'Vozvrashchenie vozhdia'; and 'Dialog Gamleta s sovest'iu' in Markov and Sparks; 'Est' v stane moem ...' in Obolensky.

Maiakovskii, Vladimir (1893–1930). 'A vsë-taki'; 'Khoroshee otnoshenie k loshadiam'; and 'Bruklinskii most' in Markov and Sparks; 'Razgovor s fininspektorom o poezii' in Obolensky.

Drama. Available anthologies include:
- Segel, H. B., ed. *The Literature of Eighteenth-Century Russia.* NY: Dutton 1967.
- — ed. *Twentieth-Century Russian Drama: From Gorky to the Present.* NY: Columbia University Press 1979.
- Reeve, F. D., ed. *Nineteenth-Century Russian Plays: An Anthology.* NY: Norton 1973.

Fonvizin, Denis (1745–1792). *The Minor* [1782]. In Segel 1967.

Griboedov, Aleksandr (1795–1829). *Woe from Wit* [1822–24]. In Reeve.

Pushkin, Aleksandr (1799–1837). *Boris Godunov* [1825]. NY: Columbia University Press 1976.

Gogol', Nikolai (1809–1852). *The Inspector General* [1836]. NY: Applause Theatre 1987.

Ostrovskii, Aleksandr (1823–1886). *The Storm* [1859]. NY: Pegasus 1969.

Chekhov, Anton (1860–1904). *The Seagull* [1896]. In *Four Plays*. NY: Hill and Wang 1969.

— *The Cherry Orchard* [1904]. In *Four Plays*. NY: Hill and Wang 1969.

Gor'kii, Maksim (1868–1936). *The Lower Depths* [1902]. In *Five Plays*. London: Methuen Drama 1994.

Maiakovskii, Vladimir (1893–1930). *The Bedbug* [1928]. In *The Complete Plays*. NY: Washington Square Press 1968.

Petrushevskaia, Liudmila (1938–). *Three Girls in Blue* [1983]. In *Cinzano: Eleven Plays*. London: Nick Hern Books 1991.

Long Narrative

Pushkin, Aleksandr (1799–1837). *Evgenii Onegin* [1833]. NY: Dutton 1963.

Gogol', Nikolai (1809–1852). *Dead Souls, Part One* [1842]. NY: Norton 1971.

Lermontov, Mikhail (1814–1841). *A Hero of Our Time* [1840]. NY: Penguin 1982.

Turgenev, Ivan (1818–1883). *Fathers and Sons* [1862]. NY: Norton 1966.

Dostoevskii, Fedor (1821–1881). *The Brothers Karamazov* [1880]. NY: Norton 1976.

Tolstoi, Lev (1828–1910). *Anna Karenina* [1877]. NY: Penguin Norton 1970.

Sologub, Fedor (1863–1927). *The Petty Demon* [1907]. NY: Random House 1962.

Gor'kii, Maksim (1868–1936). *Childhood* [1913]. NY: Penguin 1980.

Belyi, Andrei (1880–1934). *Petersburg* [1916]. Bloomington: Indiana University Press 1978.

Gladkov, Fedor (1883–1958). *Cement* [1924]. NY: Ungar 1960.

Zamiatin, Evgeny (1884–1937). *We* [1920]. London: Cape 1970.

Bulgakov, Mikhail (1891–1940). *The Master and Margarita* [1940]. NY: Vintage 1996.

Pasternak, Boris (1890–1960). *Doctor Zhivago*. NY: Random House 1957.

Nabokov, Vladimir (1899–1977). *Invitation to a Beheading* [1938]. NY: Putnam 1959.

Short Narrative. Available anthologies include:
- Proffer, Carl R., ed. *From Karamzin to Bunin: An Anthology of Russian Short Stories.* Bloomington: Indiana University Press 1969.
- Brown, Clarence, ed. *The Portable Twentieth-Century Russian Reader.* NY: Penguin 1985.

Pushkin, Aleksandr (1799–1837). 'The Queen of Spades' (1833).

Gogol', Nikolai (1809–1852). 'The Nose' (1836).

Lermontov, Mikhail (1814–1841). 'The Demon' (in verse) (1829–1839).

Turgenev, Ivan (1818–1883). *Sketches from a Hunter's Album*, Selections (1852). Read 'Khor and Kalinych,' 'Kasyan from the Beautiful Lands,' 'Hamlet of Shchigrovsky District,' and 'Living Relic.'

Dostoevskii, Fedor (1821–1881). 'The Dream of a Ridiculous Man' (1877).

Tolstoi, Lev (1828–1910). 'The Death of Ivan Ilich' (1886).

Chekhov, Anton (1860–1904). 'The Lady with the Small Dog' (1899).

Bunin, Ivan (1870–1953). 'The Gentleman from San Francisco' (1915).

Babel', Isaak (1894–1941). 'My Dove Cote,' from *Red Cavalry* (1926).

Tolstaia, Tatiana (1951–). *On the Golden Porch* (1989).

Non-Fictional Prose. Some selections will be taken from the following anthologies:
- Raeff, M., ed. *Russian Intellectual History: An Anthology.* NY: Harcourt, Brace and World 1966.
- Zenkovsky, S. A., ed. *Medieval Russia's Epics, Chronicles, and Tales.* NY: Dutton 1974.

Ilarion (11th century). 'Sermon on Law and Grace' (1037–1050), in Zenkovsky.

Nikitin, Afanasii (15th century). 'Afanasii Nikitin's Journey Across Three Seas' (late 15th century), in Zenkovsky.

Lomonosov, Mikhail (1711–1765). 'Letter on the Rules for Russian Verse Composition' (1739).

Chaadaev, Petr (1794–1856). 'Letters on the Philosophy of History; First Letter' (1829), in Raeff.

Belinskii, Vissarion (1811–1848). 'Letter to N.V. Gogol' (1847), in Raeff.

Kireevskii, Ivan (1806–1856). 'On the Nature of European Culture and its Relationship to the Culture of Russia' (1852), in Raeff.

Tolstoi, Lev (1828–1910). 'What is Art?' (1898).

Lawton, A., and H. Eagle, transll. and edd. *Russian Futurism Through Manifestoes* Ithaca: Cornell University Press 1988. Read 'Slap in the Face of Public Taste,' 'The Word as Such,' and 'Language Creation.'

Ivanov, Viacheslav (1866–1949), and Mikhail Gershenzon (1869–1925). 'A Corner-to-Corner Correspondence' (1921), in Raeff.

Terts, Abram [Andrei Siniavskii] (1925–1977). 'On Socialist Realism' (1959). In: *'The Trial Begins' and 'On Socialist Realism.'* NY: Vintage 1960.

— *Edith W. Clowes*

SCANDINAVIAN LITERATURE AND CULTURE

Medieval Iceland

Edda (13th century). Read *Völuspá, Hávamal, Locasenna, Thrymsqvifa, Sigurdarqvifa in scamma,* and *Baldrs draumar.* In Hans Kuhn, ed. *Edda: Die Lieder des Codex Regius nebst verwandte Denkmälern.* 2 volumes. Volume 1: Text. Ed. Gustav Neckel, rev. Hans Kuhn. Heidelberg: C. Winter, 5th edition 1962. Transl. Patricia Terry in *Poems of the Elder Edda.* Philadelphia: University of Pennsylvania Press 1990.

Sturluson, Snorri (1179–1241). *Prose Edda.* Read *Gylfaginning (The Deluding of Gylfi).* In Finnur Jónsson, ed. *Edda Snorra Sturlusonar udgivet efter håndskrifterne.* Copenhagen: Gyldendalske Boghandel, Nordisk Forlag 1931. Transl. Jean I. Young as *The Prose Edda of Snorri Sturluson: Tales from Norse Mythology.* Berkeley: University of Calfornia Press 1954.

Njáls saga (13th century). In Einar Olafur Sveinsson, ed. *Brennu-Njáls Saga.* Islenzk Fornrit, volume 12. Reykjavik: Hid Islenzka Fornritafelag 1954. Transll. Magnus Magnusson and Herman Pálsson as *Njal's Saga.* Baltimore: Penguin 1960.

Laxdaela saga (13th century). In Einar Olafur Sveinsson, ed. *Laxdaela Saga.* Islenzk Fornrit, volume 5. Reykjavik: Hid Islenzka Fornritafelag 1934. Transll. Magnus Magnusson and Herman Pálsson as *Laxdaela Saga.* Baltimore: Penguin 1969.

Denmark

Holberg, Ludvig (1684–1754). *Jeppe på Bjerget.* Copenhagen: Gyldendals Värkserie 1984. Transll. Gerald S. Argetsinger and

Sven H. Rossel in *Jeppe of the Hill and Other Comedies*. Carbondale: Southern Illinois University Press 1990.

Grundtvig, Nicolai F.S. (1783–1872). 'De levends Land.' In Steen Johansen, ed. *Deilig er den himmel blaa: Udvalgte digte*. Copenhagen: Gyldendal 1983. Transll. Edward Broadbridge and Niels Lyhne Jensen in *A Grundtvig Anthology*. Cambridge: James Clarke & Co. 1984.

Andersen, Hans Christian (1805–1875). *H.C. Andersen: Eventyr og historier*. Ed. Johannes Mollehave. Copenhagen: Sesam 1993. Transl. Patricia Conroy in *H.C. Anderson: Tales and Stories* (ed. Sven H. Rossel). Seattle: University of Washington Press 1980.

Andersen, Martin Nexø (1869–1954). *Pelle erobreren*. 2 volumes. Copenhagen: Gyldendal 1971. Read volume 1. Transl. Jesse Muir as *Pelle the Conqueror. Volume 1: Boyhood*. NY: Henry Holt 1915.

Dinesen, Isak [Karen Blixen] (1885–1962). *Vinter-Eventyr*. Copenhagen: Gyldendal 1970. Transl. as *Winter's Tales*. NY: Vintage 1970, 1993.

Dreyer, Carl (1889–1968). *Vredens dag*. Transl. Ole Sturm in *Four Screenplays*. Bloomington: Indiana University Press 1970. The student should also view the 1995 subtitled version of the original 1943 film, *Vredens dag/Day of Wrath* (video no. 1047, Hen's Tooth Video) dir. Dreyer.

Ditlevsen, Tove (1918–1976). *Ansigsterne*. Copenhagen: Gyldendal 1976. Transl. Tiina Nunnally as *The Faces*. Seattle: Fjord Press 1991.

Finland

Lönnrot, Elias (1802–1884). *Kalevala taikka vanhoja Karjalan runoja Suomen kansan muinoisista ajoista*. Helsinki: Suomalaisen Kirjallisuuden Seura 1985. Transl. Keith Bosley as *Kalevala*. Oxford: Oxford University Press 1989.

Runeberg, Johan Ludvig (1804–1877). Read *Fänrik Ståls sägner*, especially 'Doblen vid Jutas' and 'Lotta Svärd.' In volume 3 of

Runeberg's *Samlede arbeten*. 6 volumes. Stockholm: H. Schildt 1931. Transl. Clement B. Shaw in *The Songs of Ensign Stål*. NY: G.E. Stechert 1925.

Kivi, Aleksis [known as 'Stenvall'] (1834–1872). *Seitsemän veljestä*. In volume 2 of Kivi, *Kootut teokset*. 4 volumes. Helsinki: Suomalaisen Kirjallisuuden Seura 1984. Transl. Richard Impola as *Seven Brothers*. New Paltz: Finnish-American Translators Association 1991.

Sillanpää, Frans Eemil (1888–1964). *Hurskas kurjuus*. In volume 2 of Sillanpää, *Kootut teokset*. 2 volumes. Helsinki: Otava 1988. Transll. Alex Matson and John R. Pitkin as *Meek Heritage*. NY: P.S. Eriksson 1973.

Södergran, Edith (1892–1923). Read 'Dagen svalnar,' 'Ingenting,' and 'Jag längtar till landet som icke är' in the bilingual edition of Stina Katchadourian, ed. and transl., *Love and Solitude: Selected Poems 1916–1923*. San Francisco: Fjord Press 1981.

Waltari, Mika (1908–1979). *Sinuhe, egyptiläinen*. Porvoo: Werner Söderström Oy., 1989. Transl. Naomi Walford as *The Egyptian*. NY: G.P. Putnam's Sons 1949.

Jansson, Tove (1914–). *Trollkarlens hatt*. Helsinki: Holger Schmidts Förlag 1948. Transl. Thomas Warburton as *Finn Family Moomintroll*. NY: Farrar, Straus, Giroux 1989.

Linna, Väinö (1920–1992). *Tuntematon sotilas*. Porvoo: Werner Söderström Oy., 1957. Transl. as *The Unknown Soldier*. Porvoo: Werner Söderström Oy., 1975.

Norway

Welhaven, Johan Sebastian (1807–1873). Read 'Digtets Aand' and 'Lokkende Toner' in volume 1 of Welhaven, *Samlede verker*. 5 volumes. Oslo: Universitetsforlaget 1990. Transl. Charles Wharton Stork in *Anthology of Norwegian Lyrics*. Princeton: Princeton University Press 1942.

Wergeland, Henrik (1808–1845). Read 'Til min Gyldenlak' and 'Pigen paa Anatomikammeret' in Wergeland, *Den første gång:*

Henrik Wergelands dikt i utvalg. Oslo: Gyldendal norsk forlag 1995. Transll. G.M. Gathorne-Hardy et al. in Wergeland, *Poems.* Westport: Greenwood Press 1970.

Bjørnson, Bjørnsterne (1832–1910). *Synnøve Solbakken.* In volume 3 of Bjørnson, *Samlede vaerker.* 5 volumes. Copenhagen: Gyldendal 1900–1902. Transl. Julie Sutter as *Synnøve Solbakken.* Freeport: Books for Libraries Press 1972.

Ibsen, Henrik (1828–1906). *Peer Gynt* and *Et dukkehjem.* In volume 4 of Ibsen, *Samlede verker.* 6 volumes. Oslo: Universitetsforlaget 1993. Transll. Rick Davis and Brian Johnston in *Ibsen: Four Major Plays.* Lyme: Smith and Kraus 1995. See also the 1993 edition of *Peer Gynt* (Oslo: Universitetsforlaget) and the translation by John Northam, *Peer Gynt* (Oslo: Scandinavian University Press 1993).

Hamsun, Knut (1859–1952). *Sult.* Copenhagen: Gyldendal norsk vorlag 1990. Transl. George Egerton as *Hunger.* NY: Knopf 1920.

Undset, Sigrid (1882–1949). *Kristin Lavransdatter.* 3 volumes. Oslo: H. Aschehoug 1964. Read volume 1, *Kransen.* Transll. Charles Archer and J.S. Scott as *The Bridal Wreath.* NY: Knopf 1937.

Vesaas, Tarjei (1897–1970). *Det store spelet.* Oslo: Tanum-Norli 1951. Transl. Elizabeth Rokkan as *The Great Cycle.* Madison: University of Wisconsin Press 1967.

Sweden

Bellman, Carl Mikael (1740–1795). *Fredmans epistlar.* Read nos. 23, 40, 79. In Bellman, *Fredmans epistlar,* edd. G. Hillbom et al. Stockholm: Proprius 1994. Transll. and arr. Hendrik Willen van Loon and Grace Castagnetta in *The Last of the Troubadors: Carl Michael Bellman, 1740–1795: His Life and His Music.* NY: Simon & Schuster 1939.

Strindberg, August (1849–1912). *Fröken Julie* and *Ett Drömspel.* In Strindberg, *Fröken Julie, Master Olof, Fadren, Ett Drömspel.*

Stockholm: Bonniers 1957. Transl. Walter Johnson in *Dream Play and Four Chamber Plays*. NY: Norton 1975.

Lagerlöf, Selma (1858–1940). *Gösta Berlings saga*. Stockholm: Bonniers 1933. Transl. Robert Bly as *The Story of Gösta Berling*. NY: New American Library 1962.

Martinson, Moa (1890–1964). *Kvinnor och äppelträd*. Stockholm: Folket i Bilds 1954. Transl. Margaret S. Lacy as *Women and Appletrees*. Westbury: Feminist Press 1985.

Lagerkvist, Pär (1891–1974). *Barrabas*. Stockholm: Bonniers 1950. Transl. Alan Blair as *Barrabas*. NY: Random House 1951.

Moberg, Vilhelm (1898–1973). *Utvandrarna*. Stockholm: Bonniers 1954. Transl. Gustaf Lannestock as *The Emigrants: A Novel*. NY: Simon & Schuster 1951.

Lindgren, Astrid (1907–). *Pippi Långstrump*. Stockholm: Bonniers 1951. Transl. Florence Lamborn as *The Adventures of Pippi Longstocking*. NY: Viking 1997.

Bergman, Ingmar (1918–). *Sjunde inseglet*. Transll. Lars Malmström and David Kushner as *The Seventh Seal* in Bergman, *Four Screenplays*. NY: Simon & Schuster 1960. The student should also view the 1994 subtitled version of the original (1957) film, *Sjunde inseglet/The Seventh Seal*, dir. Bergman. Acton: Home Vision Video.

Basic Reference Works (for consultation as needed)

Clover, Carol J., and John Lindow, edd. *Old Norse-Icelandic Literature: A Critical Guide*. Ithaca: Cornell University Press 1985.

Rossel, Sven H. *A History of Scandinavian Literature, 1870–1980*. Minneapolis: The University of Minnesota Press 1982.

Laitinen, Kai. *Literature of Finland: An Outline*. Helsinki: Otava 1985.

— *Thomas A. DuBois*

SEMIOTICS

Reference Works (for consultation as needed)
Colapietro, Vincent. *Glossary of Semiotics*. NY: Paragon 1993.
Greimas, A. J., and Joseph Courtés. *Semiotics and Language: An Analytical Dictionary*. Bloomington: Indiana University Press 1982.
Nöth, Winfried. *Handbook of Semiotics*. Bloomington: Indiana University Press 1990.

Theoretical Studies
Barthes, Roland. *Elements of Semiology*. NY: Hill and Wang 1968.
— *S/Z*. NY: Hill and Wang 1974.
Clarke, D. S., Jr. *Principles of Semiotic*. London: Routledge and Kegan Paul 1987.
— ed. *Sources of Semiotic: Readings with Commentary from Antiquity to the Present*. Carbondale: Southern Illinois University Press 1990.
Culler, Jonathan. *The Pursuit of Signs*. Ithaca: Cornell University Press 1983.
— *Ferdinand de Saussure*. Ithaca: Cornell University Press, revised edition 1986.
Deely, John. *Basics of Semiotics*. Bloomington: Indiana University Press 1990.
Eco, Umberto. *A Theory of Semiotics*. Bloomington: Indiana University Press 1976.
— *Semiotics and the Philosophy of Language*. Bloomington: Indiana University Press 1984.
— *The Limits of Interpretation*. Bloomington: Indiana University Press 1994.
Greimas, A. J. *Structural Semantics*. Lincoln: University of Nebraska Press 1983.
— *On Meaning*. Minneapolis: University of Minnesota Press 1987.
— *Narrative Semiotics and Cognitive Discourses*. London: Pinter 1990.

Hawkes, Terence. *Structuralism and Semiotics*. London: Methuen 1977.

Innis, Robert E., ed. *Semiotics: An Introductory Anthology*. Bloomington: Indiana University Press 1985.

Kristeva, Julia. *Desire in Language: A Semiotic Approach to Literature and Art*. NY: Columbia University Press 1980.

Lauretis, Teresa de. *Alice Doesn't: Feminism, Semiotics, Cinema*. Bloomington: Indiana University Press 1984.

Merrell, Floyd. *Sign, Textuality, World*. Bloomington: Indiana University Press 1992.

— *Semiosis in the Postmodern Age*. West Lafayette: Purdue University Press 1995.

— *Peirce's Semiotics Now: A Primer*. Toronto: Canadian Scholars' Press 1995.

— *Peirce, Signs, and Meaning*. Toronto: University of Toronto Press 1997.

Peirce, Charles Sanders. *Philosophical Writings of Peirce*. NY: Dover 1955.

Riffaterre, Michael. *Semiotics of Poetry*. Bloomington: Indiana University Press 1978.

Saussure, Ferdinand de. *Course in General Linguistics*. NY: McGraw-Hill 1969.

Sebeok, Thomas A. *Contributions to the Doctrine of Signs*. Lanham: University Press of America 1985.

— *Semiotics in the United States*. Bloomington: Indiana University Press 1991.

— *An Introduction to Semiotics*. Toronto: University of Toronto Press 1994.

Sheriff, John K. *The Fate of Meaning: Charles Peirce, Structuralism, and Literature*. Princeton: Princeton University Press 1989.

Silverman, Kaja. *The Subject of Semiotics*. NY: Oxford University Press 1983.

— *Floyd Merrell*

SPANISH LITERATURE (Peninsular)

NOTE: All selections of lyric poetry can by found in one or more of
the following anthologies:

> Cohen, J. M., ed. *The Penguin Book of Spanish Verse*. 3rd edition
> 1988.

> Flores, Angel, ed. *An Anthology of Spanish Poetry from Garcilaso to
> García Lorca*. Garden City: Anchor Books 1961.

> Rivers, Elias L., ed. *Renaissance and Baroque Poetry of Spain*.
> Prospect Heights: Waveland Press 1988.

Mediaeval Period

Anonymous. *Poema de Mío Cid (Poem of the Cid)*.

Ruiz, Juan. Arcipreste de Hita. *Libro de buen amor (The Book of True
Love)*.

Rojas, Fernando de. *La Celestina (Celestina)*.

Manrique, Jorge. *Coplas por la muerte de su padre (Verses on the Death of
his Father)*.

Sixteenth Century

Anonymous. *Lazarillo de Tormes*.

Garcilaso de la Vega. Selected poetry:

> Sonetos:

>> 'Cuando me paro a contemplar mi estado'
>> 'Un rato se levanta mi esperanza'
>> 'Escrito está en mi alma vuestro gesto'
>> '¡Oh dulces prendas, por mi mal halladas'
>> 'Hermosas ninfas que, en el río metidas'
>> 'En tanto que de rosa y azucena'
>> 'Pasando el mar Leandro el animoso'

> Canción: 'Si de mi baja lira'

> Eglogas:

>> I: 'El dulce lamentar de dos pastores'
>> III: 'Aquella voluntad honesta y pura'

León, Fray Luis de. Selected poetry:
    Odas:
        Vida Retirada: '¡Qué descansada vida'
        A Francisco Salinas: 'El aire se serena'
        Profecía del Tajo: 'Folgaba el Rey Rodrigo'
        Noche Serena: 'Cuando contemplo el cielo'
        A Felipe Ruiz: '¿Cuando será que pueda'
    Décima: 'Al salir de la cárcel'
Cruz, San Juan de la. Selected poetry:
    Canciones:
        Cántico espiritual: '¿Adónde te escondiste,'
        La noche oscura: 'En una noche oscura'
        Llama de amor viva: '¡Oh llama de amor viva'
Jesús, Teresa de. *Vida* (*Life*).

Seventeenth Century
Góngora, Luis de. Selected poetry:
    Sonetos:
        'En este occidental, en este, oh Licio'
        'Menos solicitió veloz saeta'
        'Esta en forma elegante, oh peregrino'
        'La dulce boca que a gustar convida'
        'De pura honestidad templo sagrado'
        'Descaminado, enfermo, peregrino'
        'Ilustre y hermosísima María'
        'Mientras por competir con tu cabello'
        'Oh claro honor del líquido elemento'
        '¡Oh excelso muro, oh torres coronadas'
    Fábula de Polifemo y Galatea
    Letrillas:
        'Andeme yo caliente'
        'Aprended, flores, en mí'
    Romance: 'Angélica y Medoro'
    Romancillo: 'La más bella niña'
Vega, Lope de. *El caballero de Olmedo* (*The Knight of Olmedo*).
— *Fuenteovejuna* (*Sheepwell*).
— Selected poetry:
    Romance: 'Hortalano era Berlardo'
    Canciones populares:
        'Velador que el castillo velas'

Cervantes, Miguel de. *Don Quixote de la Mancha.*
— Entremés: 'El retablo de las maravillas' ('The Wonder Show').
— Novelas:
 'El casamento engañoso' ('The Deceitful Marriage').
 'Coloquio de los perros' ('Colloquy of the Dogs').

Nineteenth Century
Bécquer, Gustavo Adolfo. Selected poetry:
 Rimas:
 'Del salón en el ángulo oscuro'
 'Los invisibles átomos del aire'
 '— Yo soy ardiente, yo soy morena'
 'Asomaba a sus ojos una lágrima'
 'Los suspiros son aire y van al aire'
 'Olas gigantes que os rompéis bramando'
 'Volverán las oscuras golondrinas'
 'En la imponente nave'
 'No dormía; vagaba en ese limbo'
 'Cerraron sus ojos'
Castro, Rosalía de. Selected poetry:
 'Ya que de la esperanza para la vida mía'
 'Te amo ... ¿Por qué me odias?'
 'Ya no sé lo que busco eternamente'
 'Del rumor cadencioso de la onda'
 'Candente está la atmósfera'
 'Dicen que no hablan las plantas, ni las fuentes, no los pájaros'
 Las campanas: 'Yo las amo, yo las oigo'
 'Sientiéndose acabar con el estío'
 'No va solo el que llora'
 'Hora tras hora, día tras día'
Alas (Clarín), Leopoldo. *La Regenta.*
Pérez Galdós, Benito. *Doña Perfecta.*
 — *Misericordia (Compassion).*
 — *Fortunata y Jacinta (Fortunata and Jacinta).*
Pardo Bazán, Emilia. *Los pazos de Ulloa (The Manor House of Ulloa).*

Twentieth Century
Machado, Antonio. Selected poetry:
 'Daba el reloj las doce ... y eran doce'
 'Sobre la tierra amarga'

'Desgarrad a la nube; el arco iris'
'Desde el umbral de un sueño me llamaron ...'
'Llamó a mi corazón, un claro día'
A Don Francisco Giner de los Ríos: 'Como se fué el maestro'
'En plaza y los naranjos encendidos'
Cante hondo: 'Yo meditaba absorto, devanando'
'La calle en sombra. Ocultan los altos caserones'
'El casco roído y verdoso'
La noria: 'La tarde caía'
'Guitarra del mesón que hoy suenas jota'
'Desnuda está la tierra'
Retrato: 'Mi infancia son recuerdos de un patio de Sevilla'
'Caminante, son tus huellas'
'El ojo que ves no es'
Rosa de fuego: 'Tejidos sois de primavera, amantes'
'La plaza tiene una torre'
El crimen fue en Granada: 'Se le vio, caminando entre fusiles'
Canción: 'Ya va subiendo la luna'
Salinas, Pedro. Selected poetry:
    '¿Acompañan las almas? ¿Se las siente?'
    'Si la voz se sintiera con los ojos'
Guillén, Jorge. Selected poetry:
    Desnudo: 'Blancos, rosas. Azules casi en veta'
    'Ciero los ojos y el negror me advierte'
    Alamos con río: 'Frente al blanco gris del cerro'
Jiménez, Juan Ramón. Selected poetry:
    Retrato: 'Las mil torres del mundo, contra un ocaso de oro'
    Tenebrae: 'Todo el ocaso es amarillo limón.'
    Retorno fugaz: '¿Cómo era, Dios mío, cómo era?'
    '¡Inteligencia, dame'
    'Dejad las puertas abiertas'
    '¿Cómo, muerte, tenerte'
    Criatura afortunada: 'Cantando vas, riendo por el agua'
    'La calle espera a la noche'
    'Ya están ahí las carretas ...'
    'El campo duerme, temblando'
    'Doraba la luna el río'
    Amor: 'No has muerto, no'
    Hora inmensa: 'Sólo turban la paz una campana, un pájaro ...'
    Desvelo: 'Se va la noche, negro toro'

Cenit: 'Yo no seré yo, muerte'

Aleixandre, Vicente. Selected poetry:

'Ciudad del Paraíso: 'Siempre te ven mis ojos, ciudad de mis días marinos'

El viejo y el sol: 'Había vivido mucho'

El poeta canta por todos: 'Allí están todos, y tú los estás mirando pasar'

Alberti, Rafael. Selected poetry:

'Si mi voz muriera en tierra'

A un capitán de navío: 'Sobre tu nave — un plinto verde de altas marinas'

Aracelli: 'No si de arcángel triste, ya nevados'

Montes de el Pardo: 'Tanto sol en la guera, de pronto, tanta hambre'

Poema del destierro: '¿Quiénes sin voz de lejos me llamáis'

García Lorca, Federico. *Bodas de sangre* (*Blood Wedding*).

— *Yerma.*

— *La casa de Bernarda Alba* (*The House of Bernarda Alba*).

— Selected poetry:

Canción de jinete: 'Córdoba'

Romance somnámbulo: 'Verde que te quiero verde'

Llanto por Ignacio Sánchez Mejías

La guitarra: 'Empieza el llanto'

'Amparo'

'El canto quiere ser luz'

Segundo aniversario: 'La luna clava en el mar'

La casada infiel: 'Y que yo me la llevé al río'

Prendimiento de Antoñito el Camborio: 'Antonio Torres Heredia'

Muerte de Antoñito el Camborio: 'Voces de muerte sonaron'

Cernuda, Luis. Selected poetry:

Cementerio de la ciudad: 'Tras de la reja abierta entre los muros'

Primavera vieja: 'Ahora, al poniente morado de la tarde'

El arpa: 'Jaula de un ave invisible'

Buero Vallejo, Antonio. *Historia de una escalera* (*History of a Staircase*).

Valle Inclán, Ramón María del. *Luces de Bohemia* (*Bohemian Lights*).

Unamuno, Miguel de. *Niebla* (*Mist*).

— *San Manuel Bueno, mártir* (*San Manuel Bueno, Martyr*).

— Ensayo: 'Mi religión' ('My Religion').

Cela, Camilo José. *La familia de Pascual Duarte* (*The Family of Pascual Duarte*).

Martín Santos, Luis. *Tiempo de silencio* (*Time of Silence*).

Rodoreda, Mercè. *La Plaza del Diamante* (*Time of the Doves*).

Goytisolo, Juan. *Señas de identidad* (*Marks of Identity*).

Martín Gaite, Carmen. *El cuarto de atrás* (*The Back Room*).

Delibes, Miguel. *Párabola del náufrago* (*The Hedge*).

Matute, Ana María. *Primera memoria* (*School of the Sun*).

Tusquets, Esther. *El mismo mar de todos los veranos* (*The Same Sea as Every Summer*).

Ortega y Gasset, José. Ensayo: 'La deshumanización del arte' ('The Dehumanization of Art').

— *Howard Mancing*

SPANISH/AMERICAN LITERATURE

Lyric Poetry

Cruz, Sor Juana Inés de la. *Sor Juana Inés de la Cruz: Poems*, transl. Margaret Sayers Peden. Binghamton: Bilingual Press/Editorial Bilingue 1985.

Darío, Rubén. (selected poems), in *The Modernist Trend in Spanish-American Poetry*, ed. George Dundas Craig. Berkeley: University of California Press 1934.

Martí, José. (selected poems), in *José Martí: Major Poems*, transl. Elinor Randall. NY: Holmes & Meier 1982.

Castellanos, Rosario. Read the selection of poems in *A Rosario Castellanos Reader*, transl. Maureen Ahern. Austin: University of Texas Press 1988.

Neruda, Pablo. *Pablo Neruda: Selected Poems*, ed. N. Tarn. NY: Delacorte Press 1972. Read all poems selected from 'Residencia en la tierra I, II and III'; 'Canto general'; 'Odas elementales'; and 'Estravagario.'

Vallejo, César. *Selected Poems of César Vallejo*, transl. E. Dorn and G. Brotherston. NY: Penguin 1976.

Crow, Mary, ed. *Woman Who Has Sprouted Wings: Poems by Contemporary Latin-American Women Poets*. Pittsburgh: Latin American Literary Review Press, 2nd edition 1988.

Drama

Moraga, Cherríe. *Giving Up the Ghost*. Novato: West End Press 1986.

Long Narrative

Fuentes, Carlos. *La muerte de Artemio Cruz* [1962]. México: Fondo de Cultura Económica 1978. Translated as *The Death of Artemio Cruz*. NY: Farrar, Straus & Giroux 1964.

Azuela, Mariano. *Los de abajo: novela de la revolución mexicana* [1939]. Caracas: Biblioteca Ayacucho 1991. Translated as *The Underdogs*. San Antonio: Principia Press of Trinity University 1963.

Cortázar, Julio. *Rayuela*. Buenos Aires: Sudamericana 1963. Translated as *Hopscotch*. NY: Pantheon 1963.

García Márquez, Gabriel. *Cien años de soledad*. Buenos Aires: Sudamericana 1967. Transl. Gregory Rabassa as *One Hundred Years of Solitude*. NY: Harper & Row 1970.

Puig, Manuel. *El beso de la mujer araña*. Barcelona: Seix Barral 1976. Translated as *Kiss of the Spider Woman*. NY: Alfred A. Knopf 1979.

Arguedas, José María. *Ríos profundos*. Santiago de Chile: Universitaria 1967. Translated as *Deep Rivers*. Austin: University of Texas Press 1978.

Allende, Isabel. *La casa de los espíritus*. Buenos Aires: Sudamericana 1985. Transl. Magda Bogin as *The House of the Spirits*. NY: Alfred A. Knopf 1985.

Anzaldúz, Gloria. *Borderlands/La frontera*. San Francisco: Spinsters/ Aunt Lute 1987.

Molloy, Sylvia. *Certificate of Absence*. Austin: University of Texas Press 1989.

Cisneros, Sandra. *Woman Hollering Creek*. NY: Random House 1991.

Bombal, María Luisa. *House of Mist and Other Stories*. Austin: University of Texas Press 1995.

Short Narrative
Borges, Jorge Luis. *Labyrinths* [1940–60]. Edd. Donald A. Yates and James E. Irby. NY: New Directions 1962.

Quiroga, Horacio. *The Decapitated Chicken and Other Stories*. Austin: University of Texas Press 1988.

Valenzuela, Luisa. *Cambio de armas*. Hanover: Ediciones del Norte 1982. Transl. Deborah Bonner as *Other Weapons*. Hanover: Ediciones del Norte 1993.

Velez, Diana, ed. *Reclaiming Medusa: Short Stories by Contemporary Puerto Rican Women*. San Francisco: Spinsters/Aunt Lute 1988.

Non-Fictional Prose
Columbus, Christopher. *Diario del primer viaje* [1492]. Barcelona: Nauta 1965. Transl. B. W. Ife as *Journal of the First Voyage 1492*. Warminster: Aris & Phillips 1990.

Díaz de Castillo, Bernal. *Historia verdadera de la conquista de la Nueva España* [1632]. México: Espasa Calpe 1950 Translated as *The Conquest of New Spain*. NY: Penguin 1924. Read chapters i–x, xxvii–xxix, xxxi, xxxvi–xxxvii, lvii, lxxix–lxxx, lxxxiii, lxxxviii, xci, cxxvi–cxxviii, clii, ccvii.

Paz, Octavio. *El laberinto de la soledad* [1950]. México: Fondo de Cultura Económica 1959. Translated as *Labyrinth of Solitude*. NY: Grove Press 1961.

Menchú, Rigoberta. *Me llamo Rigoberta Menchú y así me nació la conciencia*. Habana: Casa de las Americas 1983. Transl. Ann Wright as *I, Rigoberta Menchú: An Indian Woman in Guatemala*. NY: Verso 1984.

— *Marcia Stephenson, Patricia Hart, and Robert S. Freeman*

UNITED STATES LITERATURE

Cooper, James Fenimore (1789–1851). *The Last of the Mohicans* [1826]. Ed. Richard Slotkin. NY: Penguin 1986.

Emerson, Ralph Waldo (1803–1882). *Selected Writings of Ralph Waldo Emerson*. Ed. William Gillman. NY: Signet 1965. Read *Nature* (1836); 'The American Scholar' (1837); 'Concord Hymn' (1837); 'The Divinity School Address' (1838); 'Self-Reliance' (1841); 'The Over-Soul' (1841); 'Circles' (1841); 'The Snow-Storm' (1841); 'The Poet' (1844); 'Experience' (1844); 'Threnody' (1846).

Hawthorne, Nathaniel (1804–1864). *The Scarlet Letter* [1850]. Ed. Nina Baym (NY: Penguin 1986).

Poe, Edgar Allan (1809–1849). *Great Short Works of Edgar Allan Poe*. Ed. G. R. Thompson. NY: Harper & Row, 2nd edition 1974. Read 'Ligeia' (1838); 'The Fall of the House of Usher' (1839); 'William Wilson' (1839); 'A Descent into the Maelstrom' (1841); 'The Masque of the Red Death' (1842); 'The Tell-Tale Heart' (1843); 'The Black Cat' (1843); 'The Purloined Letter' (1844); 'The Raven' (1844); 'The Imp of the Perverse' 1845); 'Ulalume' (1847).

Stowe, Harriet Beecher (1811–1896). *Uncle Tom's Cabin* [1852]. Ed. Ann Douglas. NY: Penguin 1986.

Thoreau, Henry David (1817–1862). *Walden and Other Writings*. Ed. Joseph Wood Krutch. NY: Bantam 1962. Read *Walden* [1854] and 'Civil Disobedience' (1849).

Douglass, Frederick (1817–1895). *The Narrative of the Life of Frederick Douglass, an American Slave* [1845]. Ed. Houston A. Baker, Jr. NY: Penguin 1986.

Melville, Herman (1819–1891). *Moby-Dick* [1851]. Ed. Charles Feidelson, Jr. (NY: Macmillan 1964) or Andrew Delbanco (NY: Penguin 1992).

Whitman, Walt (1819–1892). *Leaves of Grass* [1855]; 'Crossing Brooklyn Ferry' (1856); 'Song of the Open Road' (1856); 'Out of the Cradle Endlessly Rocking' (1859); 'As I Ebb'd with the Ocean of Life' (1860); 'Cavalry Crossing a Ford' (1865); 'The Wound-Dresser' (1865); 'When Lilacs Last in the Dooryard Bloom'd' (1866). Use either the *Viking Portable Whitman*, ed. Mark Van Doran, or the Library of America edition (published by Random House/Vintage).

Dickinson, Emily (1830–1886). *The Complete Poems of Emily Dickinson*. Ed. Thomas Johnson. Boston: Little, Brown 1960. Read Poems 249, 258, 280, 315, 448, 465, 508, 605, 616, 632, 640, 675, 712, 754, 1129, 1247, 1664.

Alcott, Louisa May (1832–1888). *Little Women* [1868]. Ed. Elaine Showalter. NY: Penguin 1989.

Twain, Mark (1835–1910) [Samuel L. Clemens]. *Adventures of Huckleberry Finn* [1884]. Use either the Mark Twain Library edition of Walter Blair and Victor Fischer (Berkeley: University of California Press 1985), or the edition by John Seelye (NY: Penguin 1986).

James, Henry (1843–1916). *The Portrait of a Lady* [1881]. Use either the edition Regina Barreca (NY: Signet 1995) or the Library of America edition (NY: Vintage 1992). Do *not* use the New York Edition version.

Chopin, Kate (1851–1904). *The Awakening* [1899]. In *The Awakening and Selected Stories*, ed. Sandra Gilbert. NY: Penguin 1986.

Wharton, Edith (1862–1937). *The House of Mirth* [1905]. Use either the Signet edition (ed. Louis Auchincloss, NY 1964) or the Scribner edition (NY 1995).

Crane, Stephen (1871–1900). *The Red Badge of Courage* [1895]. Use either the Signet edition (ed. James Dickey) or the Penguin edition (ed. Pascal Covici, Jr., 1991).

Dreiser, Theodore (1871–1945). *Sister Carrie* [1900]. Ed. Alfred Kazin. NY: Penguin 1985.

Cather, Willa (1873–1947). *The Professor's House* [1925]. NY: Random House 1990.

Frost, Robert (1874–1963). *The Poetry of Robert Frost.* NY: Henry Holt 1969. Read 'Mending Wall' (1914); 'The Death of the Hired Man' (1914); 'After Apple-Picking' (1914); 'The Road Not Taken'(1916); 'Birches' (1916); 'Out, Out —' (1916); 'Nothing Gold Can Stay' (1923); 'Stopping by the Woods on a Snowy Evening' (1923); 'A Lone Striker' (1936); 'Two Tramps in Mud Time' (1936); 'Departmental' (1936); and 'Design' (1936).

Stevens, Wallace (1879–1955). *Selected Poems.* NY: Vintage 1972. Read 'The Snow Man' (1923); 'The Monocle de Mon Oncle' (1923); 'The Comedian as the Letter C' (1923); 'The Emperor of Ice Cream' (1923); 'Sunday Morning' (1923); 'Anecdote of the Jar' (1923); 'Peter Quince at the Clavier' (1923); 'Thirteen Ways of Looking at a Blackbird' (1923); 'The Idea of Order at Key West' (1936); 'The Man with the Blue Guitar' (1937); 'Of Modern Poetry' (1942); 'Not Ideas about the Thing but the Thing Itself' (1978).

Williams, William Carlos (1883–1963). *Selected Poems.* NY: New Directions 1969. Read 'The Young Housewife' (1917); 'Danse Russe' (1917); 'Pastoral' (1917); 'Portrait of a Lady' (1920); 'Queen Anne's Lace' (1921); 'Spring and All' (1923); 'To Elsie' (1923); 'The Red Wheelbarrow' (1923); 'The Dead Baby' (1927); 'Death' (1930); 'This is Just to Say' (1934); 'The Dance' (1944); 'Burning the Christmas Greens' (1944); 'Lear' (1948); 'The Ivy Crown' (1955); 'The Dance' (1962).

Eliot, T. S. (1888–1965). *Selected Poems* (NY: Harcourt, Brace 1962). Read 'The Love Song of J. Alfred Prufrock' (1917); *The Waste Land* [1922]; 'The Hollow Men' (1925); 'Ash Wednesday' (1930); 'Burnt Norton' (1941).

O'Neill, Eugene (1888–1953). *Long Day's Journey into Night* [1956]. New Haven: Yale University Press.

Fitzgerald, F. Scott (1896–1940). *The Great Gatsby* [1925]. NY: Scribner.

Dos Passos, John (1896–1970). *The 49th Parallel* [1930]. Ed. Alfred Kazin. NY: Signet 1979.

Faulkner, William (1897–1962). *Light in August* [1932]; *Absalom, Absalom!* [1936]. NY: Vintage/Random House.

Hemingway, Ernest (1899–1961). *The Short Stories of Ernest Hemingway* [1938]. NY: Scribner. Read *In Our Time* [1925; these are the consecutive stories beginning with 'On the Quai at Smyrna' and concluding with 'L'Envoi,' pp. 87–233]; 'In Another Country' (1927); 'Hills Like White Elephants' (1927); 'The Killers' (1927); 'A Clean, Well-Lighted Place' (1933); 'A Way You'll Never Be' (1933); and 'Fathers and Sons' (1933).

Hurston, Zora Neale (1899–1960). *Their Eyes Were Watching God* [1937]. NY: Harper Perennial.

Nabokov, Vladimir (1899–1977). *Pale Fire* [1962]. NY: Vintage/Random House.

Wright, Richard (1908–1960). *Native Son* [1940]. Read the 1993 restored edition (NY: Harper Perennial).

Welty, Eudora (1909–). *The Golden Apples* [1949]. NY: Harcourt, Brace.

Williams, Tennessee [Thomas Lanier Williams] (1911–1983). *A Streetcar Named Desire* [1947]. NY: Signet.

Ellison, Ralph (1914–1994). *Invisible Man* (1952). NY: Vintage/Random House.

Bellow, Saul (1915–). *Herzog* [1964]. NY: Penguin.

Miller, Arthur (1915–). *Death of a Salesman: Certain Private Conversations in Two Acts and a Requiem* [1948]. NY: Viking 1977.

Morrison, Toni (1931–). *Beloved* [1987]. NY: Plume/Penguin.

DeLillo, Don (1936–). *White Noise* [1985]. NY: Penguin.

Pynchon, Thomas (1937–). *Gravity's Rainbow* [1973]. NY: Penguin.

Kingston, Maxine Hong (1940–). *Tripmaster Monkey* [1989]. NY: Vintage/Random House.

Erdrich, Louise (1954–). *Love Medicine* [1984]. Read the revised and expanded version (NY: Henry Holt 1993).

NOTE: You may use any accurate edition of the texts listed above, with the following caveats:

1. Most editions of Whitman are the 1891–1892 or 'deathbed' edition in which the great innovative poems of the 1855 edition, like 'Song of Myself,' are revised by the author to make them more conservative and respectable. Make sure your edition contains the original 1855 versions of these poems. The 1855 edition is available, e.g., in the Viking Portable and the Library of America.

2. Make sure your edition of Henry James's *The Portrait of a Lady* is the original 1881 edition, and not the later revised 'New York edition.' The 1881 version is available from Signet and from the Library of America. (An easy way to be sure is to check the last word of the text, which should be 'her' and *not* 'patience.')

3. For Dreiser's *Sister Carrie*, use the reconstructed edition available from either the University of Pennsylvania Press or Penguin, and not the original edition. (The last word of this text should be 'rest' and *not* 'feel.')

4. For Faulkner's *Absalom, Absalom!*, used the corrected Vintage International edition (1986), or else the Library of America edition. Do *not* use the old Modern Library edition.

5. For Wright's *Native Son*, use the new Harper Perennial edition, or else the Library of America edition (copyright 1993) and *not* any previous editions; these were badly censored.

— *G. R. Thompson and Robert Paul Lamb*

VISUAL CULTURE I: Figurative and Plastic Arts

Allert, Beate, ed. *Languages of Visuality: Crossings between Science, Art, Politics, and Literature*. Detroit: Wayne State University Press 1996.

Bal, Mieke. *Reading Rembrandt: Beyond the Word-Image Opposition*. Cambridge: Cambridge University Press 1991.

Barthes, Roland. *Image, Music, Text*. NY: Hill and Wang 1977.

Benjamin, Walter. 'The Work of Art in the Age of Mechanical Reproduction.' In Benjamin, *Illuminations*. Transl. Harry Zohn; ed. Hannah Arendt. NY: Schocken 1977.

Berger, John. *Ways of Seeing*. London: Penguin 1972.

Brennan, Teresa, and Martin Jay edd. *Vision in Context: Historical and Contemporary Perspectives on Sight*. NY: Routledge 1996.

Brunette, Peter, and David Wills. *Deconstruction and the Visual Arts: Art, Media, Architecture*. Cambridge: Cambridge University Press 1994.

Bryson, Norman. *Vision and Painting: The Logic of the Gaze*. New Haven: Yale University Press 1983.

Butler, Judith. 'Sexual Ideology and Phenomenological Description: A Feminist Critique of Merleau-Ponty's *Phenomenology of Perception*.' Pp. 85–100 in Jeffner Allen and Iris M. Young edd., *The Thinking Muse: Feminism and Modern French Philosophy*. Bloomington: Indiana University Press 1989.

Collins, Christopher. *The Poetics of the Mind's Eye: Literature and the Psychology of Imagination*. Philadelphia: University of Pennsylvania Press 1991.

Elkins, James. *The Object Stares Back: On the Nature of Seeing*. NY: Simon & Schuster 1996.

Esrock, Ellen J. *The Reader's Eye: Visual Imaging as Reader Response*. Baltimore: Johns Hopkins University Press 1994.

Gombrich, Ernst Hans. 'Image and Code: Scope and Limits of Conventionalism in Pictorial Representation.' Pp. 11–42 in

Wendy Steiner, ed., *Image and Code*. Michigan Studies in the Humanities 2. Ann Arbor: University of Michigan 1981.

Holly, Michael Ann. *Past Looking: Historical Imagination and the Rhetoric of the Image*. Ithaca NY: Cornell University Press 1996.

Hoorn, Willem van. *As Images Unwind: Ancient and Modern Theories of Visual Perception*. Amsterdam: University Press of Amsterdam 1972.

Irigaray, Luce. 'The Invisible of the Flesh: A Reading of Merleau-Ponty, *The Visible and the Invisible*, "The Intertwining — The Chiasm."' Pp. 151–184 in Luce Irigaray, *An Ethics of Sexual Difference*. Ithaca NY: Cornell University Press 1993.

Jay, Martin. *Downcast Eyes: The Denigration of Vision in Twentieth-Century French Thought*. Berkeley: University of California Press 1993.

Jenks, Chris, ed. *Visual Culture*. London: Routledge 1995.

Johnson-Laird, Philip. *Mental Models: Towards a Cognitive Science of Language Inference and Consciousness*. Cambridge: Cambridge University Press 1983.

Kosslyn, Stephen M. *Image and Brain: The Resolution of the Imagery Debate*. Cambridge MA: MIT Press 1994.

Krauss, Rosalind. *The Optical Unconscious*. Cambridge MA: MIT Press 1995.

Leppert, Richard. *Art and the Committed Eye: The Cultural Functions of Imagery*. Boulder: Westview Press 1996.

Merleau-Ponty, Maurice. *The Visible and the Invisible*. Evanston: Northwestern University Press 1968.

Messaris, Paul. *Visual 'Literacy': Image, Mind, and Reality*. Boulder: Westview Press 1994.

Mitchell, W. J. T. *Picture Theory: Essays on Verbal and Visual Representation*. Chicago: University of Chicago Press 1994.

Paivio, Allan. *Mental Representations: A Dual Coding Approach*. NY: Oxford University Press 1986.

Panofsky, Erwin. *Perspective as Symbolic Form*. NY: Zone Books 1991.

Saint-Martin, Fernande. *Semiotics of Visual Language*. Bloomington: Indiana University Press 1988.

Solso, Robert L. *Cognition and the Visual Arts*. Cambridge MA: MIT Press 1994.

Stafford, Barbara Maria. *Good Looking: Essays on the Virtue of Images*. Cambridge MA: MIT Press 1996.

Steiner, Wendy. *The Colors of Rhetoric: Problems in the Relation between Modern Literature and Painting*. Chicago: University of Chicago Press 1982.

Walton, Kendall. *Mimesis as Make-Believe: On the Foundation of the Representational Arts*. Cambridge MA: Harvard University Press 1990.

Zajonc, Arthur. *Catching the Light: The Entwined History of Light and Mind*. NY: Bantam 1993.

— *Beate Allert, Howard Mancing, and Anthony Julian Tamburri*

VISUAL CULTURE II: Film, Television, Video

Required Reading: Students are expected to read the following texts in full, except as otherwise noted.

Andrew, J. Dudley. *The Major Film Theories: An Introduction*. Oxford: Oxford University Press 1976.

— *Concepts in Film Theory*. Oxford: Oxford University Press 1984.

Besas, Peter. *Behind the Spanish Lens: Spanish Cinema under Fascism and Democracy*. Denver: Arden 1985

Bordwell, David, and Noel Carroll, edd. *Post-Theory: Reconstructing Film Studies*. Madison: University of Wisconsin Press 1996.

Corrigan, Timothy. *New German Film: The Displaced Image*. Austin: University of Texas Press 1983.

Dienst, Richard. *Still Life in Real Time: Theory after Television*. Durham: Duke University Press 1994.

Doty, Alexander. *Making Things Perfectly Queer: Interpreting Mass Culture*. Minneapolis: University of Minnesota Press 1993.

Eisener, Lotte. *Haunted Screen: Expressionism in the German Cinema and the Influence of Max Reinhardt*. Berkeley: University of California Press 1969.

Erens, Patricia, ed. *Issues in Feminist Film Criticism*. Bloomington: Indiana University Press 1990.

Friedberg, Anne. *Window Shopping: Cinema and the Postmodern*. Berkeley: University of California Press 1993.

Guerrero, Ed. *Framing Blackness: The African American Image in Film*. Philadelphia: Temple University Press 1993.

Hayward, Susan. *French National Cinema*. NY: Routledge 1993.

Hollows, Joanne, and Mark Jancovich, edd. *Approaches to Popular Film*. Manchester: Manchester University Press 1995.

Hopewell, John. *Spanish Film After Franco*. London: British Film Institute 1989.

King, John. *Magical Reels: A History of Cinema in Latin America*. London: Verso 1990.

Lawton, Anna, ed. *The Red Screen: Politics, Society, Art in Soviet Cinema*. NY: Routledge 1992.

— *Kinoglasnost: Soviet Cinema in Our Time*. Cambridge: Cambridge University Press 1992.

Lehmen, Peter. *Running Scared: Masculinity and the Representation of the Male Body*. Philadelphia: Temple University Press 1993.

Marcus, Millicent. *Filmmaking by the Book: Italian Cinema and Literary Adaptations*. Baltimore: Johns Hopkins University Press 1993.

Mast, Gerald, and Marshall Cohen. *Film Theory and Criticism: Introductory Readings*. NY: Oxford University Press, 4th edition 1992.

Mayne, Judith. *The Woman at the Keyhole*. Bloomington: Indiana University Press 1990.

McElroy, Wendy. *XXX: A Woman's Right to Pornography*. NY: St. Martin's Press 1995.

Merck, Mandy. *The Sexual Subject: A Screen Reader in Sexuality*. London: Routledge 1992.

Miller, Mark. *Boxed In: The Culture of TV*. Evanston: Northwestern University Press 1988.

Nichols, Bill, ed. *Movies and Methods*. 2 volumes. Berkeley: University of California Press 1976.

Noriega, Chon. *Chicanos and Film: Representation and Resistance*. Minneapolis: University of Minnesota Press 1992.

Pasolini, Pier Paolo. *Heretical Empiricism*. Ed. Louise K. Barnett. Transll. Ben Lawton and Louise K. Barnett. Bloomington: Indiana University Press 1988. Read pp. 167–297.

Pines, Jim, and Paul Willemen, edd. *Questions of Third Cinema*. London: British Film Institute 1989.

Renou, Michael, ed. *Theorizing Documentary*. NY: Routledge/AFI 1993.

Rosen, Philip. *Narrative, Apparatus, Ideology: A Film Reader.* NY: Columbia University Press 1986.

Sherzer, Dina, ed. *Cinema, Colonialism, Postcolonialism: Perspectives from the French and Francophone World.* Austin: University of Texas Press 1996.

Sobchack, Vivian. *The Address of the Eye: A Phenomenology of Film Experience.* Princeton: Princeton University Press 1992.

Stam, Robert, et al., edd. *New Vocabularies in Film Semiotics: Structuralism, Post-Structuralism, and Beyond.* NY: Routledge 1992.

Reference and Optional Supplementary Reading: Students are encouraged refer to the following additional materials. Some of these authors (Bazin, Bordwell, De Lauretis, Eisenstein, Metz, Mulvey, et al.) have also been anthologized in the required reading list; moreover, we have included here some general information on national cinemas, some more reference texts, and a number of studies of recent trends in film- and video-studies.

Arnheim, Rudolph. *Film as Art.* Berkeley: University of California Press 1966.

Bazin, André. *The Cinema of Cruelty.* NY: Grove Press 1982.

— *What is Cinema?* 2 volumes. Berkeley: University of California Press 1971.

Bingham, Dennis. *Acting Male: Masculinities in the Films of James Stewart, Jack Nicholson and Clint Eastwood.* New Brunswick: Rutgers University Press 1994.

Bondanella, Peter. *Italian Cinema: From Neorealism to the Present.* NY: Continuum 1995.

Bordwell, David. *Making Meaning: Inference and Rhetoric in the Interpretation of Cinema.* Cambridge MA: Harvard University Press 1989.

Brown, Nick, et al., edd. *New Chinese Cinemas: Form, Identities, Politics.* Cambridge: Cambridge University Press 1994.

Burton, Julianne. *Cinema and Social Change in Latin America: Conversations with Filmmakers.* Austin: University of Texas Press 1986.

Chomsky, Noam. *Necessary Illusions: Thought Control in Democratic Societies*. Boston: South End Press 1989.

Cook, David A. *A History of Narrative Film*. NY: W. W. Norton 1996.

Cook, Pam, ed. *The Cinema Book: A Complete Guide to Understanding the Movies*. NY: Pantheon 1985.

Deleuze, Gilles. *Cinema*. 2 volumes. Minneapolis: University of Minnesota Press 1986, 1989.

Eisenstein, Sergei M. *Film Form*. NY: Harcourt, Brace 1949.

Gerber, Martha, et al., edd. *Queer Looks: Perspectives on Lesbian and Gay Film and Video*. NY: Routledge 1993.

Giannetti, Louis. *Understanding Movies*. Englewood Cliffs: Prentice-Hall 1996.

Gledhill, Christine. *Home is Where the Heart is: Studies in Melodrama and the Woman's Film*. London: British Film Institute 1987.

Grant, Barry Keith, ed. *Film Genre Reader II*. Austin: University of Texas Press 1995.

Heath, Stephen. *Questions of Cinema*. Bloomington: Indiana University Press 1981.

Hirsch, Foster. *Film Noir: The Dark Side of the Screen*. NY: Da Capo 1981.

Horton, Andrew, and Joan Magretta, edd. *Modern European Film-makers and the Art of Adaptation*. NY: Frederick Unger 1981.

Jeffords, Susan, ed. *Hard Bodies: Hollywood Masculinity in the Reagan Era*. New Brunswick: Rutgers University Press 1994.

Kinder, Marsha. *Blood Cinema: The Reconstruction of National Identity in Spain*. Berkeley: University of California Press 1993.

Lauretis, Teresa de. *Alice Doesn't: Feminism, Semiotics. Cinema*. Bloomington: Indiana University Press 1984.

Lotman, Jurij. *Semiotics of Cinema*. Ann Arbor: University of Michigan Press 1976.

Lumet, Sidney. *Making Movies*. NY: Random House 1995.

Marcus, Millicent. *Italian Film in the Light of Neorealism*. Princeton: Princeton University Press 1986.

Mast, Gerald, and Bruce F. Kawin. *A Short History of the Movies.* Boston: Simon & Schuster 1996.

McLuhan, Marshall, and Quentin Fiore. *The Medium is the Massage.* NY: Random House 1967.

Messaris, Paul. *Visual "Literacy": Image, Mind, and Reality.* Boulder: Westview Press 1994.

Metz, Christian. *Film Language: A Semiotics of the Cinema.* NY: Oxford University Press 1974.

Mulvey, Laura. *Visual and Other Pleasures.* Bloomington: Indiana University Press 1989.

Paranaguá, Paulo Antonio, ed. *Mexican Cinema.* London: British Film Institute 1995.

Penley, Constance, and Sharon Willis, edd. *Male Trouble.* Minneapolis: University of Minnesota Press 1993.

Petro, Patrice, ed. *Fugitive Images: From Photography to Video.*Bloomington: Indiana University Press 1995.

Postman, Neil. *Amusing Ourselves to Death: Public Discourse in the Age of Show Business.* NY: Penguin 1986.

Rowe, Kathleen. *The Unruly Woman: Gender and the Genres of Laughter.* Austin: University of Texas Press 1995.

Silverman, Kaja. *The Acoustic Mirror: The Female Voice in Psychoanalysis and Cinema.* Bloomington: Indiana University Press 1988.

Sherzer, Dina. *Cinema, Colonialism, Postcolonialism: Perspectives from French and Francophone Worlds.* Austin: University of Texas Press 1996.

— *Male Subjectivity at the Margins.* NY: Routledge 1992.

Stam, Robert, and Randal Johnson. *Brazilian Cinema.* Cranbury: Associated University Presses 1982.

Telotte, J. P. *Voices in the Dark: The Narrative Patterns of Film Noir.* Urbana: University of Illinois Press 1989.

Walsh, Andreas. *Women's Films and Female Experience: 1940–1950.* NY: Praeger 1984.

Willemen. *Looks and Frictions: Essays in Cultural Studies and Film Theory.* Bloomington: Indiana University Press 1994.

Williams, Alan. *Republic of Images: A History of French Filmmakers.* Cambridge MA: Harvard University Press 1992.

Williams, Linda, ed. *Viewing Positions: Ways of Seeing Film.* New Brunswick: Rutgers University Press 1995.

Winston, Brian. *Claiming the Real: The Documentary Film Revistited.* Bloomington: Indiana University Press 1995.

Wollen, Peter. *Signs and Meanings in the Cinema.* Bloomington: Indiana University Press 1972.

— Patricia Hart, Ben Lawton, and Anthony Julian Tamburri

APPENDIX: Professional Aspects of the Discipline

While not a 'module' of the same type as the other units collected here, this appendix collects some information that I trust will be both interesting and useful to graduate students — and indeed to professional academics at all levels. All too often, graduate programs focus on the purely curricular aspect of graduate training, and students are left confused about the more 'nuts-and-bolts' aspects of the discipline.

Basic Reference Tools for Writing and Publishing

Barzun, Jacques. *On Writing, Editing, and Publishing: Essays Explicative and Hortatory*. Chicago: University of Chicago Press, 2nd edition 1985.

Booth, Wayne, et al. *The Craft of Research*. Chicago: University of Chicago Press 1995.

Braun, Eric. *The Internet Directory*. NY: Fawcett Columbine 1994.

Butcher, Judith. *Copy-Editing: The Cambridge Handbook*. NY: Cambridge University Press, 3rd edition 1991.

The Chicago Manual of Style. Chicago: University of Chicago Press, 14th edition 1993.

Cook, Claire Kehrwald. *Line by Line: How to Improve Your Own Writing*. NY: Modern Language Association of America (copublished with Houghton Mifflin) 1985.

Directory of Electronic Journals, Newsletters, and Academic Discussion Lists. Washington: Association of Research Libraries (annual).

Fowler, H. W. *A Dictionary of Modern English Usage*. NY: Oxford University Press, 3rd edition 1996.

Gibaldi, Joseph, ed. *Introduction to Scholarship in Modern Languages and Literatures*. NY: Modern Language Association of America, 2nd edition 1992.

— *MLA Handbook for Writers of Research Papers*. NY: Modern Language Association of America, 4th edition 1995.

Harner, James L. *On Compiling an Annotated Bibliography*. NY: Modern Language Association of America, revised edition 1991.

— *Literary Research Guide: A Guide to Reference Sources for the Study of Literatures in English and Related Topics*. NY: Modern Language Association of America, 2nd edition 1993.

The *Journal of Scholarly Publishing* (formerly *Scholarly Publishing*; published quarterly by the University of Toronto Press) is a constant source of interesting and useful information.

Mackesy, Eileen M., and Karen Mateyak. *MLA Directory of Periodicals: A Guide to Journals and Series in Languages and Literatures*. NY: Modern Language Association of America (biennial).

Merriam-Webster's Collegiate Dictionary. Springfield: Merriam-Webster, 10th edition 1993.

Nicholson, Margaret. *A Dictionary of American-English Usage*. NY: New American Library 1957.

The Oxford English Dictionary. 20 volumes. Oxford: Oxford University Press, 2nd edition 1989. There are also two additional volumes, in the Oxford English Dictionary Additions series, edd. John Simpson and Edmund Weiner (1994).

Pasco, Allan H. 'Basic Advice for Novice Authors.' *Scholarly Publishing* 23 (1992) 95–104.

Rodman, Hyman. 'Some Practical Advice for Journal Contributors.' *Scholarly Publishing* 9 (1978) 235–241.

Strunk, W., Jr., and E. B. White. *The Elements of Style*. NY: Macmillan, 3rd edition 1979.

Thyer, Bruce A. *Successful Publishing in Scholarly Journals*. Thousand Oaks: Sage 1994.

Webster's Third New International Dictionary of the English Language, Unabridged. Springfield: Merriam-Webster 1986.

Williams, Joseph M., and Gregory G. Colomb. *Style: Toward Clarity and Grace*. Chicago: University of Chicago Press 1990.

Practical Aspects of the Publishing Process

Clark, Charles. *Publishing Contracts: A Book of Precedents*. London: Butterworth, 4th edition 1993.

DeGeorge, Richard T., and Fred Woodward. 'Ethics and Manuscript Reviewing.' *Journal of Scholarly Publishing* 25 (1994) 133–145.

Derricourt, Robin. *An Author's Guide to Scholarly Publishing*. Princeton: Princeton University Press 1996.

Dessaur, John P. *Book Publishing: A Basic Introduction*. NY: Continuum 1989.

Forscher, Bernard K. 'The Role of the Referee.' *Scholarly Publishing* 11 (1980) 165–169.

Harman, Eleanor, and R. M. Schoeffel. 'Our Readers Report.' *Scholarly Publishing* 6 (1975) 333–340.

Hoge, James O., and James L. W. West III. 'Academic Book Reviewing: Some Problems and Suggestions.' *Scholarly Publishing* 11 (1979) 35–41.

Klemp, P. J. 'Reviewing Academic Books: Some Ideas for Beginners.' *Scholarly Publishing* 12 (1981) 135–139.

Luey, Beth. *Handbook for Academic Authors*. Cambridge: Cambridge University Press, 3rd edition 1995.

Matkin, R. E., and T. F. Riggar. *Persist and Publish*. Niwot: University of Colorado Press 1991.

Parsons, Paul. *Getting Published: The Acquisition Process at University Presses*. Knoxville: University of Tennessee Press 1989.

Powell, Walter W. *Getting into Print: The Decision Making Process in Scholarly Publishing*. Chicago: University of Chicago Press 1985.

Scarles, Christopher. *Copyright*. NY: Cambridge University Press 1980.

Smith, Datus C. 'An Anatomy of Subsidies.' *Scholarly Publishing* 6 (1975) 197–206.

Smith, John Hazel. 'Subvention of Scholarly Publishing.' *Scholarly Publishing* 9 (1977) 19–29.

Strong, William S. *The Copyright Book: A Practical Guide*. Cambridge: MIT Press, 4th edition 1993.

Historical and Theoretical Observations (Some Alarming) on the Institution

Anderson, Martin. *Impostors in the Temple: American Intellectuals Are Destroying Our Universities and Cheating Our Students of Their Future*. NY: Simon & Schuster 1992.

Barzun, Jacques. *The House of Intellect*. NY: Harper & Row 1959.

Bernheimer, Charles, ed. *Comparative Literature in the Age of Multiculturalism*. Baltimore: Johns Hopkins University Press 1995.

Blau, Peter M. *The Organization of Academic Work*. NY: John Wiley & Sons 1973.

Bloom, Allan. *The Closing of the American Mind: How Higher Education Has Failed Democracy and Impoverished the Souls of Today's Students*. NY: Simon & Schuster 1987.

Bok, Derek. *Higher Learning*. Cambridge MA: Harvard University Press 1986.

— *Universities and the Future of America*. Durham: Duke University Press 1990.

Bourdieu, Pierre. *Homo Academicus*. Stanford: Stanford University Press 1988.

Damrosch, David. *We Scholars: Changing the Culture of the University*. Cambridge MA: Harvard University Press 1995.

Douglas, Mary. *How Institutions Think*. Syracuse: Syracuse University Press 1986.

D'Souza, Dinesh. *Illiberal Education: The Politics of Race and Sex on Campus*. NY: Free Press 1991.

Ehrenberg, Ronald G., ed. *The American University: National Treasure or Endangered Species?* Ithaca: Cornell University Press 1997.

Ellis, John M. *Literature Lost: Social Agendas and the Corruption of the Humanities*. New Haven: Yale University Press 1997.

Fish, Stanley. *There's No Such Thing as Free Speech, and It's a Good Thing, Too.* NY: Oxford University Press 1994.

Ford, Laura Christian. *Liberal Education and the Canon: Five Great Texts Speak to Contemporary Social Issues.* Columbia: Camden House 1994.

Getman, Julius. *In the Company of Scholars: The Struggle for the Soul of Higher Education.* Austin: University of Texas Press 1992.

Gossman, Lionel, and Mihai I. Spariosu, edd. *Building a Profession: Autobiographical Perspectives on the Beginnings of Comparative Literature in the United States.* Albany: State University of New York Press 1994.

Graff, Gerald. *Professing Literature: An Institutional History.* Chicago: University of Chicago Press 1987.

— and Reginald Gibbons, edd. *Criticism in the University.* Evanston: Northwestern University Press 1985.

— and Michael Warner, edd. *The Origins of Literary Studies in America: A Documentary Anthology.* NY: Routledge 1989.

Grafton, Anthony. *The Footnote: A Curious History.* Cambridge MA: Harvard University Press 1997.

Greenblatt, Stephen, and Giles Gunn, edd. *Redrawing the Boundaries: The Transformation of English and American Literary Studies.* NY: Modern Language Association of America 1992.

Hallett, Judith P., and Thomas Van Nortwick, edd. *Compromising Traditions: The Personal Voice in Classical Scholarship.* London: Routledge 1996.

Johnson, Barbara, ed. *The Pedagogical Imperative: Teaching as a Literary Genre.* Special issue of *Yale French Studies* (63, 1982).

Kadir, Djelal, ed. *Comparative Literature: States of the Art.* Special issue of *World Literature Today* (69.2, Spring 1995).

Kamuf, Peggy. *The Division of Literature: Or, The University in Deconstruction.* Chicago: University of Chicago Press 1997.

Kelley, Donald R., ed. *History and the Disciplines: The Reclassification of Knowledge in Early Modern Europe.* Rochester: University of Rochester Press 1997.

Kennedy, Donald. *Academic Duty*. Cambridge MA: Harvard University Press 1997.

Kerr, Clark. *The Uses of the University*. Cambridge MA: Harvard University Press, 3rd edition 1982.

Kimball, Roger. *Tenured Radicals: How Politics Has Corrupted Our Higher Education*. NY: HarperPerennial 1991.

Levine, Lawrence W. *The Opening of the American Mind: Canons, Culture, and History*. Boston: Beacon Press 1996.

Lunsford, Andrea, et al., edd. *The Future of Doctoral Studies in English*. NY: Modern Language Association of America 1989.

Nelson, Cary. *Manifesto of a Tenured Radical*. NY: New York University Press 1997.

— ed. *Will Teach for Food: Academic Labor in Crisis*. Minneapolis: University of Minnesota Press 1997.

Nussbaum, Martha C. *Cultivating Humanity: A Classical Defense of Reform in Liberal Education*. Cambridge MA: Harvard University Press 1997.

Pelikan, Jaroslav. *The Idea of the University: A Reexamination*. New Haven: Yale University Press 1992.

Richlin, Amy. 'The Ethnographer's Dilemma and the Dream of a Lost Golden Age.' Pp. 272–303 in Nancy Sorkin Rabinowitz and Amy Richlin, edd., *Feminist Theory and the Classics*. NY: Routledge 1993.

Shils, Edward. *The Order of Learning: Essays on the Contemporary University*. New Brunswick: Transaction 1997.

Simpson, David. *The Academic Postmodern and the Rule of Literature: A Report on Half-Knowledge*. Chicago: University of Chicago Press 1996.

Smith, Anthony, and Frank Webster, edd. *The Postmodern University? Contested Visions of Higher Education in Society*. Buckingham: Society for Research into Higher Education and Open University Press 1997.

Sykes, Charles J. *Profscam: Professors and the Demise of Higher Education*. Washington: Regnery Gateway 1988.

Veysey, Laurence R. *The Emergence of the American University*. Chicago: University of Chicago Press 1965.

Woolf, Virginia. *A Room of One's Own* [1928]. NY: Harcourt Brace Jovanovich 1957.

Ziolkowski, Theodore. 'The Ph.D. Squid.' *American Scholar* 59 (1990) 177–195.

Practical Aspects of the Profession

Boufis, Christina, and Victoria C. Olsen, edd. *On the Market: Surviving the Academic Job Search*. NY: Riverhead Books 1997.

Jarvis, Donald K. *Junior Faculty Development: A Handbook*. NY: Modern Language Association of America 1991.

Schoenfeld, Clarence A., and Robert Magnan. *Mentor in a Manual: Climbing the Academic Ladder to Tenure*. Madison: Magna Publications, 2nd edition 1994.

Showalter, English, ed. *A Career Guide for PhDs and PhD Candidates in English and Foreign Languages*. With Additional Revisions. NY: Modern Language Association of America 1994.

Sternberg, David. *How to Complete and Survive a Doctoral Dissertation*. NY: St. Martin's Press 1981.

— *John T. Kirby*

CONTRIBUTORS

BEATE ALLERT is Associate Professor of German and Comparative Literature at Purdue University. The author of *Die Metapher und ihre Krise* (1987), she has edited and written the introduction to *Languages of Visuality* (1996), and has also written articles on Novalis, Berkeley, Lessing, Schiller, Eco, Cornell, and others. Her work especially links 18th-century literature with contemporary debates on verbal/visual dynamics.

MYRDENE ANDERSON is Associate Professor of Anthropology at Purdue University. She is the author of *Saami Ethnoecology* (1978) and co-editor of *On Semiotic Modeling* (1991), *Self and Society, Stereotype and Ethnicity* (1991), and *Refiguring Debris* (1994). Her published essays include 'Reindeer and Magic Numbers' (*Ethnos* 1991), 'Fat — Phatic and Emphatic' (*Semiotics* 1993), and 'A Semiotic Perspective on the Sciences' (*Semiotica* 1984).

PAUL BENHAMOU is Associate Professor of French at Purdue University. He is the author of *Index des «Lettres sur quelques écrits de ce temps» (1749–1754) d'Elie-Catherine Fréron* (1985), of *Index des «Jugements sur les ouvrages nouveaux» (1744–1746) de Pierre-François Guyot Desfontaines* (1986), and of essays on the history of the book and reading.

THOMAS F. BRODEN is Associate Professor of French at Purdue University. He is the author of *Deuil, désir et écriture chez Marguerite Duras* (1997), editor of a volume of the juvenilia of A. J. Greimas (1998) including his Sorbonne dissertation *La mode en 1830*, and author of articles in the *Yearbook of Comparative and General Literature, Recherches Sémiotiques/Semiotic Inquiry, American Journal of Semiotics,* and *Semiotica,* as well as a number of contributed book chapters.

DENIS BULLOCK is a Los Angeles-based performance-artist and writer who read Greats at Oxford. His current academic interests include Queer Theory and Gender Studies generally, and (in particular) the relationship of biological sex to gender-performativity.

EDITH W. CLOWES is Professor and Chair of Russian at Purdue University, where she previously chaired the Program in Comparative Literature. She is the author of *Maksim Gorky: A Reference Guide* (1987), *The Revolution of Moral Consciousness: Nietzsche in Russian Literature, 1890–1914* (1988), *Russian Experimental Fiction: Resisting Ideology after Utopia* (1993), and editor of *Between Tsar and People* (1991) and *Doctor Zhivago: A Critical Companion* (1995).

PAUL DIXON is Professor of Portuguese and Spanish at Purdue University. He is the author of *Reversible Readings: Ambiguity in Four Modern Latin American Novels* (1985), *Retired Dreams: Dom Casmurro, Myth and Modernity* (1989), and *Os contos de Machado de Assis* (1992).

THOMAS A. DUBOIS is Associate Professor of Scandinavian Studies and of Comparative Literature at the University of Washington, Seattle. He authored the study *Finnish Folk Poetry and the Kalevala* (1995) and specializes in Nordic folklore and literature. His research has received support from the National Endowment for the Humanities, the John Simon Guggenheim Memorial Foundation, and the Lars Hierta Fund (Sweden).

NADA ELIA is Visiting Assistant Professor at Brown University. She has published several essays on postcolonial women and women of color, and is currently writing a book-length analysis of the dynamics of subversion in the narratives of feminists of color. She is associate editor of *The Radical Philosophy Review*.

ROBERT S. FREEMAN is Assistant Professor of Library Science and Bibliographer for the Department of Foreign Languages and Literatures at Purdue University. He has special interests in the history of European books and libraries, particularly from the sixteenth to the eighteenth centuries. He is contributing an article on John Carter Brown to the *American National Biography* (1998).

CLARA GYÖRGYEY heads the Program for Humanities in Medicine at Yale University. Author of four books, twenty-four book-translations, and over three hundred articles; President of International P.E.N.'s Writers-in-Exile Center; received the NEA Drama Award and a Fulbright Fellowship; decorated with the Grand ADY Medal and the Cross of the Order of Merit by the Republic of Hungary.

PATRICIA HART is Associate Professor of Spanish at Purdue University. She is the author of *The Spanish Sleuth* (1988) and *Narrative Magic in the Fiction of Isabel Allende* (1989); has translated Isabel-Clara Simó's *Una ombra fosca, com núvol de tempesta* as *A Corpse of One's Own* (1994); and has written an original novel, *Little Sins* (1980). In addition, Hart has published numerous scholarly articles, short stories, and poems.

DANIEL HSIEH is Associate Professor of Chinese at Purdue University. He is the author of *The Evolution of Jueju Verse* (1996), and of articles on classical Chinese poetry.

SHAUN F. D. HUGHES is Associate Professor of English at Purdue University. He is the author of articles on mediaeval and post-colonial literature.

CAROLYN E. JOHNSON is Senior Research Associate and Interim Director of the African American Studies and Research Center at Purdue University., and a trustee of Bennett College. Her publications include essays in the journals *Response* and *Upper Room Disciplines*, and chapters in the anthologies *Expressively Black* (1987) and *Fanon: A Critical Reader* (1997).

JOHN T. KIRBY is Chair of the Program in Comparative Literature at Purdue University, where he was previously founding Chair of the interdisciplinary Program in Classical Studies. His publications include *The Rhetoric of Cicero's Pro Cluentio* (1990), *Landmark Essays on Ciceronian Rhetoric* (1998), and numerous essays and book-chapters.

ROBERT PAUL LAMB is Associate Professor of English at Purdue University. His publications include articles on Melville, Whitman, Norris, and literary theory in *Southern Review*, *South Atlantic Quarterly*, *ATQ*, and *Centennial Review*; articles on Hemingway in *Twentieth Century Literature*, *Hemingway Review*, *Modern Fiction Studies*, and *Midwest Quarterly*; and a full-issue monograph on southern abolitionism in *Alabama Review*.

BEN LAWTON is Associate Professor of Italian, French, and Film Studies, and Chair of Italian Studies and Film Studies at Purdue University. He is author/editor of *Literary and Sociopolitical Trends in Italian Cinema* (1975), translator of Pasolini's *Heretical Empiricism* (1988), and co-founding co-editor of *Film Studies Annual* and *Romance Languages Annual*.

VINCENT B. LEITCH holds the Sutton Chair of English at the University of Oklahoma. His books include *Deconstructive Criticism* (1983), *American Literary Criticism from the 1930s to the 1980s* (1988), *Cultural Criticism, Literary Theory, Poststructuralism* (1992), and *Postmodernism: Local Effects, Global Flows* (1996). Works in progress include the general editorship of *The Norton Anthology of Theory and Criticism*.

HOWARD MANCING is Professor of Spanish at Purdue University, where he was formerly the Head of the Department of Foreign Languages and Literatures. He is the author of *The Chivalric World of Don Quijote* (1982) and co-editor of *the Golden Age Comedia* (1994), and has also published numerous articles and book chapters.

FLOYD MERRELL is Professor of Semiotics and Spanish/American Literature at Purdue University. His numerous books include *Pararealities* (1983), *Deconstruction Reframed* (1985), *A Semiotic Theory of Texts* (1985), *Signs Becoming Signs* (1991), *Unthinking Thinking* (1991), *Sign, Textuality, World* (1992), *Semiosis in the Postmodern Age* (1995), and *Peirce, Signs, and Meaning* (1997).

PIERRE-DAMIEN MVUYEKURE is Assistant Professor of English and African/American Literature at the University of Northern Iowa. He has completed a poetry manuscript, *Give It Back to Me: My Rwanda and Other Chanted Poems from Africa*. His articles on Patricia Grace and Velma Pollard are forthcoming in a sourcebook from Greenwood Press.

NANCY J. PETERSON is Assistant Professor of English and American Studies at Purdue University. She is the editor of *Toni Morrison: Critical and Theoretical Approaches* (1997), the assistant editor of the journal *Modern Fiction Studies*, and the author of articles on Louise Erdrich.

CAROL POSTER is Associate Professor of English at Montana State University. Her scholarly essays have appeared in such journals as *American Journal of Philology*, *College English*, *Philosophy and Rhetoric*, *Phoenix*, and the *Victorian Newsletter*. Her verse translations include Plautus' *Stichus*, Aristophanes' *Clouds*, and *Selected Poems of Jacques Prevert*. She edits the journal *Disputatio*.

APARAJITA SAGAR is Associate Professor of English at Purdue University, where she teaches anglophone postcolonial studies. She has published essays on Caribbean and postcolonial literatures, Jamaica Kincaid, and Nawal el-Sa'adawi. Her book-length study on Caribbean women writers is forthcoming from Duke University Press in 1998.

EDWARD SCHIAPPA, formerly Associate Professor of Communication at Purdue University, is now Associate Professor of Communication at the University of Minnesota. He is the author of *Protagoras and Logos* (1991), and editor of *Landmark Essays on Classical Greek Rhetoric* (1994) and of *Warranting Assent: Case Studies in Argument Evaluation* (1995).

CALVIN O. SCHRAG is George Ade Distinguished Professor of Philosophy at Purdue University. He is the author of numerous books, including *Radical Reflection and the Origin of the Human Sciences* (1980), *Communicative Praxis and the Space of Subjectivity* (1986), *The Resources of Rationality: A Response to the Postmodern Challenge* (1992), and *The Self after Postmodernity* (1997).

MELISSA DEUTSCH SCOTT is an Assistant Professor at University of Hawai'i at Hilo, where she teaches rhetoric, pedagogy, and creative writing. Her current research is in the history of feminist rhetoric and the politics of textual recovery.

EIJI SEKINE is Associate Professor of Japanese and Chair of Chinese and Japanese at Purdue University. He is the author of *Tasha no shôkyo* [*Eliminating the Other*] (1993) and editor/author of *Uta no hibiki, monogatari no yokubô* [*Echo of Poems, Desire for Narrative*] (1996), and has published articles both in English and in Japanese.

BOŻENA SHALLCROSS is Assistant Professor of Polish Literature at Indiana University. She is the author of *Cien i forma. O wyobraźni plastycznej Leopolda Staffa* [*Shadow and Form: On Leopold Staff's Visual Imagination*] (1987), *Dom romantycznego artysty* [*Homes of the Romantic Artists*] (1992), and of articles both in Polish and in English.

T. DENEAN SHARPLEY-WHITING is Assistant Professor of French and African American Studies at Purdue University. She is author of *Frantz Fanon: Conflicts and Feminisms* (1997) and co-editor of *Spoils of War: Women of Color, Cultures, and Revolutions* (1997) and of *Fanon: A Critical Reader* (1996).

MARCIA STEPHENSON is Associate Professor of Spanish at Purdue University. She is the author of *Subject to Relocation* (1998) and of articles in *MLN*, *Dispositio*, and *Chasqui*. She specializes in Bolivian gender and cultural studies.

ANTHONY JULIAN TAMBURRI is Professor of Italian and Comparative Literature, and Chair of Classics and Italian at Purdue University. He is the author of several books, including *Of Saltimbanchi and Incendiari* (1990), *To Hyphenate or Not to Hyphenate* (1991), *Per una lettura retrospettiva* (1994), and *A Semiotic of Ethnicity* (1998).

G. R. THOMPSON is Professor of English and Comparative Literature at Purdue University. He is the author of *Poe's Fiction: Romantic Irony in the Gothic Tales* (1973) and *The Art of Authorial Presence: Hawthorne's Provincial Tales* (1993), and the editor of *Essays and Reviews of Edgar Allen Poe* (1984) and *The Gothic Imagination: Essays in Dark Romanticism* (1974).

ERDMUTE WENZEL WHITE is Associate Professor of French and Comparative Literature at Purdue University, where she previously chaired the Program in Comparative Literature. She is the author of *Les années vingt au Brésil: Le modernisme et l'avant-garde internationale* (1978), *The Magic Bishop: Hugo Ball, Dada Poet* (1998), and of numerous essays and book-chapters.

YINGJIN ZHANG is Assistant Professor of Chinese, Comparative Literature, and Film Studies at Indiana University. He is the author of *The City in Modern Chinese Literature and Film* (1996), co-author of *Encyclopedia of Chinese Film* (1998), and editor of *Engaging Texts: Essays in Chinese Comparative Literature and Cultural Studies* (1998) and *Romance, Sexuality, Identity: Cinema and Urban Culture in Shanghai* (1998).

VINCIT QVI PATITVR.